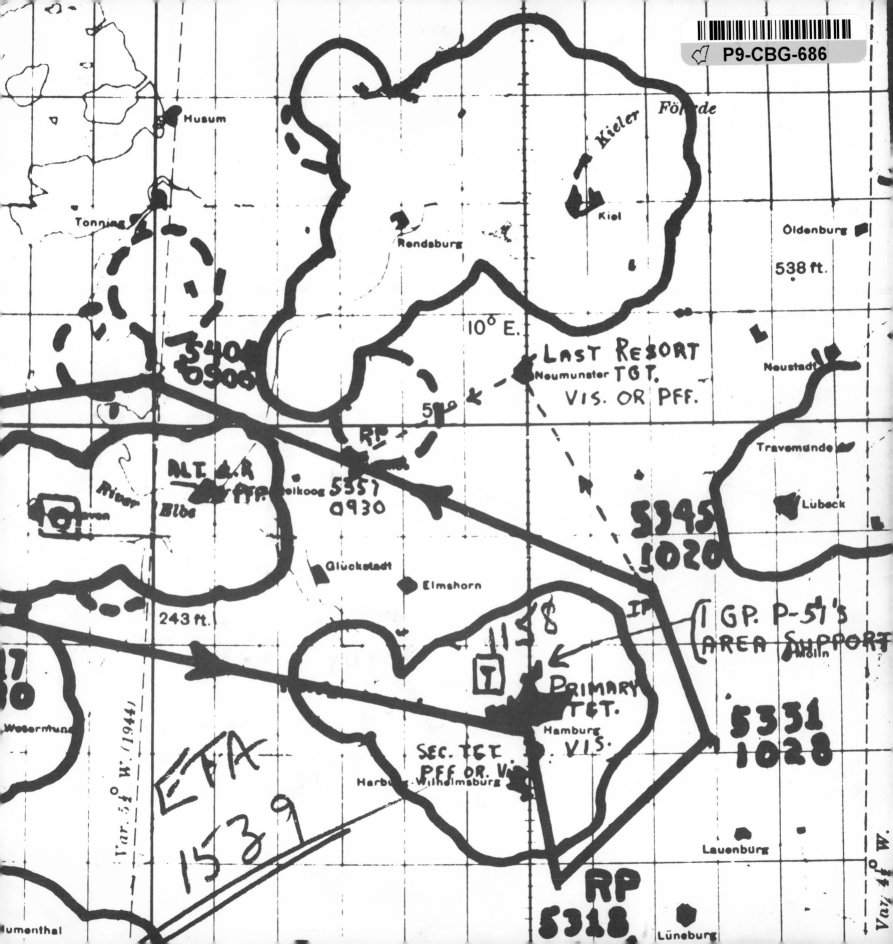

ONE LAST LOOK

ONE LAST LOOK

A SENTIMENTAL JOURNEY TO THE EIGHTH AIR FORCE
HEAVY BOMBER BASES OF WORLD WAR II IN ENGLAND

ABBEVILLE PRESS · PUBLISHERS · NEW YORK

BY PHILIP KAPLAN
AND REX ALAN SMITH

For Ray Wild

The authors wish to thank the various authors, publishers, and agents for permission to reprint various poems and prose selections. For the convenience of readers, these acknowledgments are listed by author or poet.

George Barker: to Faber & Faber, Ltd., for "To My Mother" and "Allegory of the Adolescent and the Adult" from *Collected Poems*.

Robert Graves: to Robert Graves and A. P. Watt, Ltd., for "Warning to Children" and "The Naked and the Nude" from *The Collected Poems of Robert Graves*.

A. E. Housman: to the Society of Authors, Jonathan Cape, Ltd., and Holt, Rinehart and Winston, Inc., for "The Chestnut Cast His Flambeaux" from *Complete Poems*. Copyright © 1922 by Holt, Rinehart and Winston, Inc., copyright © 1936 by Barclays Bank, Ltd., copyright renewed 1950 by Barclays Bank, Ltd.; to the Society of Authors and Jonathan Cape, Ltd., for "When I was One-and-twenty" and "Reveille" from *Collected Poems*.

Randall Jarrell: to Farrar, Straus & Giroux, Inc., and Faber & Faber, Ltd., for "Losses" from *The Complete Poems*, copyright © 1948 Randall Jarrell, copyright renewed © 1975 by Mary Von Schrader Jarrell; "The Death of the Ball Turret Gunner" from *The Complete Poems*, copyright © 1945, 1969 by Mrs. Randall Jarrell, copyright renewed © 1973 by Mrs. Randall Jarrell; "Stalag Luft" from *The Complete Poems*, copyright © 1947 by Mrs. Randall Jarrell, copyright renewed © 1974 by Mrs. Randall Jarrell.

D. H. Lawrence: to The Viking Press, Inc., William Heinemann, Ltd., Laurence Pollinger, Ltd., and The Estate of Mrs. Frieda Lawrence for "The Ship of Death" from *Last Poems*, copyright © 1933 by Frieda Lawrence; and to Laurence Pollinger, Ltd., William Heinemann, Ltd., and The Estate of Mrs. Frieda Lawrence for "Don'ts."

D. H. Lawrence: To Viking Penguin, Inc., and to Lawrence Pollinger Agency for selections from the *Complete Poems of D. H. Lawrence* by Vivian De Sola Pinto and F. Warren Roberts. Copyright © 1964, 1971 by Angelo Ravagli and C. M. Weekley, Executor of the Estate of Frieda Lawrence Ravagli.

Edwin Muir: to Oxford University Press, Inc., and Faber & Faber, Ltd., for "The Bridge of Dread," "The Child Dying," and "The Voyage" from *Collected Poems*, © 1960 Willa Muir.

Wilfred Owen: to New Directions Publishing Corporation for "Spring Offensive," "Apologia Pro Poemate Meo," "Exposure," and "Miners" from *Collected Poems of Wilfred Owen*, copyright © Chatto & Windus, Ltd., 1963.

W. B. Yeats: to Michael B. Yeats, Anne Yeats, Macmillan, London, Ltd., and Macmillan Publishing Co., Inc., for "When You Are Old," "The Song of the Wandering Aengus," and "The Second Coming" from *The Collected Poems*, copyright © 1924 by Macmillan Publishing Co., Inc., renewed 1952 by Bertha Georgie Yeats.

Library of Congress Cataloging in Publication Data   Editor: Walton Rawls
Kaplan, Philip.
    One last look.
    Bibliography: p. 208
    Includes index.
    1. World War, 1939–1945—Aerial operations, American.
2. United States. Army Air Forces. Air Force, 8th—
History. 3. United States. Army Air Forces—Military
life. 4. World War, 1939–1945—Personal narratives,
American. I. Smith, Rex Alan. II. Title.
D790.K36 1983   940.54′4973   83-8777
ISBN 0-89659-404-1

MEMORIES
By Andy Rooney

LONDON — There's just so much sentimental baggage you can carry through life. I'm not much for reunions. Anyone who has reached the age of 60 could easily spend the rest of his days just sitting around, remembering.

I'm here at this old U.S. 8th Air Force Base near Bedford, England, though, because members of the 306th Bomb Group are having a reunion and I flew with them on the first U.S. bombing raid on Nazi Germany in February 1943. It's sentimental baggage I carry easily and with great pride.

It's been 40 years now since these men flew their four-engined B-17 Flying Fortresses out of here. They're the kind of men Americans like to think are typical Americans, but they're better than typical. They're special. A lot of World War II Air Force men are.

It was a terrible war for them although during this reunion they're managing to recall a lot of the good things about it. It would be too sad if they didn't. It was terrible because so many of them were killed. One evening they'd be sitting around their huts talking, worrying, playing cards and writing letters home. The next evening, if there had been a bombing mission that day, the bed next to theirs or the one next to that — and maybe both — might be empty, its former occupant, their pal, dead. Perhaps he had gone down in a parachute that caught fire. "Who burned Bailey?" MacKinley Kantor wrote. "Was it you?"

It was a great and terrible war for me because, as a young reporter for the Army newspaper, The Stars and Stripes, I was in a strange position. I came to this base often when the bombers went out, and when they returned — if they returned — I talked to the crews about what had happened. Then I'd return to London and write my story. I often felt ashamed of myself for not being one of them. I was having the time of my life as a newspaperman and they were fighting and dying. That's how I came to fly with them just that once to Wilhelmshaven. It made me feel better about myself.

Looking out at the crumbling remains of the old runways at this airfield, I'm haunted by flashes of memory. Often the bombers came back badly damaged and with crew members dead or dying. In April 1943, I was here when they came back from a raid deep in Germany and one of the pilots radioed in that he was going to have to make an emergency landing. He had only two engines left and his hydraulic system was gone. He couldn't let the wheels down and there was something even worse. The ball turret gunner was trapped in the plastic bubble that hung beneath the belly of the bomber.

Later I talked with the crewmen who survived that landing. Their friend in the ball turret had been calm, they said. They had talked to him. He knew what they had to do. He understood. The B-17 slammed down on its belly ... and on the ball turret with their comrade trapped inside it.

There are funny stories, too. Everyone here remembers the eccentric gunner Snuffy Smith, Sgt. Maynard Smith. He was an oddball kind of guy, but he did his job well in the air. The Air Force loved to give medals and they had good reason in Snuffy Smith's case. On one occasion, Henry Stimson, then called secretary of war, came to England, and officials, thinking this would be a good time for publicity for the Air Force and the secretary, arranged to give Snuffy Smith the Medal of Honor. The whole entourage came to this base with the secretary and a dozen generals, but the hero was nowhere to be found. It turned out he was in the kitchen washing dishes. He was on KP, being disciplined for some minor infraction of the base rules.

This reunion is a bittersweet experience. Last evening I had a drink at a bar where there was a gathering, and a strong-looking weather-beaten man came over and quietly said he'd like to buy me a drink. He's a Nebraska farmer now. He had been the tail gunner on the Banshee, the B-17 I flew in over Wilhelmshaven. We'd been hit that day and it was a terrifying trip, but it made a good story for me. We laughed and talked together and he paid for the drink. As we lifted our glasses in a mutual toast, I noticed that two fingers on his right hand were missing. It often happened to crewmen who stuck by their guns while their hands froze.

And he was buying me a drink.

right and below:
A crumbling brick
and stucco shell is all
that remains today of
the control tower at
Deenethorpe (401st
Bomb Group [H]).

At a quarter-past-one on a sunny afternoon in August 1943, 230 B-17 bombers, flying high and still climbing, crossed the eastern coast of England outward bound. They were United States Eighth Army Air Force "Flying Fortresses," and they were traveling in a neatly organized formation composed of three-ship vee's gathered into squadrons, groups, and wings. From the ground they looked much like a flight of migrant geese.

Four hours later the bombers recrossed the coast of England, this time flying low and inward bound. They were fewer than before, and their formation was no longer neat. Battered, disorganized, trailed by straggling cripples, the formation now resembled a flight of geese that had passed over too many hunters' blinds—which was precisely what it had done. Going to and from its target deep into Germany, it had flown through seven hundred miles of fire from German fighter planes in the air and from anti-aircraft guns on the ground. As a result, in the words of one of the fighter-escort pilots who had met the returning bombers over Belgium, "You could see machines with one, sometimes two stationary engines . . . lacerated tail-planes, gaping holes in fuselages, wings tarnished by fire or glistening with black oil from gutted engines . . . stragglers, making for the coast . . . [and] flying only by a sublime effort of the will. . . ." Another escort pilot recalled: "There were gaping holes in their precise formations . . . more than half the bombers we nursed over the North Sea were shot up. One or two ditched in the sea. Others, carrying dead and badly wounded crew members, had to make crash landings."

By the time the returning formation had

10

S/Sergeant Clarence
Johnson, a waist gunner
on the crew of an Eighth
Air Force B-24 Liberator
bomber.

reached the coast, fire trucks and ambulances were manned and standing by at the various home bases of its nine component groups, which lay scattered across southeastern England from Ridgewell, thirty miles from the sea, to Grafton-Underwood, sixty miles further inland. At each base ground crews, staff officers, and others were gathering in quiet clusters around the operations towers and the mood was apprehensive and sober. As was always the case when a mission was returning, this was when everyone sensed that barring a miracle, tonight there would be empty hardstands where last night bombers had parked and empty bunks where men had slept. It was also the time of listening for the distant rumble of homing ships and waiting to count them in to see who had made it home and who had not. It was the time, in Air Force parlance, of "sweating out" a mission. This mission's target, the ball-bearing factories at Schweinfurt, lay deeper in Germany than American bombers had ever gone before, so today's "sweating out" was especially intense.

As the formation moved inland—and the groups peeled out to land at their various bases—it began to dwindle away. The 381st dropped out at Ridgewell, the 91st at Bassingbourn, and so on until, with the landing of the 384th at Grafton-Underwood, all were home that were coming home.

Several of the landing aircraft came in firing double red flares, which signaled the waiting ambulances that wounded men were aboard. Some of the ships that had suffered little apparent damage carried dead men, while others that were so battered they appeared incapable of flying brought home crews not even scratched.

One of these was the 384th's "El Rauncho," piloted by Randolph Jacobs. There were holes in its tail and both wings, its landing gear was unusable, and on final approach for a belly landing, two of its engines suddenly quit. Even so, Jacobs managed to put it on the runway where, after a long spark-showered metal-shrieking slide, it finally came to rest, and its ten-man crew climbed out unhurt. Thereupon, Jacobs lit a cigar, looked at the remains of his airplane, and observed, "Guess they just didn't want us to bomb their ol' nuts and bolts factory."

Once the ships were down and the cost of the mission could be counted, it turned out to be high. In some groups a miracle had happened; although many of their planes had been hit, all of them had come home, and none was carrying dead or wounded. In other groups, however, the news was grim. At Ridgewell, where twenty-one ships had gone out and only eleven had returned, there were now ten empty hardstands and a hundred empty bunks. At Bassingbourn it was even worse. Although "Bad Penny," named for the old saying about a bad penny always returning, had indeed returned, as had nine other ships, eleven had not. At Grafton-Underwood the ground crews waited in vain for the return of "Deuces Wild," "Powerhouse II," "Snuffy," "Vertical Shaft," and "M'Honey." All told, sixty bombers were lost and their 600 crewmen were either killed or captured. There were eight dead and twenty-one wounded in the ships that did come home, and more than a hundred aircraft were seriously damaged—some so badly they had to be scrapped.

That was only part of the cost, however; the rest could not be computed. The accountants of

12

06-5-1 WILL BE CONSULTED
OR EMERGENCY ACTION.
FUEL
PRESSURE
OIL
PRESSURE
LEFT ENGINE
RIGHT ENGINE
FLAP
POSITION
DOWN

war have no keys on their calculators for adding up the cost of fear, or of seeing a best friend's ship going down in flames, or of that weird feeling produced by joy mixed with guilt on returning unharmed from a mission from which so many others would never return.

What had been purchased at this price was not known for a long time. There was much disagreement about it, in fact. Air Force analysts were inclined to believe the mission had not accomplished much; Air Force public relations officers, however, played it up as a huge success. The truth, according to German records captured at the end of the war, lay somewhere between. Neither a complete failure nor a complete success, the raid had damaged German ball-bearing production somewhat, and thereby hastened Germany's defeat a bit.

All of this happened a long time ago. Only about two out of ten Americans now living are old enough to remember clearly the time when that war began, and four out of ten had not yet been born when it ended. Most of the future personnel of the Eighth Air Force were in their teens when that war began. Since then, they have grown thicker in the middle and thinner on top. All of them are old enough now to be grandparents and some are great-grandparents. They have become, as their British friends might have put it, a bit long in the tooth. The aircraft they flew have long since gone to scrap and the fields they flew them from have long since gone to grass or factories or housing subdivisions.

In the minds of the Eighth's veterans, however, these things are still fresh, for their experiences were not of a kind to be forgotten. In their minds they can still see the aircraft as they were, and the airfields as they were, and hear the engines and the sound of bursting flak, and smell the burnt cordite from the guns and the ale in an English pub.

Human nature often seems to prod a man into returning later in life to the scene of some meaningful event of his youth. That event may have been of such significance as to alter the course of his life. And while the imprint of the event is permanent, the experience itself remains in the backwaters of his mind, receiving little consideration over the years. Then, in maturity, he begins to focus on the times of his life that were most influential, the experiences that helped to shape his character. And a need in him surfaces, to return to the scene of the event, to recall the experience as it really happened, to have one last look at the place where it happened.

In *One Last Look* members of the U.S. Eighth Army Air Force who served in World War II recall life in a Nissen hut, the routine on the base, the food, their relationships with the British, their off-duty hours at the Officers' and EM clubs. They describe, in vivid detail, their preparation for a raid, the briefing, and the raid itself, the flak and the fighter attacks, the losses, being shot down and taken prisoner in Germany, the songs and the jargon, the girls they knew, the USO shows and celebrity visitors, the "ground grippers" who didn't fly but labored with little recognition to keep the air crews flying, how they spent their 48-hour passes in the "liberty towns," the nearby villages, the mud, boredom and fatigue . . . and the fear of the experience that was to become, for most of them, the one great adventure of their lives.

left: part of the instrument panel of a B-17 Flying Fortress bomber. *overleaf:* one of the larger Nissen huts remaining at Deenethorpe.

15

THE AIR CREWS

"In 1955 I went back [to Shipdham]...seams in the concrete sprouting weeds...shells of buildings....Out on the main runway stood an abandoned farm machine....Up in the control tower broken glass covered the floor, a door swung eerily in the breeze...."

"...faces flitted through my mind, faces of men—boys, really, [who had become] men before their time....Where were they those wonderful kids?...kids who did not speak of patriotism, love of country, fear of death, but who went out and did the best they could, clumsily at times, perfectly sometimes, but always the best they could."
Jacob T. Elias, waist gunner, 44th Bomb Group, Shipdham

"We were not children fired with a vision....We were merely young men accepting our times. Some of us fancied the role we played; others did not. In any case we did not go off into the sky shouting hosannas."
Elmer Bendiner (navigator, 379th Bomb Group, Kimbolton), in Fall of the Fortresses

"Less than two months after joining my Group I became at age seventeen the oldest gunner in my Squadron."
John A. Miller, waist gunner, 100th Bomb Group, Thorpe Abbotts

Many of them looked like children when they first went to the war, and some of them no doubt could have been called children. Veteran pilot Ernest K. Gann encountered many of them at Goose Bay, Labrador, on their way to England, and saw, as he wrote in his classic book *Fate is*

1st Lt. J. M. Smith of Austin, Texas, gives his final instructions to the crew of "Our Gang," a B-17, just before takeoff on a bombing mission on 24 June 1943. They are members of the 91st Bomb Group (H) based at Bassingbourn.

right: In full flying gear, a crew member of a 91st Bomb Group (H) B-17.

the Hunter, "earnest young men with peachfuzz beards . . . brave aerial children who would go down in flame and history as the Eighth Air Force." But because aerial warfare is, to say the least, a ripening experience, once they flew a few combat missions they were children no longer. As Gann put it, "the innocence was gone from their eyes." In age, however, they were still absurdly young and but little removed from childhood. Most were in combat before the age of twenty-two; some, such as gunner Miller, were as young as seventeen, and the few graybeards among them who were twenty-five or older were known more often than not to their fellow crewmembers as "Dad" or "The Old Man."

Their training, when compared to the complexity of their duties, was brief. So brief, in fact, that most found themselves doing battle in airplanes within a year (and often much less) of first having been in an airplane. The bombers they manned were among the largest, heaviest, most complicated aircraft then in existence. Yet, despite their youth and inexperience and the briefness of their training, they managed to lift those huge craft overloaded with bombs and gasoline from foggy, tree-rimmed fields whose runways were no longer than they had to be, to assemble them in neat formations in the air, and to keep the formations tight while being harassed by fighters and flak; to navigate them accurately over hundreds of miles of alien land and trackless sea; to drop bombs that usually landed on or reasonably near their targets even after a four-mile fall through windswept space, and to shoot with reasonable hope of success at enemy fighters streaking past at relative closing speeds of up to ten miles per minute.

That thousands of crews, most of whose members were not yet old enough to vote, should have learned in so short a time to do all of this successfully is remarkable enough. But the fact that they also found within their souls the steel required for doing it under the conditions in which it had to be done is more than remarkable. It is astonishing! In his book, *Serenade to the Big Bird*, pilot Bert Stiles described those conditions with wry understatement, when he said of a sortie over France: "I can say that I have been to Paris, but travel by Flying Fortress is a hell of a way to go anywhere. . . . The welcome is so surly. No one is ever glad to see us."

And it was indeed a surly welcome to the European continent—unfailingly offered by Germans who, said Stiles, "did not want us over there at all." They delivered it from the muzzles of airborne guns in Messerschmidt 109s and 110s, Focke-Wulf 190s and assorted other aircraft, and from ground-based guns that peppered the heavens with the airplane-breaking, man-killing explosive shells called flak. It was a welcome the Germans never neglected. On deep penetration missions, such as to Berlin or the notorious target called Schweinfurt, unwilling beneficiaries of that welcome were forced to accept it for as much as four hours at a time, and it was a nerve-wracking thing to endure.

Combat is never comfortable, of course. But aerial combat is probably the most frightening warfare of all, because for man the air is an unnatural habitat through which he travels uneasily at best. Regardless of other distractions, he must keep his airplane moving and under control, or it will fall. In case he is hit, he cannot just park it somewhere while making repairs or attending to the wounded. And worst of all, he cannot run and he cannot hide. He is simply *there*, marooned aloft in an aluminum capsule that seems to creep as slowly across the hostile sky as a fly across a wall, nakedly visible and vulnerable to all who wish to swat it down.

The American bombers were armed for their own defense. In fact, they were the best-armed bombers then in existence, but they were vulnerable nonetheless. B-17s and B-24s each carried at least ten fifty-caliber machine guns, and their gunners used them well. Even so, they could not stop all enemy fighters, and against flak, of course, machine guns were useless. This is why most Eighth veterans will tell you their greatest fear in combat was of flak. "You couldn't do a darned thing about it," they will say, "all you could do was plow through it and figure that either it would get you or it wouldn't."

On every raid some bombers suffered battle damage, and on almost every raid some were lost—exploding in midair, or falling from the sky in pieces or in tears of flame. On some raids both the damage and losses were dismally heavy. Out of the 315 bombers sent by the Eighth to Schweinfurt and Regensburg on August 17, 1943, for instance, sixty were shot down, seventeen came home so badly shot up that they had to be scrapped, and another 121 were so damaged that only after major repairs were they able to fly again. Out of thirteen B-17s in the October 10, 1943, raid made by the 100th Bomb Group on Munster, twelve were shot down over the target within a period of seven minutes, and the lone survivor—"Rosie's Riveters," piloted by Brooklyn Law School graduate Robert Rosen-

21

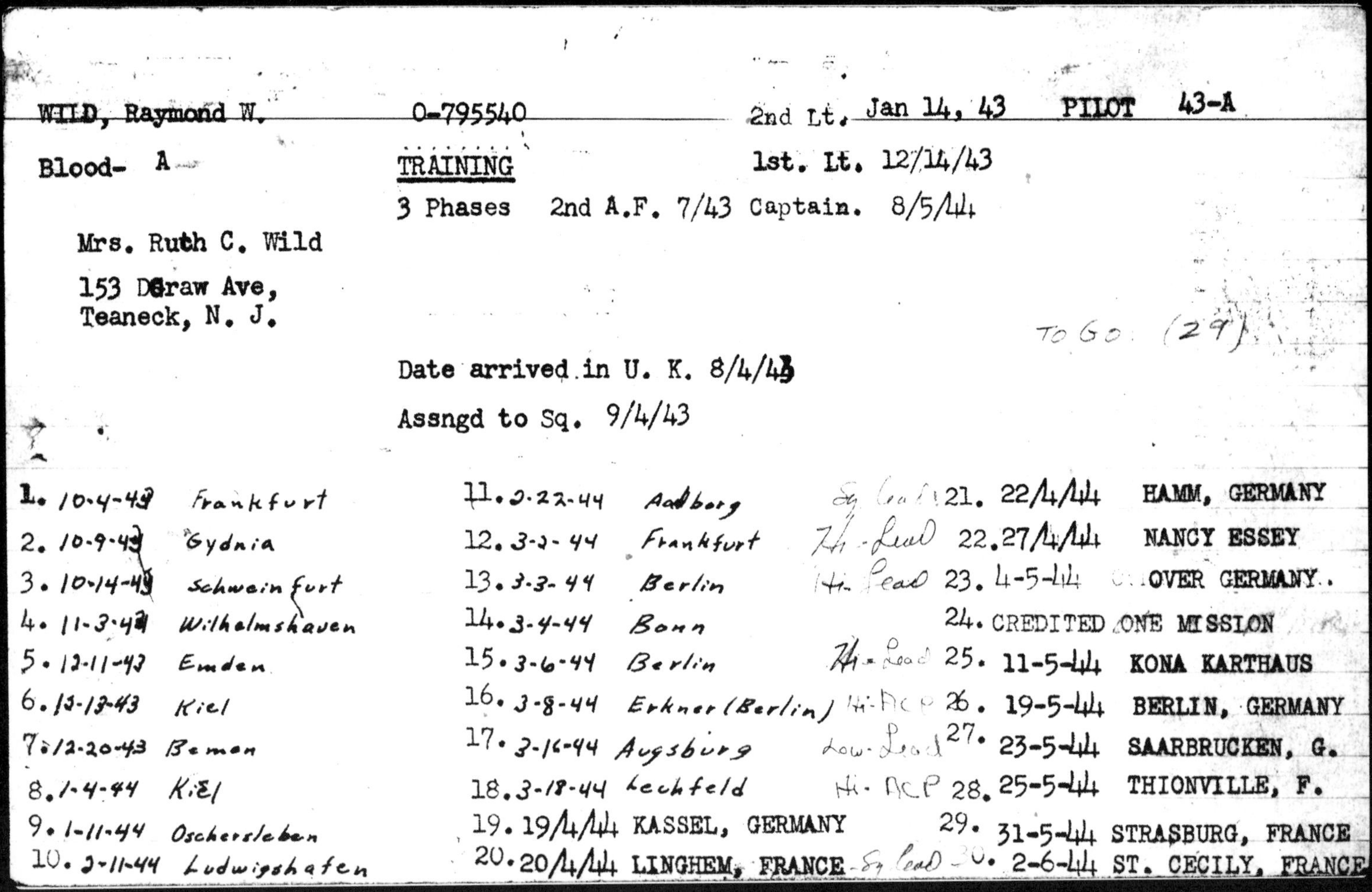

WILD, Raymond W. 0-795540 2nd Lt. Jan 14, 43 PILOT 43-A

Blood- A TRAINING 1st. Lt. 12/14/43

3 Phases 2nd A.F. 7/43 Captain. 8/5/44

Mrs. Ruth C. Wild

153 DeGraw Ave,

Teaneck, N. J.

TO GO (29)

Date arrived in U. K. 8/4/43

Assngd to Sq. 9/4/43

1. 10-4-43	Frankfurt	11. 2-22-44	Aalborg	Sq Lead	21. 22/4/44	HAMM, GERMANY
2. 10-9-43	Gydnia	12. 3-2-44	Frankfurt	Hi-Lead	22. 27/4/44	NANCY ESSEY
3. 10-14-43	Schweinfurt	13. 3-3-44	Berlin	Hi-Lead	23. 4-5-44	OVER GERMANY.
4. 11-3-43	Wilhelmshaven	14. 3-4-44	Bonn		24.	CREDITED ONE MISSION
5. 12-11-43	Emden	15. 3-6-44	Berlin	Hi-Lead	25. 11-5-44	KONA KARTHAUS
6. 12-13-43	Kiel	16. 3-8-44	Erkner (Berlin)	Hi-ACP	26. 19-5-44	BERLIN, GERMANY
7. 12-20-43	Bemen	17. 3-16-44	Augsburg	Low-Lead	27. 23-5-44	SAARBRUCKEN, G.
8. 1-4-44	Kiel	18. 3-18-44	Lechfeld	Hi-ACP	28. 25-5-44	THIONVILLE, F.
9. 1-11-44	Oschersleben	19. 19/4/44	KASSEL, GERMANY		29. 31-5-44	STRASBURG, FRANCE
10. 2-11-44	Ludwigshafen	20. 20/4/44	LINGHEM, FRANCE	Sq Lead	30. 2-6-44	ST. CECILY, FRANCE

The personnel records file of every Eighth Air Force air crew member contained a mission card like the one above which credits Captain Raymond W. Wild with his required thirty combat missions thus completing his tour of duty in the ETO. Captain Wild was a member of the 92nd Bomb Group (H) based at Podington.

thal—came staggering home with two engines shot out, a gaping hole blasted in one wing, countless smaller holes in the fuselage, and both waist gunners seriously wounded. And when seventeen-year-old John Miller suddenly found himself the oldest gunner in his squadron, it was because of a raid on which his Group had sent out eighteen ships and got back only two. "I was living in the spare gunners' hut at the time," he later recalled, "and for fifteen days following the March 6th, 1944, raid on Berlin I was *alone* in that hut! Everyone I knew was either killed or taken prisoner that day. . . ."

What it all boiled down to, according to the statistics-keepers of that time, was this: In 1943 and 1944, the average life of an Eighth Air Force bomber and crew was fifteen missions. The assigned tour of duty for crew members, however, was twenty-five missions, and out of this grew a set of odds most discouraging to anyone interested in longevity. These odds especially impressed navigator Lou Bober, who had been trained as an insurance actuary, and who was moved to say to his pilot, Keith Newhouse, "Skipper, mathematically there just ain't any way we're gonna live through this thing."

Actually there was a way of living through it, or at least of making sure that however one might meet his end, it would not be in aerial combat. The way to do it was to request a transfer from flying status to some other kind of duty. Because all air crew service was voluntary, such requests were granted and with no resulting stigma on the record of the applicant. As it happened, however, such applications were few. Following that bad day over Munster, Robert Rosenthal went on to finish his tour, then volun-

teered for another, and at war's end he had flown and survived something like sixty missions. John Miller overcame the shock of suddenly finding himself the sole survivor in a hut where "those empty bunks almost drove me to the 'tapioca farm,' " and went on to complete thirty-five missions. Newhouse and Bober continued to fly (and by surviving cast some doubt on Bober's mathematics), as did thousands of others—going on until they had finished their allotted missions or had been killed, wounded, captured . . . whichever came first.

Why did they do it? Why, when they knew they were not required to do so, did they keep going back? After reading their history, a string of tales about bombers setting out in the morning whole and healthy and returning in the evening as flak-battered wrecks, often piloted by wounded men and carrying dead ones, and after seeing pictures of other bombers on those missions exploding in air, or falling in pieces, or trailing exclamation points of smoke, one must ask, why did they do it?

In the diaries and letters they wrote then and in the statements they make now, the men themselves explain it rather simply. And even while their words differ, their meanings are almost always the same. Back then, they would have told you they were doing it simply because "it's our job," or, "somebody's got to do it," and they would have said little more. Not because there wasn't anything more to be said but because in the service at that time (as, perhaps, in all times) it would not have been fashionable to say it. It was true, as Bendiner said, that they were not "fired with a vision," but it was also true that most of them did have a deeply felt

Oft have I struck those that I never saw / and struck them dead.

(from *Henry VI*, Act IV, by William Shakespeare)

above: Decorated A2 leather flying jacket typical of those worn by air crew members of the Eighth's heavy bombers. *right:* The flying jacket of Sidney Rapaport, a B-17 navigator with the 94th Bomb Group (H) based at Bury St. Edmunds.

sense of purpose, the expression of which would have embarrassed them then but which, in the mellowness that comes with years, they will acknowledge now. Navigator Frank W. Nelson of the 487th Bomb Group at Lavenham recently put it this way: "We really thought we had a job to do. You betcha we did! And I know I wouldn't have been happy if I hadn't been helping to do it." And as Ira Eakin has expressed it: "I really believed in what I was doing. If we hadn't of stopped that Hitler cat over there, why, he'd of taken over the whole cotton-pickin' world."

It was one thing, however, for a man to believe he was fighting in a virtuous cause, and it was quite another for him to get into an airplane day after day and make himself a target for the German gunners who had tried but failed to kill him the day before.

Each man crossed his personal moat of fear by various bridges, and probably the strongest of these was personal pride—the determination of each to let his fellows know that if they could do it, he could do it too. "I was a devout coward," said Ray Wild, pilot of the lead ship on the first American raid on Berlin: "But what happens is, *pride* makes you get into that airplane, and pride makes you stay there and keep going when what you really want to do is to turn back while you still can. They had that tradition that an Eighth Air Force sortie never turned back from a target. So, hell!, you didn't dare turn back!"

Another of the bridges they used to overcome fear was pride in the organization—pride in their Group and in the Eighth, itself. "When we took off from Miami and I could then open our sealed orders and find out where we were

going," said one pilot, "and when I then announced over the intercom that we were on our way to the Eighth in England, everybody cheered. They figured if we were going to the Eighth it was because we were considered good enough to play in the big leagues." And Sidney Rapaport, navigator and radar expert with the 94th Bomb Group at Bury St. Edmunds, put it this way: "Morale was very high. . . . A book like *Catch 22* is just an absolute mockery of how things really were because you had this marvelous morale, a marvelous esprit d'corps, and everybody on the flight crews flew because they really *wanted* to fly."

Important also was that inner sense we all have (and that creates so much difficulty for life insurance agents) of our personal immortality, and our inability to imagine a world without ourselves in it. Veterans of the Eighth speak of this time and again with comments that can be summed up in a remark by ball-turret gunner Ken Stone of the 381st Bomb Group at Ridgewell: "You know it's gonna happen to somebody, but it's not gonna happen to you. It's gonna happen to the other guy, not you."

Finally, and more important than it may sound, was the conquering of fear through rituals and symbols. Ken Stone remembers that in his hut: "We were superstitious. When we dressed we'd put on our clothing in exactly the same order as the time before. One fellow had a little doll he always carried on raids, and the one time he forgot it he didn't come back."

In *Fall of the Fortresses*, Elmer Bendiner wrote: "I knew some of them would that day die. Still, I was certain I would survive . . . but only if I followed my private ritual. Only if I went out

Few air crewmen brought cameras along on the bombing raids they flew, but many recorded their combat experiences in personal diaries. Here is a page from the diary of Harold Haft, a B-17 pilot of the 351st Bomb Group (H), Polebrook.

and found a poppy to put in my buttonhole. I had worn poppies before and survived. I am a reasonable man, but in matters of life and death I do not exclude talismans."

Ray Wild described his own private ritual thus: "I remember that just before my first raid—the one where you are really frightened to death—I went into the john in the operations tower. Didn't have to go, but just went in and sat on the john. That was when the song 'Paper Doll' had just come out and somebody had written all the words on the wall. Well, just through nothing but being nervous I sat there and memorized those words." The mission was the October 8, 1943, raid on Frankfurt, and it proved to be a rough one. Wild's ship returned with a two-foot hole in one side, one engine out, three of its six elevator control cables shot in two, and its radio operator wounded (though not fatally). But because the ship did get back and all its crew did survive, said Wild, "From then on I sat in that same john every morning. And you know, even to this day I know every word of 'Paper Doll.' "

Learning their craft, conquering their fears, enduring the eerie loneliness of doing combat in an aluminum cocoon four miles above the earth—these were things these young men managed to do not because they were extraordinary, but because they were ordinary young men responding to extraordinary circumstances. They were, like the other armed services, a mixture of the shy and the bold, sophisticated and naive, refined and crude, gentlemen and hoodlums. They differed from those in the other services in only two respects. First, Air Force medical examiners found they

possessed the eyes of eagles and reflexes of cats; organs and passages in their bodies not likely to collapse, explode, plug up, or otherwise cease to function in the thin air at thirty thousand feet; and an emotional stability that allowed them to keep their heads, do their jobs, and not become screaming claustrophobics when confined in an airplane under fire. Second, they were in an assignment of their own choosing. This was a thing to be prized at a time when in most of the other services the man who could shoot like Annie Oakley, and liked to do it, was apt to wind up as a mess cook, and the one who was happiest when baking bread was most likely to find himself inhabiting a foxhole and holding a rifle.

Still, men do not voluntarily undergo such traumatic experiences as aerial combat without reason. They will pay that kind of price only in the expectation that they will get correspondingly equal material or psychological benefits. And, of course, flight duty did have its benefits.

One of these was the extra pay they received for flying. Although certainly welcome, this apparently was not what induced most crewmen to fly; it seems to have been merely the extra icing on an already desirable cake.

Another inducement for flying, or so many veterans of the Eighth say now, was the quality of Air Force life, as compared to that of the other services. Bombardier A. D. McAllister, Jr., of the 448th Bomb Group at Seething, recalls having begun his military career as a second lieutenant in infantry training at Fort Benning, Georgia, where, "A notice on the bulletin board said that infantry officers could apply for transfer into air force flight training with no loss in rank, but I hadn't paid much attention to it be-

26

cause the air force physical exam was supposed to be a real booger and I doubted I could pass it. Then one day they marched us about fifteen miles out into the boonies and then demonstrated the way we should disperse our troops when under a strafing attack. The instructor said, 'Look to your right front and up about a thousand feet and you will see an approaching aircraft.' Well, I looked, and there it was, and I thought to myself, 'Now, that fella didn't get up nearly as early as I did, and he didn't have to march fifteen miles either. He'll make a couple of passes at us, and a few minutes after that he'll be back at the base having a hot lunch. Then he'll probably get a pass and spend the afternoon in town. And tonight he'll sleep in his own comfortable bunk while I'm out here with the chiggers and ticks and mosquitoes and sleeping on the ground.

"So-o-o, as soon as we got back to the base I applied for transfer to the air force.' "

It is true that life was more comfortable in the Air Force than in most of the other services. Infantry and marines in combat were in it twenty-four hours a day and they lived "on the job," occupying foxholes, enduring rain and snow, eating cold canned rations, sleeping in sand and mud. Pilots and air crews, on the other hand, were commuter-warriors. They flew to and from their work as other men commute to and from their offices. And whereas theirs was probably the most intense and frightening "work" in the war, they were only engaged in it for a few hours at a stretch, and at other times they enjoyed a relatively comfortable and civilized life. But it is also true that Air Force ground units enjoyed the same kind of life as

March 18 — I visited Berlin for the third time. Mike and I flew section lead together for the first time today. The leading job was nothing to brag about. Bombing altitude was 27,000 through a partial undercast. Vapor trails were very heavy, especially over the target and it really made it rough over the target. 'Flak' was pretty heavy and very accurate. I saw a couple of planes go down, but we were lucky and only picked up a couple of small holes. On the way back bandits were reported in the area and we really socked it in.

March 19 — Went after the same target at Leipzig for the third time and I don't think we hit today either. Bombing was done at 24,000' through a partial undercast. The vapor trails were extremely dense and made formation flying very difficult. Over the target I could hardly see my wingmen. At that time our squadron leader lost all sense of direction and our squadron went all over the sky. It was a mad house and I don't see how the planes didn't come crashing into one another. After bombs away I became separated from the rest of the group. Just about the time I was going to ask for fighters we spotted

On the Kiel job I got my first close-up of a Fort blowing up. The flak tightened up on the group just ahead of ours, and right out at ten o'clock, not very far away, a great red wound opened up, and then the drifting pieces, and ten men and a couple of hundred thousand dollars' worth of airplane, powdered in a hundredth of a second. And while we were watching the streamers of flame from that one, another Fort nosed over straight down and started for the ground by the shortest road. It must have dived five thousand feet, and then by some miracle it pulled out, level and into a straight-up climb. It stalled out somewhere below us, and fell off on the right wing and spun in.

(from *Serenade to the Big Bird*, by Bert Stiles)

flying personnel without paying the price of aerial combat. This means there must have been still another reason why those who flew chose to do so, and there was. McAllister acknowledged it when, after giving his practical reasons for transferring to the Air Force, he then grinned and added, "And ... well, y'know I'd always wanted to fly anyhow. Back then it was considered a pretty glamorous thing to do."

Indeed it was considered a glamorous thing to do, and of course he had wanted to fly. So had the others in the flight crews, and so had the thousands more who had applied but failed to qualify for flying duty. And they had good reason for wanting to. Most of them were born within twenty years after the Wright Brothers first flew at Kitty Hawk. While they were growing up, aviation was still an exciting new frontier, the sky was considered a habitat for heroes, and small boys dreamed of becoming fliers just as their grandfathers as boys may have dreamed of becoming railroad engineers. They were at about kindergarten age when Lindbergh flew the Atlantic, and in the following winter there was hardly a tyke in the land who did not go about with his head proudly encased in a "Lucky Lindy" helmet complete with goggles. It was a time when young boys saw *Wings* and other films glorifying the army pilots in World War I, then shattered their mothers' nerves by racing through the house waving toy airplanes in grubby fists and shouting, "Eeeerrrowww! Ah-ah-ah-ah! I'm Eddie Rickenbacker chasing the Red Baron! Ah-ah-ah-ah!" And it was a time when barnstormers worked the carnivals and county fairs—first giving demonstrations of aerial acrobatics and wing-walking, then giving

rides at a penny per passenger-pound. Rarely could a youngster overcome his parents' objections ("If God'd wanted you to fly He'd of given you wings ...") and also wheedle from them the eighty cents or so necessary for a ride, although many certainly attempted it. But whether they succeeded (and thereby received both the thrill of a lifetime and at least six months' worth of schoolyard bragging material) or failed, they usually came away from these affairs determined that one day they, too, would be fliers.

Given this background, it is small wonder that in 1940, when the United States reinstituted the draft and began building up its armed forces, young men by the tens of thousands applied to become pilots if they could qualify, or for other flying duty if they could not. And it is also small wonder that those who did manage to qualify for some kind of flying duty gained instant prestige in the eyes of their communities and a dashing desirability in the eyes of young women.

This was heady stuff for a young man—this sudden leap from the ranks of students or from a usually less-than-significant job into the select, sheepskin-clad fraternity of airborne warriors. It tended to create a certain cocky self-importance among many of even the most modest, and to introduce a certain swagger into the steps of some who previously had only shambled. This cockiness, however, proved to be only temporary—a juvenile snakeskin that they promptly shed as soon as they grew up—that is, after their first day of heavy combat. There is no glamour in an airplane that is plowing through a field of flak, and there is no desire to swagger there. On the contrary, the airman's only wish is to be as little noticed as possible by those who wish to press their deadly attentions upon him. And so among these crews, as always with young men who go to war, the first combat casualty they experienced was their own cockiness.

For many, said Allan Healy, "the first few [missions] were an unreality like a movie you saw but weren't in." But by the tenth mission, if not before, "almost all became effective fighters, quiet and cool on the ground and in the air, took responsibility and acquired *esprit de corps*." By this time also, most were acquiring a new sense of importance that was sober and real rather than cocky and superficial, that was hard-earned, and that would become one of the true and enduring rewards of their work. It was the feeling that by their efforts as groups, crews, and even as individuals, they were making a difference—that instead of merely being a few insignificant ants among millions of others in the anthill of war, they actually were influencing the course of the war and shortening it.

This is a feeling that rarely comes to ground troops, no matter how much they may have earned it. The view of war from the ground, in the words of correspondent Ernie Pyle, is a "worm's-eye view" of a war "a hundred yards wide." Accordingly, even when they take a hill that may be the most important hill in the entire war, it usually looks just like any other hill—and a poor bargain in terms of the blood that was spent in buying it. Airmen, on the other hand, have a bird's eye view, a lofty perch from which they may see the results of their work. And this was especially true for the men of the Eighth because they flew daylight missions and had a daylight view. Also, they were told in

their premission briefings the importance of their work, but they were told this so often that they were inclined to make fun of it and to pretend not to believe it. "The Colonel would get up there and sell the mission," said pilot Lawrence Drew. "He'd let you know the entire war hinged on the job you did on that particular target." As Elmer Bendiner wrote of a briefing the 379th Group had before a bloody day at Schweinfurt, "I was to be one of those who on that day—August 17, 1943—were to strike the blow that would destroy Hitler and win the war."

But even while they professed not to believe in the importance of what they were doing, they did believe it. They could, after all, see the evidence. Smoke and flame billowing from a raided refinery told them of millions of gallons of gasoline they had prevented from reaching German tanks and planes, and smoldering factories told them of machines and equipment the Wehrmacht would never receive.

The price they paid for these accomplishments was high—for every thousand tons of bombs delivered, the bomber and fighter escort groups together lost sixty-seven men killed, wounded, missing, or captured, and thirteen airplanes destroyed. But because, unlike most ground troops, they could see immediately the results of their efforts, they could at least take sober satisfaction in knowing the price had not been paid in vain.

The adventure of aviation, extra pay, the prestige of wearing wings, the advantages of Air Force life over that of other services—these appear to have been, in various degrees and combinations, the anticipated rewards by which men were drawn to volunteer for combat flying duty

Ken Stone, ball-turret gunner on the crew of a B-17 called "Big Time Operator" in January of 1944 and again in 1982. Stone was a member of the 381st Bomb Group (H) based at Ridgewell.

in World War II. Indeed, they *were* rewards, and were well enjoyed. But Eighth Air Force veterans who speak of them now usually do so with a grin, recognizing them as merely tinsel on the tree of memory. For, as is so often the case in life, the true rewards of their service turned out to be far different and more valuable than those they originally expected. Discovery of the power within themselves to master fear and assume responsibility in times when the degree of responsibility exercised by one meant the difference between life and death for many; the feeling that they truly did affect the course of the war, and to an extent far out of proportion to their numbers; the *esprit de corps* and close comradeship developed among men joined together in doing a job that was dangerous, often deadly, but necessary, and doing it well—when the Eighth's veterans speak of these things now, they do it with feeling, and they do not grin. In recalling his days as a pilot with the 445th Bomb Group film star Jimmy Stewart recently said: "It was a strange, exciting, sometimes wonderful, sometimes terrifying time. I don't talk about it much but I think about it a lot. I'm glad to have had the experience. It helped me to develop as a person." And in an account written in 1978, Jacob T. Elias concluded his reminiscences by saying: "Many a time, in those moments before I fall asleep, I return to that Nissen hut. Again we are making tea on that little stove, and there is teasing and laughing . . .

"I don't want my sons to experience war. But I wish they could experience that complete camaraderie that I had at Shipdham-in-the-Mud. . . . my mind often goes back to Shipdham . . . and most likely will keep going back. . . ."

At Hardwick, the ground crew of "Exterminator," a 93rd Bomb Group (H) B-24, greet the air crew on their return from a raid over Germany. *overleaf:* Captain Howard Slaton and the crew of the B-24 called "Arise My Love and Come With Me" after a bombing mission.

THE BASES

Louise

Bill

OUT
OF
BOUNDS

KEEP
THIS PLACE
CLEAN

If you were a serviceman going overseas in World War II, you were presumed by the folks at home to be a warrior who by the very act of going had already become something of a hero. In response, you usually assumed an air of nonchalance that implied the trip you were embarking on was of no more interest or consequence than a visit to the barber shop. To have revealed that you were actually eager and excited and a little bit frightened would have been "square," and embarrassingly improper for the kind of laconic, hard-bitten troopers you and your fellow pink-cheeked military fledglings liked to think you had become. But even though you concealed it under a pretended indifference, the excitement was there. You were at the age of adventure, as interested in new things as a half-grown pup, probably had traveled very little before going into military service, and now you were on your way to some exotic faraway place you had never expected to see. Accordingly, your mental baggage was packed with preconceived notions and imaginary pictures of your destination, and you were as eager as any tourist to find out how well it matched with your mental pictures.

If you were serving in the United States Eighth Army Air Force, your faraway place was England. And if you flew there you could see immediately that in at least two respects it not only matched but exceeded your imaginary pictures of it. You had expected England to be green, even your childhood storybooks had told you that, but you had not expected it to be *this* green—actually to be, well . . . *storybook* green. And you had expected England, especially in the south and east, to be a land of airfields. Dur-

ing the two-and-a-half years they battled alone in the air war against Germany, the English had been busy building fields for their own air forces, and after the United States entered the war they continued just as busily to build them for their American cousins. You had seen these fields on your flight charts, their circles dotting the surfaces like measles, but only after seeing them from the air—scattered across the landscape like dozens of toy triangles that had been carelessly tossed out upon a green and yellow carpet—could you realize how many there really were and how closely they lay to each other. Because of the route you had flown, the sight of all those airports as you came in made you feel like a beggar who had suddenly come into an inheritance. You came either by way of Trinidad, Brazil, West Africa, and the Sahara Desert, or via Newfoundland, Greenland, and Iceland. Either way you had come nervously and with palms slightly damp, for if trouble had forced you to land unexpectedly on one of those routes, at points where airfields were hundreds and sometimes thousands of miles apart, you would have experienced an eruption of flying sand, snow, seawater, or jungle foliage, and it probably would have been a permanent landing. Here in England, however, it appeared that it would be hard for an airplane in trouble *not* to find a field to land on. Which indeed was true, and many lives were saved because of it. It was also true that when inbound pilots of the Eighth became frustrated in trying to determine which field among so many was their own, or when the air traffic around their field became entangled with that around neighboring fields, they often roundly cursed the closeness of the English

left and above: All that remains of "Louise" and "Eileen," creative self-expression on the wall of a crumbling hut at Knettishall, home to the 388th Bomb Group (H).

35

bases. More often, however, they blessed it. As remembered by Ray Wild, a pilot with the 92nd Bombardment Group at Podington: "There were always runways somewhere in the neighborhood. If you were coming back from a raid in trouble and needed a field in a hurry, or if you were in soupy weather and couldn't find one, you'd just fly a circle while giving your code and call letters on your radio. Then this English voice would come on and say 'Hello, Yank!' and in thirty seconds he'd have you on radar and in two minutes more he'd have you right over a field."

And Ira Eakin, a crew chief with the 91st BG at Bassingbourn recalls: "In a twenty-five- or thirty-mile radius around us there must have been twenty-five or thirty bases. If you had some kind of trouble, an engine failure or something, why, all you had to do was hop over a hedge and set down on one. Man! We had bases in every direction around there!"

By the spring of 1944 there were more than 130 military airfields crowded into an area of southeastern England no larger than the state of Vermont and smaller than some counties in Texas or California. Forty-two of these were homes for Eighth Air Force B-17 and B-24 Bombardment Groups and fourteen were occupied by their fighter escorts—the P-47 and P-51 Fighter Groups whom the bomber people referred to as their "Little Friends." Five of these bases were permanent installations built for the Royal Air Force before the war, and they were fairly comfortable. The other fifty-one were new, temporary, hastily built, and they were not comfortable.

No matter which of these bases you were

assigned to, you discovered immediately that in only one respect did it resemble the bases you had served on back in the States. Its runways were similar, and that was only because when it comes to runways it is airplanes not men that dictate the terms, and the airplanes will punish you if their terms are violated. They demand runways that are of at least a certain length, that do not bend, that remain firm under wheels that are heavily burdened, and that are laid out in directions reasonably related to those of the prevailing winds. Because of the rigidity of these requirements, the runway portions of the English bases were much like those of the ones back home. In all other characteristics, however, they were unlike any bases you had ever seen before, and were one aspect of England for which both experience and imagination had left you unprepared.

The bases you had come from were located, more often than not, upon land previously occupied only by sand, salt, or sagebrush, and that was good for little else *but* an air station. More often than not, also, they were located out in what the troops in the Pacific had begun to call by a word borrowed from the Filipinos, though the Filipinos would no longer recognize it. The word was *bundok*, which the Americans had converted to "boondocks" and then to "boonies," and used to describe places dismally distant from the comforts and temptations of civilized life. But wherever bases in the States were located, their geometry was almost always as simple and crisp as the grids on a waffle iron. Their boundary fences were straight lines and their boundary corners were right angles. The buildings within their boundaries were

in blocks and rows neatly aligned with the cardinal points of the compass, and were grouped so that all buildings having a similar function, such as, say, barracks, or hangars and shops, were to be found in one area. As a result of this geometric tidiness, these bases usually appeared not to have been fitted into the surrounding landscape but to have been dropped upon it after having been manufactured elsewhere, and if the two did not fit, it was the landscape more often than the base that got rearranged.

On the Eighth's English bases these things were all exactly reversed. They were not located on the worst of land but on the best, for in that corner of England nearest the Continent—which was where the bases were needed—there was no other kind. Nor were they located in uncivilized emptiness, for in this densely populated corner of England there wasn't any. The Eighth's combat groups were all contained in a forty-by-eighty-mile strip that lay north and northeast of London and south and southwest of The Wash and extended from Northampton eastward to the sea, and this area of England was the seat of a civilization whose age was hard for the American mind to grasp. If your home was in St. Augustine, Florida, which was the United States' oldest settlement, you came from a place less than four hundred years removed from primeval wilderness. If you happened to be from western South Dakota, which was the most recently settled part of the States, your home area was but seventy years removed from wilderness. Upon arriving in England, however, you suddenly found yourself in a gentle, age-mellowed, long-tamed land where structures younger than five hundred years were referred

The trumpet sounds retreat, the day is ours. Come, brother, let us to the highest of the field, to see what friends are living, who are dead.

(from *Henry IV, Part One*, by William Shakespeare)

top left: The control tower at Bovingdon. *left:* The late summer sky of Northhamptonshire from a window in the Deenethorpe tower. *overleaf:* one of the remaining runways at the 487th bomb group's field near Lavenham.

ATTLEBRIDGE
SCHEDULE OF BUILDINGS

1 Blister Hangar
2 G.P. Hut
3 Latrine
4-5 Latrine A/Ms
6-11 Barrack Huts
12 Latrine A/Ms
13 M & E Plinth
14 Hangar
15 Link Trainer
16 Do Do
17 Latrine Tech. RAF
18 R.U. Pyro Store
19 Office and Store
20 Latrine Tech.
21 Squadron and Flight Office
22 Armory Maintenance and Maintenance Unit
23-24 Do Squadron
25 Free Gunnery Teacher
26 Fuel Compound
27 Maintenance Staff Block
28 Maintenance Office & W/T
29 Latrine Tech.
30 Store
31 Fire Party Hut
32 Guard House & Extension
33 Picket Post
34 MT Shed USAAF
35 M & E Plinth
36 Gas Respirator Store
37 Main Stores
38 Do Do USAAF
39 Technical Latrine RAF
40 Do Do WAAF
41-48 Main Workshops
49 Dinghy Store
50 Parachute Store
51 MT Sheds
52 MT Office
53 Bulk Petrol Installation
54-55 AMWD
56-62 Do
63 Static Water Tank
64 Latrine Technical
65 Gas Defense Center
66 Fire Tender House
67 Speech Broadcasting Bldg
68 Petrol Installation MT
69 Do Compound Do
70 Lubricant & Inflam. Store
71 Bulk Petrol Installation-Aviation
72 Photographic Block
73 Latrine Technical
74 Crew Locker & Drying Room
75 Armory
76 Sleeve Streamer Mast
77 Control Tower
78 Fire Tender Shelter

79 Floodlight Trailer & Tractor Shed
80 NFE Store
81 Petrol Installation-Aviation
82 Squadron Offices
83 Latrine Officer's Defense Unit
84 Officers' Quarters
85-88 Barrack Huts
89-90 Latrines
91 Crew Locker & Drying Room
92-93 Flight Offices
94 Do Do
95 A.M. Bombing Teacher
96 R.U. Pyro Store
97 Gas Chamber
98 Sub-Station
99 Do Do—Main
100 Radar Workshop
101 G.P. Hut
102 Latrine
103 Do
104-105 Barrack Huts
106 G.P. Hut
107 Latrine
108 Barrack Hut
109 Latrine
110 G.P. Hut
111-112 M & E Plinth
113 Shooting-In Butt
114 Latrine
115-116 G.P. Huts
117 Latrine
118-119 Barrack Huts
120 Latrine
121 Latrine
122 G.P. Hut
123-124 M & E Plinth
125-126 Barrack Huts
127-128 Do Do
129 Maintenance Unit Armory
130 Squadron Armory
130a Maintenance Unit Armory
131 Dump
132 Latrines—RAF
133 Hangar
133a Maintenance Unit
134 Latrine—WAAF
135 Maintenance Staff Block
136 Bulk Petrol-Aviation
137 Picket Post
138 M & E Plinth
139-140 G.P. Hut
141-142 Latrines
143 G.P. Hut
144 M & E Plinth
145-147 Barrack Huts
148 Latrine
149-150 Barrack Huts
151 Latrine
152-153 Barrack Huts
154 G.P. Hut
155 Latrine
156 Picket Post

157 M & E Plinth
158-160 Barrack Huts
161-162 Latrine
163-164 G.P. Hut
165 M & E Plinth
166 G.P. Hut
167 Latrine
168-169 Barrack Huts
170 MT Shed
171 G.P. Hut
172 Latrine
173 Battle Headquarters
174 Pump House
175 M & E Plinth
176 Beam Approach-Main Beacon
177 Do Do Inner Marker
178-186

Administrative Site
187 Picket Post
188 Bomb Sight Store & Special D.C. Test Facilities
189-189a Station Offices
190 Latrine WAAF
191 Do RAF Officers & O.R.s
192 Operations Block
193 Office Annex
194 Crew Briefing Room
195-199

Bomb Store Site
200-202 Bomb Stores
203-204 Fused & Spare Bomb Stores
205 Components Store
206 Do Ex S.A.A. Store
207-208 Fusing Point Bldg Ultra Heavy
209 Do Heavy Light
210 Sea Marker & Flame Float Store
211-213 S.A.A. Store
214-215 Fusing Points
216 Incendiary & Pyro Store

The layout of a typical Eighth Air Force bomber station. This one is Attlebridge, home of the 466th Bomb Group (H)

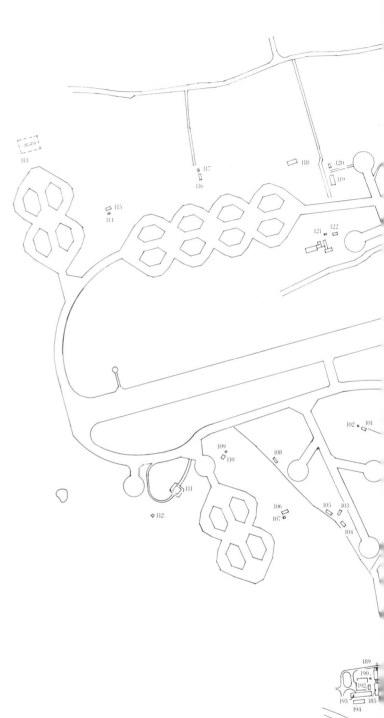

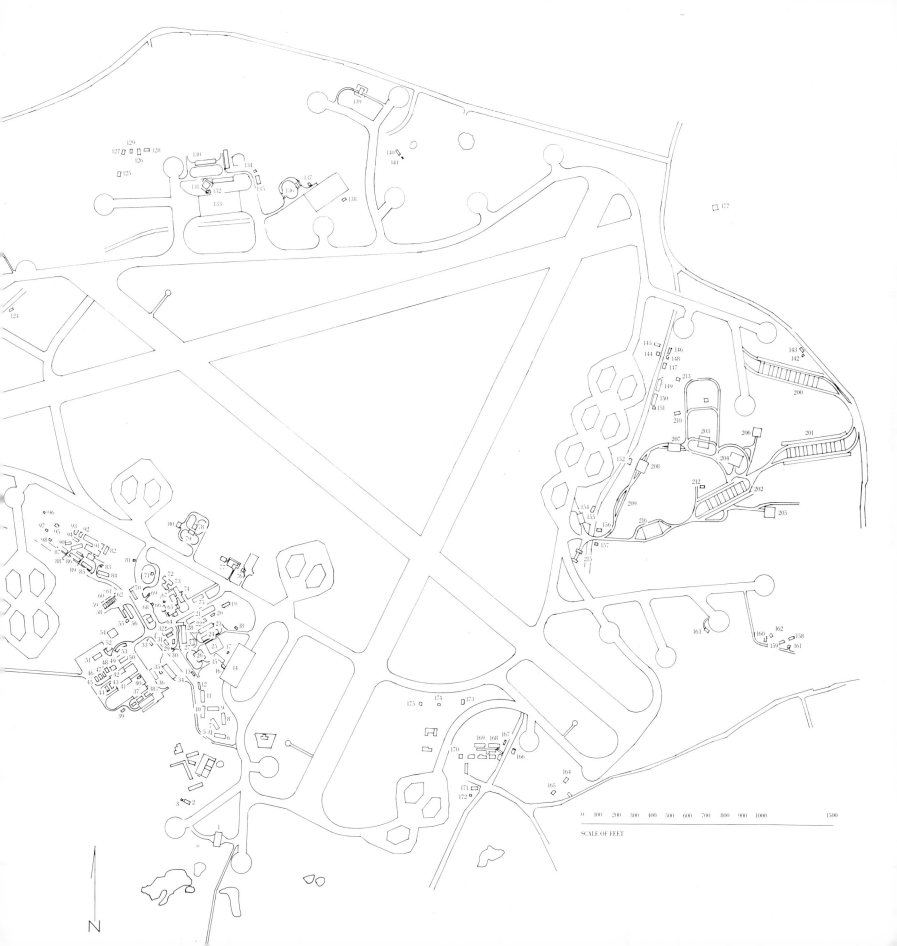

SCALE OF FEET

0   100   200   300   400   500   600   700   800   900   1000   1500

N

far right: A training site at Deenethorpe; *below:* Rackheath, home of Sir Edward Stracey during the war, as it appeared in the summer of 1982. Most of Sir Edward's estate was occupied by the 467th Bomb Group (H).

to as "new." The landscape bristled with towers of churches and cathedrals that had seen more than thirty generations of worshipers come and go. Some of the towns you visited and roads you traveled had been established by Roman colonists before the start of the Christian era. And for young men who had grown up in a young land that was still sharp-edged and raw with youth, and where the "new" was valued far above the "old," these things took some getting used to.

But the most striking feature of these English air stations was the seeming irrationality of their design. They did not sit upon the land neatly, as American bases did. They sprawled upon it, were entangled in its features, and some of their parts were entirely disconnected from the rest. A typical example was Thorpe Abbotts, home of the "Bloody Hundredth" Bomb Group. The largest area at Thorpe Abbotts—the main base area—was shaped like an old-fashioned powder flask with badly dented edges, and contained the runways, tower, firehouses, two hangars, and a few other flight-related buildings. Off to one side of the main base area but connected to it were two smaller areas, one of which was occupied by (among other things) the Operations Block, base offices, a mess hall, and the briefing rooms, and the other was where the bombs were stored. Scattered about in the countryside between and beyond these two areas, and connected to the main base only by narrow roads and country lanes, were ten still smaller areas called "dispersed sites." Seven of these were occupied by clusters of the Nissen huts that served as barracks, one by the hospital and morgue, another by mess halls, and one by the

sewage disposal plant.

When seen on a map, Thorpe Abbotts appeared to make no sense. It looked dismembered and haphazard, and in shape was so ragged that the boundary fence around the main base area alone contained sixty-six angular corners and another six that were curves.

As might be expected, however, these bases were not laid out mindlessly. They were designed as they were for two very good reasons— air raid safety and food production. German raiders from the Continent needed only about a half-hour in the air to reach any of the Eighth's combat bases, and could reach some in as little as fifteen minutes. As it happened, the Germans did not make many serious efforts to bomb these bases, but they could have. And had the barracks and other base facilities been neatly clumped together instead of being scattered as they were, the damage from a bombing raid could have been enormous. As for food production, perhaps 40,000 acres of good English farmland was occupied by the bases of the Eighth Air Force alone—to say nothing of the additional amount occupied by bases of the RAF—and there was no sense in allowing any base to occupy more of it than absolutely necessary. Not in that hungry time of war when all food was scarce and farm products were in such short supply that parks in the cities had been converted into gardens, and vegetables were even being grown at the foot of the Albert Monument next door to Buckingham Palace. Also, there was the future to think of. These bases were temporary, built on land that was to be returned to the plowshare when the need for swords had passed. Accordingly, they were molded into the landscape in

whatever way that would do least damage to present and future farming. The dispersed sites, for example, were placed whenever possible in copses of trees, for this not only would help to conceal them from German raiders but also would keep them from taking up land that otherwise could be farmed. And wherever putting a zigzag in a boundary fence would help preserve a farmer's field or buildings without interfering with the base's purpose, the zigzag was put in.

The effect of this kind of arrangement was recounted by Ray Wild in his description of the base at Podington: "The runways were built right into the farm, and the farmer was still farming it. He'd be there farming when we left on a raid, and he'd still be farming when we came back." And Allan Healy, in his history of the 467th Bomb Group, said of Rackheath: "The air base was completely mingled with farm, field and spinney.... Its plan was far different from that of American bases. There were no serried rows of bleak buildings with grass and trees scraped from the ground and everything barren, efficient, and a scar on the landscape.... [our] Nissen huts were grouped under tall trees at the edges of woods and in and under them. Roads passed under rows of fruit trees. The farm croft and byre were left untouched. One [dispersed] site was far down a rhododendron drive, another across [a] field where sheep and tame deer grazed. You walked through a bluebell carpeted wood ... from Site 1 to the Operations Block, and past straw ricks from there to the Briefing Building. A hedgerow lined the lane of a civilian-traveled road right through the base, where, on Sundays, the children stood and asked, 'Any gum,

chum?'"

That civilian road through the Rackheath base brings up another thing about English bases that took some getting used to. Air Force bases in the States were strictly off-limits to all but those who were stationed there or were there on Air Force business. Base commanders sometimes boasted of keeping security so tight that even the base mice had to show identification cards. But this was not so in England. Lawrence Drew, a pilot with the 384th Bomb Group at Grafton-Underwood, remembers: "It was the estate of some Duke.... He'd come around on a horse to inspect his property. He'd have a couple of other people with him on very fine horses, and they'd all come trotting around right through the high-security areas and everywhere else."

They were unusual bases built to fill the needs of unusual times. Now those bases and times are both long gone and their kind will not be seen again. But to recall a little of the feel and flavor they had then, let us for a moment turn back the clock to the spring of 1944, when the Eighth's operations in England were at their height, and visit, say, the newly activated Rackheath base....

Rackheath is the estate of Sir Edward Stracey, Baronet, and is located some ninety miles northeast of London and perhaps fourteen miles inland from the North Sea shore. It lies on the English coastal plain where Norfolk's fields are spread level and green as the top of a billiard table, and it is one of those timeless, tranquil places that inspire passersby to murmur, "There'll always be an England." Rackheath's gates are much admired by travelers on the

Norwich-Wroxham road for they are of French ironwork custom-made in Paris and are elaborate and lacy, and the gateposts from which they swing are lacy ironwork towers. Behind the gates there is a lawn, smooth and tree-studded and perhaps ten acres in size. It is said that someone once asked an English gardener what was needed for the creation of an English lawn, and this was his reply: Regular mowing, regular fertilizing, and at least 300 years. That is the kind of lawn that Rackheath has, and at the back of it—1,000 yards or so in from the gate—is Sir Edward's house. It is an English country manor; square, flat-roofed, three stories tall, built of squared and finished gray stone blocks. If you removed its columned porticoes, it would look remarkably like a courthouse in some small American town, and it is fully large enough to serve as one. Behind the house there is a grove of towering beech and chestnut trees, and beyond the trees are the lands of the estate—a vast crazy quilt of little pastures and little fields outlined by hedgerows and punctuated here and there by the clumped outbuildings and thatched houses of Rackheath's tenant farmers.

Before the war—until recently in fact—this is where a description of Rackheath might have ended. But not now. Since the twelfth of March the estate has been not only the home of Sir Edward and his farmers but also of the 467th Heavy Bombardment Group, United States Eighth Army Air Force. Now Sir Edward is awakened almost every morning by a heavy rumbling that surges at intervals of less than a minute to a bellowing thunder that rattles his bedroom windows and sets dishes atinkling in their dining room racks, and sounds as if it were coming from his very back yard. And indeed it almost is. It is the sound of heavy bombers taking off one behind the other to make another raid on the Nazi war machine, and their runways lie not far past the trees behind his house.

The airfield looks jarringly out of place, especially when seen from the air. Its three runways lie in a triangle overlapped at the corners. They slash ruler straight through fields and hedgerows and the edges of farmyards, and from the air the runways and the combination road and taxi-strip (called the perimeter track) that encloses them look as absurdly improper against the green countryside as strips of adhesive tape on a green velvet gown.

Just to one side of the runways is a small cluster of buildings. A few are of stuccoed concrete, square-built and homely as cardboard boxes. The others are corrugated metal half-cylinder structures that look like halves of tin cans split lengthwise and are known as Nissen huts. And in this ancient and soft-edged landscape the buildings, too, look jarringly out of place.

These highly visible runways and buildings are the only parts of the Rackheath base that boldly announce themselves to the eye. Its other buildings are scattered in tree-shielded clusters and dispersed sites. They are tucked so unobtrusively into the landscape that neither from the ground nor the air can an observer realize how large the base really is—that it contains more than 400 buildings (mostly Nissen huts, of which 165 serve as barracks), has a population of 3,000 and is, in fact, a small city. And because its bombing missions are flown by day and the planning of them, the crew-briefing preparation,

left: A field defense pillbox at Grafton-Underwood. *above:* Fire Tender Shelter at Bodney. *overleaf:* The control tower at Polebrook (now demolished).

right: One of the original Maycrete huts at Old Buckenham.

the bomber servicing, the fueling and loading, must therefore be done by night, it is a city that never sleeps.

Life on the base is spartan at best, and during cold weather it is downright miserable. The barracks are heated only by little stoves that are, in the words of pilot Keith Newhouse, "little more than a bulge in the stovepipe." Even when the stoves are lit, according to Allan Healy, "the wet North Sea cold" still lies about them "like wolves about a dying doe"—and they are not lit nearly as much as their customers would like. The coal ration is one bucket per stove per day, with the result that at Rackheath, and at all the other bases as well, attempting to steal coal from the closely guarded base stockpile is considered not an adventure but a necessity.

Another problem is mud. When it rains, all unpaved roads, paths, and barracks areas become gooey quagmires, and it rains a lot. Also, the latrines and showers are in Nissen huts separate from the barracks; the mess halls and other such base facilities are, in most cases, at a considerable distance from the housing sites, and especially in cold or muddy weather this inconvenience is the inspiration for a good deal of inventive and colorful language.

Base life does, however, have its compensations. There are recreational facilities and softball diamonds and softball teams. There are monthly dances, to which English girls come by the load in army trucks. And men, when off duty, can get passes to go in to nearby Norwich.

That was Rackheath in 1944, and the Eighth's other English bases were just about the same, except that the few built before the war and inherited by the Eighth from the RAF were

considerably more comfortable. Charles Bosshardt, a navigator with the 458th Bomb Group, recalls: "We were among the lucky ones. We had nice brick two-story barracks with two men to the room. We had steam heat, the latrine was just down the hall and the mess hall was on the first floor. After going to Nuthampstead to see one of my buddies, and finding him living in a crowded Nissen hut with an outside latrine, I was real happy that I had been sent to Horsham St. Faith."

They were not resorts by any means, those English bases, but the men of other American services—the sailor living amid stacks of steel-pipe bunks in a crowded fo'csle, the soldier or marine in a tent or foxhole in the sands of North Africa or a steamy Pacific jungle—would have said they were. The men of the Eighth knew this and even while griping felt fortunate—and, indeed, it was why many of them had chosen the Air Force instead of some other service. In the worst of times base life was more uncomfortable than it was harsh. And in the best of times, when it was neither raining nor cold, again to quote Allan Healy: "On bikes we rode the old lanes to Coltishall, Wroxham, or Horning Ferry, through that beautiful village—Woodbastwick . . . many of us rented boats on Wroxham Broad and sailed dinghies on that pocket handkerchief of a lake, or had parties aboard with the girls we had met. . . . We smelled the perfume of English hedgerows and saw woods blanketed in bluebells. Poppies grew in profusion on the sides of the air raid shelters . . . pheasants crowed near the barracks sites and rabbits came out in late evening around the Operations Block. It was a lovely spot, even to homesick Americans."

IN QUARTERS

On all but a handful of the Eighth's English bases, officers and enlisted men alike lived in scattered clusters of Nissen huts. Nissens came in three sizes, of which the housing Nissens were the smallest—sixteen feet wide, eight feet high at the center, twenty-four or thirty feet long— and when veterans of the Eighth recall those huts now it is seldom with kindness. They were dark, their concrete floors usually were littered with tracked-in mud, and their mingled odors of cigarettes and cigars both past and present, damp woolen clothing, and socks too long unlaundered gave them, said one pilot, "the heady aroma of a goat-barn."

Each hut was heated by one small stove aptly called a "tortoise" by the English. "When cherry red," recalled one veteran, "it would keep you warm if you were within five feet of it, and because a week's coal ration would keep you warm for about one evening, it wasn't cherry red too often."

Accordingly, the barracks heroes were not men who had distinguished themselves in combat, but in pilfering coal from the base's closely guarded stockpile.

In most of the housing clusters the washroom or "ablution centre" was in one place, the latrine was in another, and the showers often as not were not in the housing areas at all, but in the base's various "communal sites." In describing this arrangement to the folks at home, a Rackheath pilot wrote: "Celebrated this warm afternoon by taking my first shower since arriving here. Went down to the cleansing center, which is about four blocks away and contains only showers. The ablution center, with tubs for washing and shaving, is a block away. Our la-

There was a whispering in my hearth, / A sigh of the coal, / Grown wistful of a former earth / It might recall.

(from "Miners," by Wilfred Owen)

left: Keeping the fire going in a Nissen hut coal stove on an Eighth Air Force base.

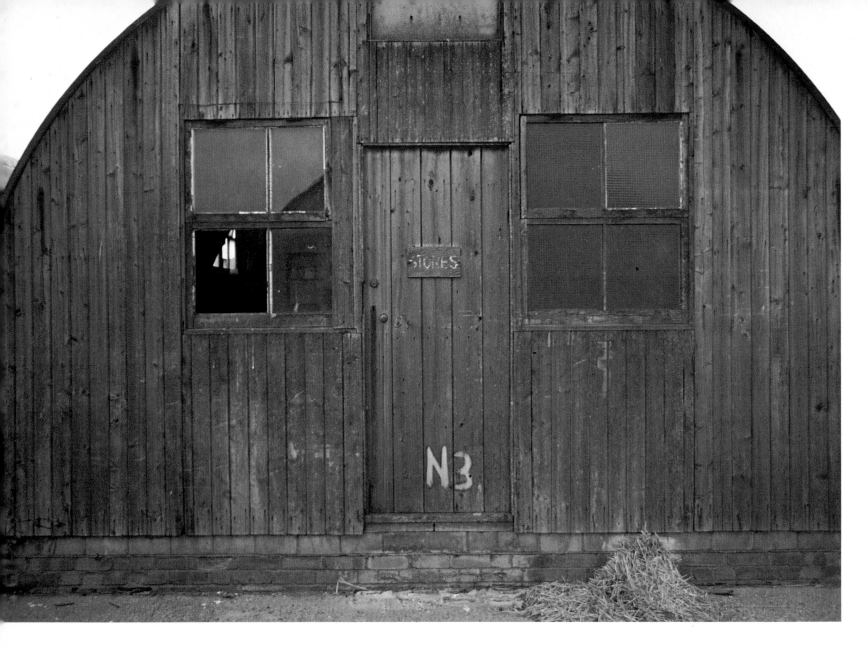

right: Photographed at Podington in 1965, this cat's mother arrived in England during WW2 in a 92nd Bomb Group "Fort." *far right:* A stenciled reminder of the ever-present "blackout" condition on the airfields. This one is at the 390th Bomb Group (H) base.

trine (with running water instead of the usual "honey buckets") is next door. So, a complete toilet is spread over quite an area, and when the cold wind doth blow a shower is easily discouraged."

In most cases, enlisted men's and officers' quarters differed only in that the enlisted men's huts had double-deck bunks (and were therefore more crowded), whereas the officers slept on

above left and above: Nissen huts in a company street of the 384th Bomb Group (H) station at Grafton-Underwood. *left:* Order of Dressing stenciled on the brick wall of a hut at Grafton-Underwood.

53

below: An 8AF officer's living quarters in a Maycrete hut. *right:* "Pin-up" girls warmed the drab interior of this 401st Bomb Group (H) officer's billet at Deenethorpe.

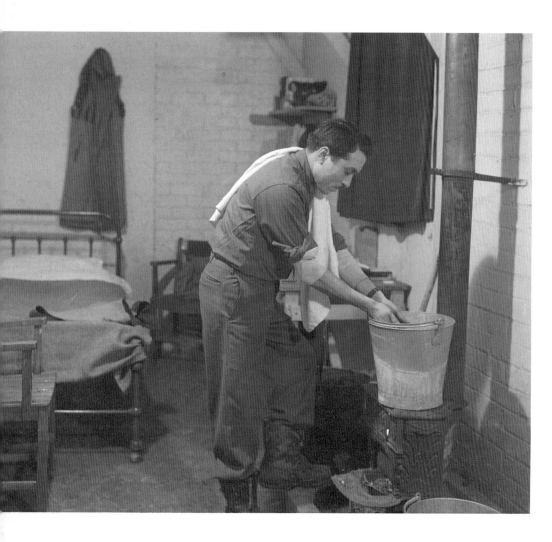

right: 8-ball symbol of the 44th Bomb Group (H) on its headquarters wall at Shipdham. *far right:* A barracks hut on the 34th Bomb Group (H) base at Mendlesham. *center left:* Beth and David Alston whose efforts have made Lavenham the best preserved 8AF base in England today. *center right:* A barracks hut at Molesworth, home of the 303rd Bomb Group (H). *bottom:* Farm equipment is stored in many of the remaining huts on the bases of the Eighth, like this one at Twinwood Farm near Bedford. The plane in which Major Glenn Miller is believed to have disappeared departed from Twinwood on its final flight.

left: GI humor in a Shipdham mural captioned "HEY PAW, TELL ME AGAIN HOW YOU AND THE BOYS WERE SWEATIN IT OUT IN THE E.T.O. BACK IN 42, 43, 44, 45!" *bottom:* Interior of a Maycrete hut at Lavenham. *above:* Peter Rix, owner of the huts at Shipdham which contain a few of the surviving examples of 8AF artwork.

cots. Their cots, however, were a dubious blessing at best: "Narrow, and made up of two frames of angle-iron, they were sheer torture. The frames were about three feet long, and the iron crossbars where they joined would hit you right about the hips. Your mattress was three separate, unforgiving little biscuits stuffed with excelsior, and the middle one would teeter on those crossbars and let in cold air where it was separated from the other two. You tried to arrange your blankets to hold the things together and keep the cold air out, but nobody ever succeeded."

As compared to this, the men at the five or so prewar RAF bases taken over by the Eighth lived in palaces. Bassingbourn, for example, was relatively so luxurious that it was called "the country club." And at Horsham St. Faith, said Charles Bosshardt, officers had brick barracks with steam heat, two-man rooms, and "a latrine just down the hall," and enlisted men lived in "nice two-plex and four-plex structures." However, at these "country club" bases as much as at the spartan ones, the men griped about the food.

The Eighth's menus, like those of the other U.S. forces in World War II, included a good deal of those tinned meats known as Spam (though most were not actually of that brand); chipped beef on toast, known to all the armed forces as something-or-other "on a shingle"; orange marmalade, of which one pilot wrote, "The Eighth must have bought the entire U.S. output"; and powdered eggs. All of these, except the powdered eggs, were good at first and became offensive later only because they had been served so often. Thus, Dave Shelhamer's diary

comment that at Molesworth "the quarters aren't too good but the food is excellent" can be explained by the fact that when he wrote it he had been in England only twenty days and at Molesworth only two.

The powdered eggs were another matter. Leathery, sulphurous, and often stale as well, "they would," said one pilot, "gag a buzzard."

Appearing with great frequency on the Eighth's tables, also, were mutton and Brussels sprouts. And because even at home these had been less than popular with America's young, when served up by army cooks they were even more unpopular. Said one sergeant: "I never cared for mutton, and we had a whole lot of it. First they'd serve it as chops, then a couple days later it'd come back at you as stew, and by the time it got to be stew you could smell it a quarter-mile away."

As for Brussels sprouts, "At Seething we had a lot of 'em and I like 'em," recalled Sam Burchell. "So the other guys were always saying I was the only red-blooded American boy they knew of who'd have anything to do with a Brussels sprout."

Still, despite their griping about their living quarters and their food, in comparison to the army "dogfaces" in their muddy foxholes and the marine "grunts" in their steaming jungles, the men of the Eighth lived well and they knew it. As Bert Stiles summed it up in his *Serenade to the Big Bird*: "Most people in the army could not boil eggs on an electric heater any time of night, nor lie on the sack and look at [a picture of] Chili Williams who was right where [roommate] Sam could pat her. We were lucky to live in such a place."

above: Made of
corrugated iron roofs with
brick and stucco
endwalls, many of the
remaining Nissens at
Podington are used as
workshops for the
construction of racing
cars. *below:* The design
of this door is common to
nearly all of the Nissens
used by the Eighth. *right:*
Late-summer twilight
at Twinwood Farm,
Bedfordshire.

60

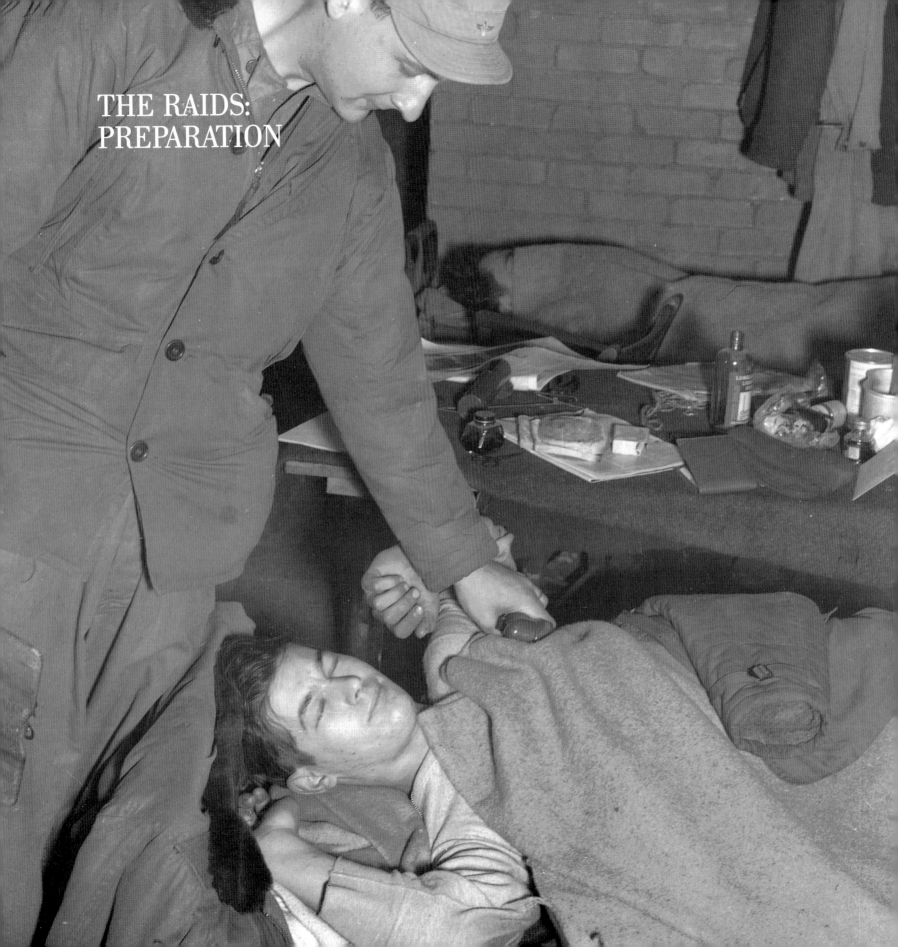

THE RAIDS:
PREPARATION

"Sitting on the edge of the bed, yawning and shivering, a man thinks, 'Here we go again,' and tries to convince himself that all those aches and stomach flutters are only in his mind. But he still can't help wondering why the hell he didn't take a job that would keep him on the ground." But, fortunately, there was little time for cogitation because, as pilot Lawrence Drew of the 384th Bomb Group at Grafton-Underwood has pointed out: "They just didn't tolerate you being late for briefing, so you'd get your clothes on real quick. . . . You had to take time to shave, though, because you wore your oxygen mask real tight against your face, and the mixture of breath condensation and gunsmoke would irritate your face badly enough even if you had shaved."

But even though for the flight crews this was when the preparation for a raid began, the overall preparation for it had been started several days earlier in a beautiful old mansion-like building standing among great green lawns in High Wycombe, near London. Code named "Pinetree," this was now the Eighth's General Headquarters. Until recently, however, it had been a girls' boarding school and in its bedrooms, to the amusement of their present military occupants, were bell-buttons labeled "Ring for mistress." And it was at "Pinetree" that the Eighth's high command, working from a priority list supplied by Supreme Allied Headquarters in London, had selected the target for today's raid. Once that was done, the various Headquarters sections—Personnel, Intelligence, Operations and Planning, and Supply—had begun weaving together the myriad threads of detail essential to the tapestry of a successful mission. This required them to provide answers to such questions as: How many bombers should be used on this target, what fighter protection should they be given, and by which Groups should the bombers and fighters be furnished? What kind of bombs should be used—high explosive, fragmentation, incendiary, or some combination of these? Should the bombers be sent to the target by the shortest route, which would give them the shortest time of exposure to enemy resistance, and by requiring less gasoline would also allow them to carry a heavier "payload" of bombs? Or should they be sent by a more circuitous route that, although longer, would keep them away from some of the heavier concentrations of enemy flak and fighters? Do the chosen Groups have enough bombs and fuel on hand, or must they be resupplied? What do the latest spy and European underground reports show to be the best methods to be used by airmen downed over the Continent when attempting to avoid capture and to make their way back to England?

Once the various Headquarters sections had answered these and a number of other similar questions, the mission was planned and orders for it were drawn up. But execution of those orders now rested upon a matter which Headquarters could neither plan nor control—the capricious European weather. The mission required a day when England's morning weather would be clear enough to permit the bombers to take off and to assemble in formation, and its afternoon weather clear enough to permit them to return and land. It also required a day when over the Continent the bombers could fly clear of clouds at eighteen thousand feet or higher be-

Up, lad, up, 'tis late for lying: / Hear the drums of morning play; / Hark, the empty highways crying / 'Who'll beyond the hills away?' / Clay lies still, but blood's a rover; / Breath's a ware that will not keep / Up, lad: when the journey's over / There'll be time enough to sleep.

(from "Reveille," by A. E. Housman)

left: The CQ's ritual awakening of this 303rd Bomb Group air crewman who is scheduled to participate in his group's mission on this morning of 9 December 1944.

cause at lower levels the German flak would be truly murderous, and attempting to fly in formation while in the clouds and "blind" would be even more murderous. Finally, it required a day when clouds over the target would be broken enough to permit visual bombing. So, once the mission was planned and organized, the decision to execute it rested with the Weather Officer—who more often than not was known as "Stormy"—and his job was not an easy one. Western Europe and eastern England, where on the average there was rainfall on fourteen days of every month, had some of the world's most unpredictable weather and the best of forecasts was usually no more than an educated guess. Accordingly, the decision to execute a mission was not made until the evening before it was to be flown. Then, teletypes began to chatter, passing the orders and corollary information down from Headquarters to the affected Divisions, Wings, and Groups.

When the Group commanders received the orders, they immediately listed and alerted those crews scheduled to go on the raid. "They usually did this by squadrons," recalled navigator Frank Nelson. "Before going to bed we'd check at Operations to see if a mission was on, and if our squadron was listed for it."

And Lawrence Drew recalls that: "In the officers' club at Grafton-Underwood we had three lights—red, amber, and green. They were behind the bar and vertical, just like a traffic light. When the bar opened at five or six in the afternoon the light would be on amber. If it later went to green it meant the group was "stood down" and there'd be no mission. Then we usually had a party of some kind and the bar would

64

stay open as long as there were customers. But if the light went to red it meant we were gonna have a mission the next day, so they would close the bar at eight o'clock and everybody who was scheduled to fly would try to get some sleep."

While the crews alerted for the mission were sleeping, or trying to, most of the other base personnel were not. Throughout the night lights burned behind the blackout curtains of the Operations building, where the various section officers and their staffs were assembling and organizing information to be given to the combat crews in premission briefing, were typing and mimeographing "flimsy" sheets of specialized information to be given to pilots, navigators, and radio operators, and were seeing to the thousand-and-one other details involved in getting the Group's aircraft aloft on time and in an organized manner.

On the airfield, meanwhile, trucks with blackout-dimmed headlights could be seen moving along the perimeter track like so many fireflies, delivering bombs and fuel to the fifteen to thirty-six or so aircraft scheduled for the mission. As Sam Burchell, an ordnance man in the 448th Bomb Group at Seething, remembers it: "We Ordnance crews would go out to our particular planes, where they would tell what kind of bombs were to be loaded; fragmentation or five-hundred pounders or whatever. The loading took from, say, eleven at night until four or five in the morning. It was usually freezing cold, but because of putting shackles on the bombs and doing other delicate work we couldn't wear gloves." Glenn R. Matson, a combat gunner in the 458th Bomb Group at Horsham St. Faith, has written of the men in Burchell's line of work:

"Those Ordnance guys were something else. They worked their tails off under the most miserable conditions, yet seemed to take delight in their labors. . . . It is my opinion their job was more dangerous than flying combat. For instance, there was the time when [due to poor visibility from blackout headlights] a bomb-hauling truck with about ten guys on it catapulted over an antiaircraft pit while going about forty miles an hour. When it came to earth on the other side the only person still on it was the driver." And Burchell had reason to agree that bomb-handling was a dangerous business: "The truck drivers unloaded their bombs by backing up real fast and then slamming on their brakes. That would make all the bombs roll off the truck at once, but in the ordinary course of events this caused no problems because the bombs before they were fused were perfectly safe. But then one day a truck driver unloaded that way without knowing he was hauling a new type of bomb that went off on impact without a fuse. He blew up quite a bit of the base, and himself with it.

"There was an outside lavatory not too far from where that happened, and the top sergeant was in it sitting on the pot when those bombs went off. Well, the explosion blew down all four walls of that lavatory, but left the sergeant still sitting there on the pot in the middle of the field."

While the Ordnance crews were loading bombs, men from the Armament section, wrote Allan Healey, "were working at the planes, placing fifty caliber links of cartridges aboard and checking gun turrets and bomb sights."

"All through the night," Healey continued, "crew chiefs and their crews worked on the

left: Wycombe Abbey, a girl's school that was commandeered by the Eighth Air Force to be its headquarters in England. Located at High Wycombe, the facility has reverted to its former role. *above:* Major General James H. Doolittle who commanded the Eighth from 6 January 1944 to 9 May 1945, with Brigadier General Robert B. Williams during their visit to the 379th Bomb Group (H) at Kimbolton, March 1944.

planes, repairing and tuning engines, patching flak holes, readying the ships for their long mission." And Will Lundy, a member of such a crew in the 44th Bomb Group at Shipdham, remembers: "[walking] around the hangars, eastward along the perimeter track, then around the bend and across the end of the main runway . . . and finally there she is, *Miss Diane*, in a cul-de-sac back by the fence. [Then] it's up through the rear hatch, forward and open the bomb-bay doors . . . then up on the wing to remove the canvas [engine] covers. Have to do a balancing act here to keep from sliding off that high, frosty wing.

"George Baccash, Crew Chief, climbs into the pilot's seat and I follow him into the co-pilot's seat while Stoddard and Bailey are 'pulling through' the propellers. . . . Stoddard [then] starts the APU [Auxiliary Power Unit], a gas driven generator that provides auxiliary power for lights, instruments, starting engines, etc.

"No matter how many times I experience the starting and run-up of those engines, the feel of all that harnessed horsepower gives me a tremendous thrill. But when all four engines have passed their instrument checks we quickly shut them down to conserve that precious 100 octane fuel.

"When our immediate jobs are done, the waiting begins. There is still feverish activity all over the airfield, however, as other pre-flight checks are progressing, minor repairs are being completed, bombs loaded, etc. The sounds are there but nothing is visible except an occasional flash of light where someone becomes careless with his flashlight.

"Time drags on . . . no place to go to escape the bone-chilling dampness . . . each in his own way tries to keep warm by slapping his hands, jogging in place on the hardstand, etc., but still shivering. Finally, with the arrival of dawn come the . . . jeeps and trucks bringing the combat crews, and the discomforts of the night are forgotten. Now it's the business of getting the mission under way."

The combat crews, after they had dressed and shaved, were taken by truck from their quarters to the mess halls, where, on mission mornings, they were able (at least in theory) to enjoy fresh eggs instead of the usual powdered ones. "At Bury St. Edmunds," recalls Sidney Rapaport, "the food on mission mornings was absolutely marvelous. Fresh eggs, ham, corned beef hash—you name it and we had it." At Grafton-Underwood, said Lawrence Drew: "We ordinarily had 'square eggs'—powdered eggs made in a large GI pan and then cut into squares, and with a little cheese added so we could tolerate them. But on mission mornings we got 'combat eggs,' fresh and very delicious." But at Rackheath, according to Keith Newhouse, things were different. "They talk a lot about the crews getting fresh eggs on mission mornings, but we, at least, didn't get them all that often. More often than not we got scrambled powdered eggs. We had toast, too, and a lot of coffee in heavy white mugs." And when speaking of those breakfasts in a 1944 letter, Newhouse said: "A lot of the guys stumble around, still trying to wake up. Others are over-animated and talk a lot. Some can eat heartily while others have butterflies in the stomach and can't eat at all. The air is heavy with cigarette smoke. . . .

"Then, with chow finished, we again pile into trucks and go to briefing."

Since all the secrets of the day's mission were brought to the briefing room, it was well guarded and all who entered had first to be cleared by white-legginged MPs who stood at the door. Even so, there was cynicism among the crews as to how well those secrets were kept. Pilot Bob Mallick of the 453rd Bomb Group at Old Buckenham recalls that: "We sat there and squirmed around on those rock-hard benches ... waiting for the moment when the curtain would be drawn back from the mission board to show the secret route and mission that the Krauts had been busily preparing for the whole damned night."

Most Eighth veterans remember the briefing room as a place of odors. There was the smell of shaving lotion, hair oil, and sweat. "We had on heavy boots, heavy pants, heavy jackets—and when we opened these jackets up there was body smell." And, of course, the air was heavy with cigarette smoke. "We put up a haze in that room that rivaled a Pittsburgh smog. . . ."

The briefing room, unlike a church or classroom, always filled from front to back: "When you went in you'd always go toward the front where the maps were. Everybody wanted to be down forward, as close as possible to what was going on." "The wall map was covered with a white sheet," said Bert Stiles in *Serenade to the Big Bird*: "The course was all drawn out up there with a piece of yard ... but we couldn't see it.

"Every guy coming in checked the position of the yarn pulley at the left side of the map. If

Raid preparations include *(left)* making pancakes at Bassingbourn, *left below:* bombs to be loaded, *below:* crew briefing, *below right:* synchronizing watches and the "time hack."

above: A maintenance hut at Podington.
right: A mess hall at Framlingham. *center right:* Shipdham humor discovered in a mess hall.
far right: The entrance of a Horham mess hall at the 95th Bomb Group (H) airfield. *far right above:* Offices in a J-type hangar on the 305th Bomb Group (H) station at Chelveston.

PUB
Ye Silent Woman

NO UNAUTHORISED PERSONS ALLOWED IN THIS SECTION

REGULAR MEAL HOURS
BREAKFAST 6:45 TO 7:45
DINNER   11:15 TO 1300
SUPPER   1715 TO 1845

By Order Mess Officer

the pulley was near the top and the yarn was all used, everyone got set for Berlin or Posen or Munich and a long rugged time of it. But if the pulley was way down, we were probably going to Cherbourg or Calais, and we'd be home in time for early chow." While waiting for briefing to begin, said Bob Mallick, "We shuffled our feet, coughed up phlegm, threw butts on the floor, and groused...."

At precisely the scheduled minute, the commanding officer would enter the room. The first man to see him would call, "Tenn-hut!" Then all would rise and remain standing until he had reached the front of the hut and said, "Be seated, gentlemen." Then came the dramatic moment when the CO nodded to his S-2 (Intelligence) officer, who, in turn, withdrew the curtain from the mission map. If the mission thus revealed happened to be a long one, there would be hoots, jeers, and catcalls, and someone (quoting a well-known civilian gasoline conservation slogan) was sure to call out, "Is this trip really necessary?!" But underneath the catcalls and nervous badinage, there was fear that clutched like a cold hand at one's vitals. "You'd think, 'Oh boy! I'm not going to go on this one. This one will kill me!' " remembers Ray Wild, "But you'd go anyhow. Pride made you go."

Once the mission map had been unveiled, the briefing proceeded with well-organized, clinical detachment. As Allan Healey described it: "By map, picture, and diagram the whole operation was explained. S-2 put on the route, target, and expected reaction from flak and fighters; S-3 (Operations and Planning) gave the operational data; Weather told of conditions to and from the target ... all cut and dried; an opera-

tion of death told like a commuter's timetable." And because the operation did indeed run on a timetable, the last act of the briefing was the synchronization of watches, or "time-tick." "The CO would say something like, 'Gentlemen, it is now three-forty-five minus twenty seconds ... ten seconds, nine ... two, one, Hack!' When he announced the time, you set your watch to the time it was going to be when he called 'hack!' Then when he called 'hack' you started the watch again."

Before or immediately after this main briefing many crew members would pause for a moment of conversation or prayer with the Group chaplains. "Chaplain Duhl and Father Sharbaugh were always at the [Rackheath] briefings," wrote Allan Healey, "and the crews had the opportunity, which many took, to have a word with their Chaplain and the comfort of prayer."

After the main briefing navigators went to a special navigation briefing, bombardiers and radio operators lined up to receive "flimsy" sheets of information pertinent to their particular duties, and copilots lined up to receive for their crews the "escape kits" provided for use by airmen downed over enemy-occupied territory. The sergeant gunners, meanwhile, had gone on ahead—first to the flight-line locker rooms to dress for the frigid air at high altitude, and to pick up their parachutes, flak suits, etc.; and from there to the armament shop where, said 493rd Bomb Group gunner Paul Sink, "... you'd pick up your guns, then go out to your particular airplane. Then you'd get your guns ready and mount them in their receivers in the airplane ... get everything ready." Bert Stiles,

62 FI SQ	PLATFORM	338 FI SQ	ACORN	360 FI SQ VORTEX
63 FI SQ	DAILY	343 FI SQ	TUDOR	361 FI SQ CHINWAG
56 B FI GP	SUBWAY	55 B FI GP	GRAPHIC	356 B FI GP NOTEBOOK
61 B FI SQ	HOUSEHOLD	38 B FI SQ	PROGRAM	359 B FI SQ BUCKET
62 B FI SQ	ICEJUG	338 B FI SQ	RICHARD	360 B FI SQ DEANSGATE
63 B FI SQ	YORKER	343 B FI SQ	SAUCY	361 B FI SQ WEBBER
56 C	PANTILE	55 C	KODAK	356 C SEAWEED

STEEPLE MORDEN-TWOROOM

355 FI GP	UNCLE	P51
354 FI SQ	FALCON	
357 FI SQ	CUSTARD	
358 FI SQ	BENTLY	
355 B FI GP	HORNPIPE	
354 B FI SQ	CHIEFTAIN	
357 B FI SQ	MOSES	
358 B FI SQ	BEEHIVE	
355 C	BORAX	

FOWLMERE-GASPUMP

339 FI GP	ARMSTRONG	P51
503 FI SQ	BEEFSTEAK	
504 FI SQ	COCKSHY	
505 FI SQ	UPPER	
339 B FI GP	STUDENT	
503 B FI SQ	UNIQUE	
504 B FI SQ	GLUEPOT	
505 B FI SQ	SLAPJACK	
339 C	PRETEND	

BODNEY-BEACHHOUSE

352 FI GP	PACKLOAD	P51
328 FI SQ	SCREWCAP	
486 FI SQ	ANGUS	
487 FI SQ	TRANSPORT	
352 B FI GP	BEARSKIN	
328 B FI SQ	TARMAC	
486 B FI SQ	ROCKET	
487 B FI SQ	VICAR	
352 C	CLOISTER	

T. WALDEN-DARKFOLD

361 FI GP	GLOWBRIGHT	P51
374 FI SQ	AMBROSE	
375 FI SQ	DECOY	
376 FI SQ	YORKSHIRE	
361 B FI GP	FILLY	
374 B FI SQ	RIPPER	
375 B FI SQ	DISHCLOTH	
376 B FI SQ	SKYBLUE	
361 C	MAGPIE	

RAYDON-COCKLE

353 FI GP	JONAH	P47
350 FI SQ	SELDOM	
351 FI SQ	LAWYER	
352 FI SQ	JOCKEY	
353 B FI GP	KEYLOCK	
350 B FI SQ	PERSIAN	
351 B FI SQ	SQUIRREL	
352 B FI SQ	BULLRING	
353 C	MUFFIN	

EAST WRETHAM-WOODBROOK

359 FI GP	CHAIRMAN	P51
368 FI SQ	JIGGER	
369 FI SQ	TINPLATE	
370 FI SQ	RED CROSS	
359 B FI GP	CAVETOP	
368 B FI SQ	HANDY	
369 B FI SQ	EARNEST	
370 B FI SQ	ROLLO	
359 C	RAGTIME	

WATTISHAM-HEATER

479 FI GP	HIGHWAY →	P51
434 FI SQ	NEWCROSS	
435 FI SQ	LAKESIDE	
436 FI SQ	BISON	
479 B FI GP	SNOWHITE	
434 B FI SQ	REFLEX	
435 B FI SQ	HADDOCK	
436 B FI SQ	SPRINGBOX	
479 C	FLAREUP	

LEISTON-EARLDUKE

357 FI GP	DRYDEN	P51
362 FI SQ	DOLLAR	
363 FI SQ	CEMENT	
364 FI SQ	GREENHOUSE	
357 B FI GP	SILAS	
362 B FI SQ	ROWNTREE	
363 B FI SQ	DIVER	
364 B FI SQ	HAWKEYE	
357 C	EYESIGHT	

HONINGTON-OUTSHINE

364 FI GP	SUNHAT	P51
383 FI SQ	ESCORT	
384 FI SQ	GOLDFISH	
385 FI SQ	EGGFLIP	
364 B FI GP	WEEKDAY	
383 B FI SQ	TANTRUM	
384 B FI SQ	ZEETA	
385 B FI SQ	PILLOW	
364 C	HARLOP	

SCOUT FORCE

2ND DIV. BOOTLEG......S'MORDEN
3RD DIV. KODAK......W'FORD
1ST DIV. CAVALRY-BASSINGBORNE BUCKEYE.....H'GTON

	DEST.	PROB.	DAM.	
4 GP	984	44	445	1473
56 GP	1003½	65	689½	1758
355 GP	855	24	577	1456
361 GP	328	10	137	475
479 GP	437	10	197	644
65TH W. TOT.	3605½	153	2045½	5806
78 GP	688½	28	451	1167½
55 GP	578	24	234	836
339 GP	692	17	319	1028½
353 GP	722	40	356½	1118½
357 GP	690½	24	175	889½
66TH W. TOT.	3371	133	1535½	5039½
20 GP	416	12	207	635
356 GP	271	22	185	478
352 GP	755½	29	260	1044½
359 GP	356	23	180	559
364 GP	462½	26	275	763½
67TH W. TOT.	2261	112	1107	3480
8AF. TOT.	9237½	398	4688	14325½

AIRDROME	ST	AMT	CEL	VIS	REMARKS
4 DEBDEN	○	8	9?	7M	
56 BOXTED	○	5	08	8M	
355 S'MORDEN	○	5	15	10M	
361 L'WALDEN	○	5	08	8M	
479 W'SHAM	○	6	20	6M	
55 W'FORD	○	9	18	7M	
78 DUXFORD	○	3	15	10M	
339 F'MERE	○	5	35	15M	0900
353 RAYDON	○	8	17	6M	H
357 LEISTON	○	5	10	10M	
20 K'CLIFFE	○	9	15	10M	
352 BODNEY	○	8	20	8M	H
356 M'SHAM	○	3	1.0	5M	
359 E'W'HAM		5	12	6M	
364 H'GTON		8/6		10M	
WOODBRIDGE					
MANSTON					
ASR H'WORTH					

ONLY LOW CLOUD WELL BROKEN

SOLID TO 20,000

LET-DOWN WILL BE O.K. OVER CHANNEL. ONLY LOW CLOUD PRESENT, AND THIS IS WELL-BROKEN. VIS GOOD 0900

right: Tailfin units are fitted to these bombs prior to loading aboard this B-17G at its hardstand. Ground crew personnel attend to routine premission maintenance at this dispersal on an 8AF field in the Midlands. *overleaf:* The interior of a B-17 of the 381st Bomb Group, looking forward toward the bomb bay, from the waist gunners' crew station. Clearly detailed are the airplane's control cables, .50 caliber machine guns with linked ammunition belts and the ball-turret housing structure.

in his book, recalled that when the rest of the crews then went to their lockers, "The equipment hut was a mess, with everyone trying to dress in the same place at the same time. I decided to wear an electric suit because I hate long johns. I put my OD's on over that, a summer flying suit over that, and a leather jacket on top. A Mae West comes last. I was sweating before I got into all my clothes, and by the time I had heaved my flak suit and parachute onto the truck I could feel sweat rolling down my knees." Keith Newhouse—who never wore the electrically heated blue "monkey suit" because, "When I sweated I'd short the damn thing out"—recounted the "razzing and corny jokes" in the locker-rooms in a 1944 letter to his wife: "Fellows greet each other with, 'Joe, which do you get when those ME 109s come at you—constipation or dysentery?'

'Boy! That Focke-Wulf puckered me up for a week with that pass he made at us yesterday.'

'If we get too near Paris it'll be *goodby crew* cause we'll all bail out and go after those French chicks! Ooh, la la—ze Frrrench!'

'If we get thick flak I'm gonna put my tin helmet on the seat and then crawl under it.'

'I'm gonna quit this damned flyin' an' become a mess officer, by God!'

When all members of the crew had arrived at their particular airplane and had then run all their preflight checklists, they usually faced a tedious time of waiting. The preflight checking made for "a kind of busy time," recalled Lawrence Drew, but once it was done, "You'd get into the airplane and just sit. Many a time we sat as long as an hour and a half, ready to go but waiting on clearance from the weather man. . . .

"If then they decided to scrub the mission they'd fire red flares from the Operations building. Wouldn't use the radio, just flares. But if they fired a green flare, that told you to start engines and be ready to taxi out."

Upon seeing the green flare, pilots and copilots began together to run through yet another of the checklist liturgies peculiar to their particular priesthood. This one began with, "Alarm bell" . . . "*Checked,*" included such things as "Master switches" . . . "*On*" and "Carburetor filters" . . . "*Open*" and, a dozen items later, concluded with "Energize . . . Mesh!" Whereupon on hardstands all around the field dozens of airplane propellers twitched, turned, then spun as the engines driving them coughed, snorted blue smoke, then caught and settled down to a combined roar that seemed to shake the very air. Then the great ships crept, one by one, from their hardstands onto the perimeter track surrounding the runways. "You had a [flimsy sheet] telling you which plane to follow, so you waited for him to come by, then taxied out to follow him."

When your turn came to take off, said Ray Wild, "you lined up so that one guy would take off from this side of the runway, and the next guy from the other side. That way you had a better chance of avoiding each others' prop wash."

Then, as Keith Newhouse wrote to his wife: "Airspeed builds up until the pilot shouts 'Wheels up!' and the mission is really on. Invariably there is a tussle with propwash and some nervous moments until some altitude and airspeed are gained. Then the whole crew silently sighs and settles down . . . to getting the job done and over with."

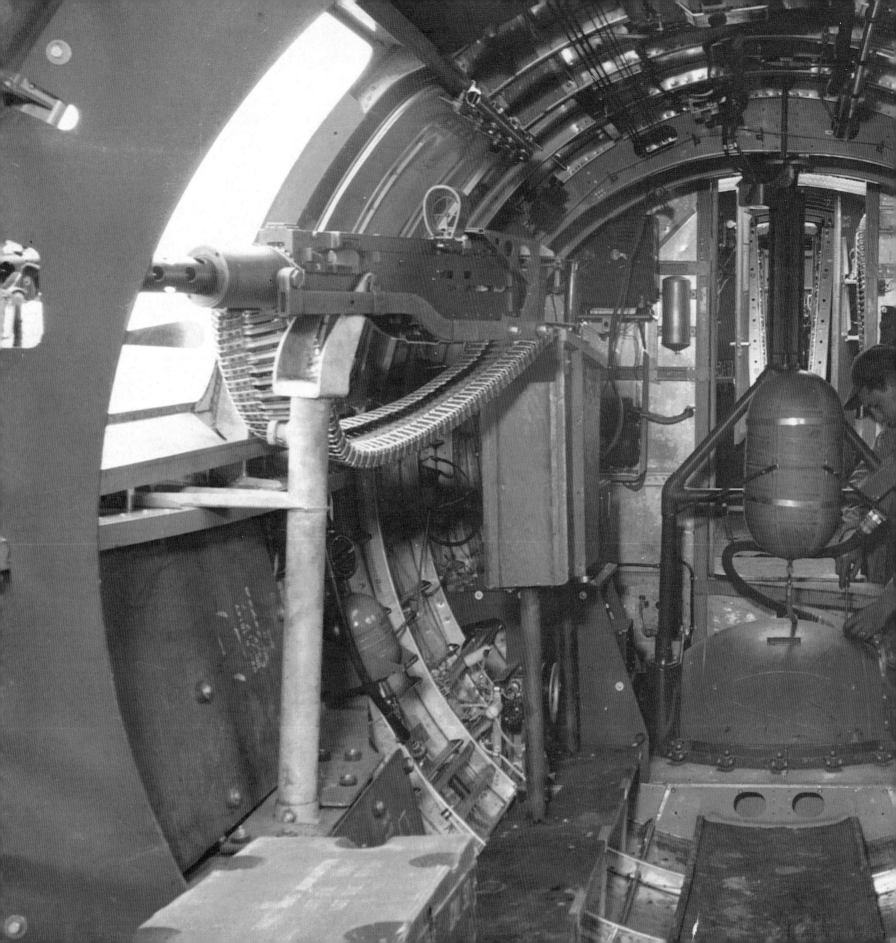

"On the evening of 12 May, 1943," wrote an English girl whose family's farm was partially occupied by a newly built air base at Framlingham, "we saw a truck with a white star on it come down our road, followed by another and another. . . . We were very excited; they just kept coming and coming. . . . From our garden we watched the boys get out, while the road beside the huts became one great mass of khaki. . . . The Yanks had arrived!"

It was the same at most of the Eighth's other bases. The Americans were not there, and then they were—3,000 boisterous youngsters abruptly dropped into a placid countryside of fields and lanes lined by hedgerows and of village streets lined with picture-book, half-timbered cottages.

The English children, of course, were delighted by this sudden Yankee invasion. At the bases they peered through hedgerows to watch the Americans and their airplanes, and on the roads and streets they asked, when they met them, "Any gum, chum?" Recalled Englishman Neil Shakery, who was a child at that time, "We kids saw the Americans as romantic figures, as sort of super-heroes." But, Shakery added dryly, "This view was not always shared by our parents." Which was true, and for good reasons. Once the Americans had occupied a base, the surrounding countryside was quiet no longer. The lanes and roads became crowded with bicycles and motor vehicles operated by khaki-clad young men who had trouble remembering to stay on the left side of the road, and the villages became crowded with wise-cracking airmen who whistled at all the local girls and invaded all the local pubs. "When they stormed into . . . an un-

above: A pub well known to the men at Lavenham. *right:* The Great Cathedral at Peterborough.

THE VILLAGES

Children, if you dare to think / Of the greatness, rareness, muchness, / Fewness of this precious only / Endless world in which you say / You live, you think of things like this: / Blocks of slate enclosing dappled / Red and green, enclosing tawny / Yellow nets, enclosing white / And black acres of dominoes, / Where a neat brown paper parcel / Tempts you to untie the string. / In the parcel a small island, / On the island a large tree, / On the tree a husky fruit. / Strip the husk and pare the rind off: / In the kernel you will see / Blocks of slate enclosed by dappled / Red and green, enclosed by tawny / Yellow nets, enclosed by white / And black acres of dominoes, / Where the same brown paper parcel— / Children, leave the string alone!

(from "Warning to Children," by Robert Graves)

right: Men of the 390th Bomb Group (H) entertain English children at a Christmas party given at their Framlingham base 23 December 1943.

suspecting pub," wrote 392nd Bomb Group pilot Myron Keilman, "it was like a Wild West scenario where the cowboys . . . came to town and stormed the Longhorn Saloon."

Not only did the Americans thus at first strike their English neighbors as a rowdy, cheeky lot disrupting community life, but, wrote Air Force veteran John T. Appleby in his book, *Suffolk Summer:* "By British standards, we were pampered. Our food was much better than theirs. Our pockets bulged with candy and chewing gum, and we gave the impression of having more money than we knew what to do with."

A few Americans, unfortunately, boasted of this American affluence and gave the impression of having come from homes that, in Appleby's words, "had a private bath for every member of the family." "The British," Appleby added sarcastically, "were very fortunate in [thus] . . . learning about the American way of life." And Ira Eakin remembers being similarly disgusted by some of his fellows who "used to really burn me by telling the English, 'We've come over to win the damned war for you.'"

Among the English, on the other hand, there were some who made known their opinion that Americans were relatively uncivilized, and were johnnies-come-lately in a war they ought to have been in from the beginning.

Had there been no more to their association than this, the Eighth and its English neighbors obviously could not have gotten along together at all. Fortunately, there was more. Beneath their boisterous flippancy, the Americans were much impressed and felt a sense of "homecoming" in this land from whence had sprung their own language and much of their customs,

literature, and laws. The English, though fond of saying, "The trouble with Yanks is, they're overpaid, oversexed, and over *here*," were grateful for the Americans' assistance in the war, and realized they were really just lonesome youngsters hungry for a touch of normal life. Accordingly, as one veteran put it, "They would come to the bases and invite GIs to their homes, where they would fix them a good meal." They did this, moreover, without revealing that in this time of strict rationing it was at considerable sacrifice to themselves. "We thought then that they could get rations for us too," said tail gunner Paul Sink, "and only when the war was over did some of us discover they'd been splitting their own rations with us."

In response, the Americans shared with their English friends their own far more liberal rations of such niceties as candy and cigarettes, and "some of them," wrote the Framlingham farm girl, "came and helped us in the fields." Also, the Americans gave parties. At the 390th's Hundredth Mission party, recalled the English girl: "Hangar Number 2 was beautifully decorated . . . with bales of straw around the sides to sit on, and a great many blue lights. There were thousands of persons there from the neighboring villages. . . . Glenn Miller's band played for the dance." At Christmas, almost every Group gave a party for the local children. "The boys all saved up their candy rations so each child would have something to take home," the English girl wrote. And armorer Sam Burchell, who one Christmas at Seething was assigned to kitchen police duty, has said: "Because of the war, some of the smaller children had never seen some of the things we gave them—oranges and bananas

and the like—and everyone was touched. GIs usually complain about KP duty, but on that day no one did."

As time passed and associations such as these grew, the Eighth's English neighbors may have continued to have strong reservations about Yanks in general. But where their neighborhood Air Force group was concerned, they seem to have come to feel as did the family of the Framlingham farm girl. "When the boys were returning from a raid," she wrote, "we never felt at ease until all of them had landed. We called those boys 'our boys,' and their ships 'our ships.'"

Then the war was over, and as abruptly as the men of the Eighth had come, they departed. "They went shouting and singing and waving," wrote the Framlingham girl: "We could hear them as they went along the road to the station ... farther and farther away, then everywhere became silent. The Yanks had come—and now they were gone!

"One moment it was all noise, then dead silence, with everything deserted. We walked back home across the runway. There was no one in sight. It was just as if everyone had fallen asleep. We shall never forget the 390th, the boys who had come so far from their homes in America, many of them never to return. . . ."

Neither did the men of the Eighth ever forget the English. Many friendships formed between them then still exist now. And when asked about the English, veterans of the Eighth interviewed in connection with this book agreed almost unanimously with Ira Eakin, who said: "The English? There's *nothin'* bad I could say about those people. They were really great!"

SMALL TALK

ALL OF THESE WORDS AND PHRASES, NAMES AND PLACES WERE A PART OF THE LIVES OF EIGHTH AIR FORCE PERSONNEL IN ENGLAND DURING WW2.

Ack ack
Achtung!
Aero club
AGO card
Air medal
Air raid
Alert
Allies
"All or Nothing At All"
"All the Things You Are"
"A Lovely Way to Spend an
    Evening"
Ammo
Ann Sheridan
Any gum, chum?
Arc-lamp
Army convoys
Avalon cigarettes
AWOL
Axis Sally
A2 jacket
Baby Ruths
Bail out
Bandits
Barrage balloons
Battle fatigue
Beaverboard
"Be Careful, It's My Heart"
Belgravia
Benny Goodman
Berets
Berlin
Betty Grable
Betty Hutton
Bicycles
Big Ben
Bing Crosby
Bitter
Black bakelite

Blackout
Black Underwood typewriters
Blitz
Blockbuster
Bluie West One
"Blues in the Night"
Bob Hope
Bomber Command
Boogie Woogie
Bovril
Bremen
British double summer time
Brown leather
Browned off
Brussel sprouts
Bub
Bubble and squeak
Buck slip
Buncher
Burnt cordite
Buzz bombs
BBC
Cambridge
Camouflage
Canteen
Canvas lorries
Carole Landis
Carole Lombard
Chaff
Chain smoking
Channel, the
"Chattanooga Choo Choo"
Cheeky
Cheerio!
Chelsea cigarettes
Chesterfield cigarettes
Chum
Cigarettes
Civilians
Civvies
Clark Gable
Class As
Coal stoves
CocaCola
Coin-operated gas meters
Colder than a polar bear's ass
Colder than a witch's tit
Cole Porter
Corktips
Covent Garden
Crap game
Crewcut
Daddy
Dames
Darts
Day room

D-Day
Debs cigarettes
Deuce-and-a-half
DFC
Dicey
Ditch
Ditty bag
"Do Nothin til You Hear From
    Me"
Dodgy
Dogtags
Domino cigarettes
"Donchaknow there's a war on?"
"Don't Get Around Much
    Anymore"
"Don't Sit Under the Apple Tree"
Doodlebugs
Doubledeckers
Dull tool
East Anglia
East End
Edward G. Robinson
Embarcation
Ersatz
Escape kit
ETO
Euston station
FDR
Fighter Command
Firestorm
Fish and chips
Fleece-lined
Flit
Flying Control
Fog
"Fools Rush In"
For the duration . . .
Fort
For Whom The Bell Tolls
Fountain pens
Frances Langford
Fred Allen
"Frenesi"
Furlough
FW (190)
Gander
Garbled
Gene Tierney
Gerry
Get hep
G.I.
Glenn Miller
Good show!
Gooseneck lamps
Got a fag?
Greer Garson

Gremlins
Gumpopping
Hack
Hampstead Heath
Hannover
Hardstand
Harrod's
Hedy Lamarr
Helmet
Hemo
Hep (cat)
Hershey bars
He's had it!
Hildegarde
Home guard
Homerun cigarettes
Hubba hubba!
Hun
"I Can Dream, Can't I?"
"I Concentrate on You"
Idaho
"I Don't Want to Walk Without
    You"
"If I Didn't Care"
"I Get Along Without You Very
    Well"
"I Hear a Rhapsody"
Ike (jacket)
"I Left My Heart at the Stagedoor
    Canteen"
"I'll Be Around"
"I'll Be Seeing You"
"I Love You"
Incendiary
"In the Mood"
"Intermezzo"
Invasion stripes
Ipana
"I Remember You"
I remember we had . . .
"I Should Care"
Isinglass
"It's Been a Long, Long Time"
"I've Heard that Song Before"
Jack Benny
Janet Blair
Jerry Colonna
Jersey Bounce
Jinx Falkenburg
Jitterbug
Joe
Johnny Walker
Jolly Good!
Jug
Julep cigarettes
Jump

Kassel
Kidney pie
Killer diller
Kilroy was here!
Kings College
Kings Cross station
Knightsbridge
K-rations
Kraut
Kreml hair tonic
Kriegie
Lanc
Leaflets
Lib
Liberty
Life magazine
Lift
Lightning
Little friends
Limey
London
"Long Ago and Far Away"
Lord Haw Haw
Lord Salisbury cigarettes
Lorry
"Love Letters"
Love letters
Luckies (Lucky Strikes)
Luftwaffe
Mac
Mapleton cigarettes
Marvels cigarettes
Mayfair
Merseberg
ME (109)
Mickey
Milk run
Mission
Molotov cocktail
"Moonlight Serenade"
Motor pool
Mud
Munster
Musette bag
Mustang
"My Devotion"
"My Reverie"
Nannies
Nazi
NCO club
Nissen hut
Northhampton
North sea
Norwich
O club
Off limits

Old Gold cigarettes
"One Dozen Roses"
"Once in a While"
Ops block
Out-of-bounds
Overcast
Oxford street
Paddington station
"Paper Doll"
Parties
Pass
Paulette Goddard
Pavement artists
Perspex
Perimeter track
Peterborough
Petty girls
Philip Morris cigarettes
Piccadilly commando
Pillbox
Pint of the prime
Planter's peanuts
Player's cigarettes
Plexiglas
"Polka Dots and Moonbeams"
Pompadour
Powdered eggs
Power settings
P.O.W.
Practice missions
Prestwick
Pub-crawling
Purple Heart
PX
Queue
Quid
Radar
Radio channels
RAF
Raid
Rain
Rainbow club
Rationing
Red Cross (girls, clubmobiles)
Regent cigarettes
Regents Park Zoo
Regensburg
"Right in Der Führer's Face"
Rita Hayworth
Rotten weather
Round-about
R&R
Rubble
Rum and Maple cigarettes
Sandbags
Sausages

Schweinfurt
Scrubbed
Searchlights
Sector
"Sentimental Journey"
"September Song"
"Serenade in Blue"
SHAEF
Shaving lotion
Shelters
Shellshocked
Sherlock Holmes
Shit
Shortages
Short snorter
Shuttle raids
Sirens
Skylark
Smashing!
Smokestacks
SNAFU
Snood
Soho
So long . . .
"Speak Low"
Spit (Spitfire)
Splasher
Stagedoor canteen
Stand-down
Stars and Stripes
St. John's Wood
St. Pancras station
St. Paul's
Sweat
Sweating 'em out (in)
"Swinging on a Star"
Synthetic
Ta ta
Tallyho cigarettes
"Tangerine"
Tannoy
Tea
Teel dentifrice
Thank you, love . . .
"That Old Black Magic"
The Andrews Sisters
The Broads
The Fens
"The Horst Wessel Song"
The Midlands
"There Are Such Things"
"There Will Never Be Another
    You"
The Tivoli
The Wash
"This Love of Mine"

"This Is the Army, Mr. Jones"
"Til the End of Time"
Time, gentlemen, time!
"Tonight We Love"
Tour
Trafalgar Square
Traffic patterns
Training manuals
Trams
Treacle
Trolley
Tunbridge Wells
Tweak
Twilight Time
Twit
U-boats
Undercast
Underground
Used carbon paper
Utterly
Varga girls
Vector
Vera Lynn
Veronica Lake
Verry pistol
V-E Day
Viceroy cigarettes
Victory roll
Victoria station
VD
V-1, V-2
V-bombs
V for Victory
V-weapons
WACs
War Department
"Warsaw Concerto"
Waterloo station
W.C.
Wearing watch on inside of wrist
    . . . WW2-style
When the war's over . . .
"Where or When"
"White Christmas"
"White Cliffs of Dover"
Wings cigarettes
Winston Churchill
Wizard!
WRENs
Yank
You cawn't miss it . . .
"You'd Be so Nice to Come
    Home to"
"You'll Never Know"
"You Stepped Out of a Dream"
Zippo

THE AIRCRAFT

They were not easy to fly. The fighters were as touchy and headstrong as half-broken horses, the bombers when loaded had to be alternately bullied and coaxed, and both had to be flown with a firm hand, alertness, and *respect*. The bombers had their disconcerting quirks, one of which was an understandable reluctance to leave the ground when overloaded. On the long runway—which at most English bases measured about 6,000 feet—this could be trying. On either of the short runways—usually a little over 4,000 feet—it was, as one pilot said, "a real nail-biter." This was especially true because of the high penalty for failure. A loaded bomber carried more than 20,000 pounds of bombs and gasoline, which meant that a crew that failed to get one off the ground before reaching the end of the runway would be spoken of thereafter only in the past tense. It is therefore understandable that every such takeoff had the rapt attention of the three men charged with bringing it off—the pilot, copilot, and engineer.

To get an idea of how it felt to conduct such a takeoff, imagine for a moment that you are a pilot of a B-17 or B-24, that your ship is heavily loaded, and that you have just now taxied it into position for takeoff from one of your field's short runways . . .

With less distance for gaining takeoff speed than you would like, you are eager to seize every advantage you can. Accordingly, you set the brakes and hold the airplane stationary on the very end of the runway and at the same time advance the throttles to full takeoff power. The engines thunder, the airplane begins to shiver, as someone once crudely but aptly put it, "like a dog shitting peach pits," and if the airplane is a

B-24 (which has a nose-wheel) its accelerating propellers pull it down into a belligerent crouch. Now, there is much argument about whether this raucous procedure actually helps a takeoff run, but it certainly *feels* as if it does, so you run up the engines until the airplane strains to be released and to race bellowing down the runway. Then you release the brakes . . . and find the airplane to have been a liar. Instead of leaping forward, it waddles. What had promised to be a charging bull is actually a fat lady beginning a languid Sunday stroll. You knew this would happen. It always happens. Even so, it exasperates you and you unconsciously hunch back and forth in your seat in an attempt to nudge the airplane forward.

Slowly, the heavy ship accelerates and becomes lighter on its feet. Standing behind and to the right of your seat, the engineer watches instruments reporting the engines' health and is ready to make instant corrections if he detects malingering. Sitting to your right, the copilot watches the airspeed indicator and calls out its advancing numbers, and you listen for those announcing arrival at certain critical speeds. The first of these is the speed beyond which you can no longer stop the airplane on the remaining runway and are committed to take off no matter what. It is a variable number determined by aircraft weight, runway length, and wind direction and speed, and today you figure it at about ninety miles per hour. Next is stalling speed, the speed above which the airplane will fly once it is in the air, and below which it will retire from flying and become a thirty-five ton rock. It, too, is a variable that at today's weight and with landing gear and flaps extended you calculate to be be-

Oh build your ship of death. Oh build it! / for you will need it. / For the voyage of oblivion awaits you.

(from "The Ship of Death," by D. H. Lawrence)

left: B-17Gs of the 381st BG (H) flying low over the manicured landscape of the English Midlands. *overleaf:* In the cockpit of a forty-year-old B-24 Liberator bomber.

Butch

U.S. ARMY — MODEL B-17G-30-BO
AIR FORCES SERIAL NO. 9-2-31200

Dog Breath

tween 105 and 110 mph. Finally, there is takeoff speed. For a safe (or even successful) takeoff, this needs to be well in excess of stalling speed. You figure today it ought to be at least 120 mph, and you will be very grateful for more if you can get it.

With movements so automatic you are not aware of them, you hold the accelerating ship straight on the runway, and you listen to the numbers . . . "seventy . . . eighty . . . *ninety*. . . ." Now you are committed. Even if you lose an engine you must still try to take off.

The airplane is rushing now. Objects beside the runway whip past in blurred flashes. "Hundred 'n five . . . *hundred 'n ten*. . . ." Now you have passed stalling speed and thereby have been led into temptation. The end of the runway is fast approaching. So, too, are the trees beyond the field. Instinct urges you to get the ship up *now*, before it is too late. You *could* get it up now. But would it stay up? The energy that lifts an airplane is robbed from its airspeed. Your margin of speed above stalling is still thin and if the act of lifting off consumes it all, the airplane will rise, then wallow and stagger and fall back to earth in a booming, pyrotechnic bankruptcy seen and heard by everyone in the neighborhood excepting, of course, you and your crew. So, you master the temptation, and wait.

"*Hundred 'n twenty* . . ." You'd like more, but the end of the runway is too near. This will have to do. Easing the control wheel back, you lift the ship from the runway. It rises so heavily that you feel you've lifted it with your own hands, but it rises, and to get rid of landing gear drag you immediately call to the copilot, "Wheels up!"

Now, even though you are off the ground you are not out of the woods. Not yet. Now you have additional problems, as described by one Eighth pilot: "You really had to walk a tightrope. If you didn't build up additional airspeed before starting to climb you were liable to stall out. On the other hand, you had to climb enough immediately to get over whatever obstacles lay just beyond the field. Trying to do enough of each and not too much of either, you really could work up a quick sweat—especially if at the same time you ran into propwash from the plane ahead of you. Once, I remember, we seemed certain to fly right through a farmhouse just beyond the field. Somehow we got over it, but I'll swear we dragged our tail on the roof as we went by!"

You nurse the airplane carefully upward and the treetops flash past just beneath you. Now you can build up some airspeed, reduce the punishing power you've had on the engines, and begin the tedious climb to assembly altitude.

Now you feel a sudden wave of affection for your airplane—B-17 or B-24 as the case may be—even though moments ago you were thoroughly exasperated by it. Again, you've asked it to lift from a short runway a load that the book says it can't lift in that distance, and again the airplane has done it. Moreover, you've seen many of its kind become so battle-damaged they seemed held together only by their control cables, and yet still managed to get their crews safely home. "These are tough old birds," you think, "the best bombers ever built," and you'll defend their honor against anyone who tries to claim otherwise.

For me, the naked and the nude /
(By lexicographers construed / As synonyms that should express / The same deficiency of dress / Or shelter) stand as wide apart / As love from lies, or truth from art.

(from "The Naked and the Nude," by Robert Graves)

left: Many 8AF air crews wanted to personalize the airplanes in which they flew and often they chose to have unclad or lightly clad females, a la Varga or Petty girls, painted on the noses of their B-17s and B-24s. Others elected to make a different sort of statement. Witness "DogBreath."

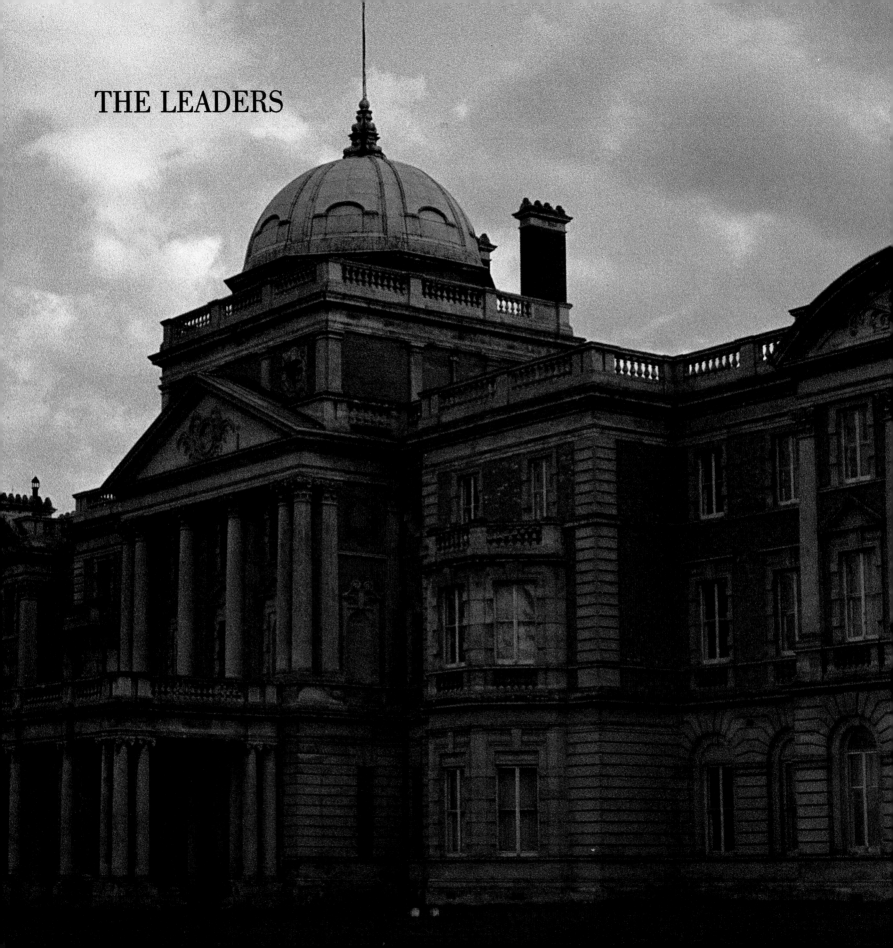

THE LEADERS

In 1938 the Army Air Corps strength was about 20,000 men and fewer than 500 first-line aircraft. By mid-1944 it had grown, as the Army Air *Force* (the name was changed in 1941), to a strength of two-and-a-third million men and nearly 50,000 aircraft.

The growth of that part of it known as the Eighth Army Force was even more dramatic. First activated in January, 1942, it grew in thirty months from nothing to a strength of 200,000 men and about 4,000 aircraft.

Such quick expansion—such swift molding of thousands of youngsters who knew nothing about airplanes into the world's most powerful air force—demanded strong leaders who understood organization and airplanes and human nature, and in whom lack of patience was a virtue. Fortunately, many such leaders were found. Among them:

General Henry "Hap" Arnold, who never commanded the Eighth itself, but who, as chief from 1938 to 1946 of all the Army air forces, was responsible for its creation and welfare.

A career army airman who had first begun flying in 1911, Arnold, with his white hair and habitually benevolent expression, looked like a kindly grandfather. He did not, however, act like one. In his mid-fifties, he was demanding, dynamic, and had a talent for picking the right man for a job and then seeing that the man had what he needed to get the job done.

A 1943 letter from one of his generals, said Arnold, "summed up the mail from all of them. It said, 'I need everything!' " And Lockheed Aircraft president Robert Gross has told how Arnold set about getting "everything": "He made you do better than you could because he demanded more than you had in you. He got his suppliers to promise more and do more than they thought they could do. . . . He pressured us with his own dedication."

General Carl "Tooey" Spaatz assumed command of the Eighth in May, 1942; he took its first units to England in July, and there commanded it until he was sent, on November 30, 1942, to command Allied air operations in the Mediterranean. Then, on January 6, 1944, he was returned to England as the overall commander of U.S. Air Forces in both England and the Mediterranean.

Spaatz also was a career army airman and had served in the Air Corps in France in World War I. A quiet, scholarly looking man, he was, said General Eisenhower, "so modest and retiring that the public never became fully aware of his value." Eisenhower knew his value, though, and wrote: "On every succeeding day of almost three years of active war, I had reasons for thanking the gods of war and the War Department for sending me 'Tooey' Spaatz."

General Ira Eaker, deputy commander of the Eighth under Spaatz, was appointed to its command when Spaatz was sent to the Mediterranean. He remained its commander until January 6, 1944.

Eaker, too, had had long experience as an army pilot. He was, said war correspondent Ernie Pyle, "one of the most thoughtful men about doing little things for people," and he got along with the British better, perhaps, than any other American general. Pilot Max Pinkerton of the 351st Bomb Group, who later served as copilot on Eaker's official airplane, remembers him as being "very calm, very articulate, very low key,

. . . Reminiscently I consider our first St. Nazaire mission. The pilot right behind me, leading the second element, was too far back after we left the target. I saw him in that position and gave him hell for it. He said, "Well, maybe I was further back than I should have been; but I would have been hit if I was up there where you wanted me to be. Because that flak was right on your tail all the way through." I told him, "Doesn't make any difference. You get up there next time. You can't tell exactly where the flak is bursting, anyway. You concern yourself with staying in formation, and let someone else worry about the flak."

(from *Mission With LeMay,* by General Curtis E. LeMay)

left: Elveden Hall was taken over by the USAAF to be the headquarters for the Third Air Division. Elveden is a few miles to the west of Thetford.

"Pettingill." "Yes sir." "We're plenty lucky to have only one loss on this strike. Why did you break formation?" "Well, sir, Ackerman was in trouble . . . two engines on fire, and we were getting enemy fighters. I figured I'd better stay back with him and try to cover him going into the target . . . but he couldn't make it."

"Ackerman a pretty good friend of yours?" "My roommate, sir."

"So for the sake of your roommate you violated group integrity. Every gun on a B17 is designed to give the group maximum defensive firepower. That's what I mean by 'group integrity.' When you pull a B17 out of a formation you reduce the defensive power of the group by ten guns. A crippled airplane *has* to be expendable. The *one thing* which is never expendable is your obligation to this group. THIS GROUP! THIS GROUP! *That* has to be your loyalty, your only reason for being! Stovall!" "Yes sir." "Have the billeting officer work out a complete reassignment of quarters so that every man has a new roommate." "Very well sir." "Gately." "Yes sir."

"Baxter is promoted out of the *Leper Colony*. Pettingill is your new co-pilot."

(from *Twelve O'Clock High*, by Sy Bartlett and Bierne Lay, Jr.)

92

quite a writer and a master in the use of the English language."

Actually, it may have been Eaker's mastery of language that saved the American program of daylight bombing. The British were at first opposed to daylight raids, with one newspaper declaring it was "a great pity" that the Americans hadn't seen fit to build "Lancasters, Britain's finest bombers," and "fly them by night" instead of clinging to the "discredited theory" of daylight raids. Winston Churchill, being of the same opinion, persuaded President Roosevelt to halt daylight bombing. Thereupon, General Arnold called Eaker to come and try to turn the Prime Minister around. Eaker came, and gave Churchill a one-page argument for daylight bombing. "Sort of half reading aloud," Eaker wrote later, Churchill "came to the paragraph that said, 'If the RAF bombs by night and we bomb by day, bombing around the clock, the German defenses will get no rest.' He repeated the 'bombing around the clock' phrase . . . and said, you have not convinced me . . . but when I see your President I will tell him that I withdraw my objection."

Not only did the Prime Minister do as he had promised but, being a lover of well-turned phrases, he continued to speak of bombing around the clock until it became a stock expression of the time.

A later Churchill–Roosevelt conference, according to Pinkerton, led Eaker again to demonstrate his mastery of words. As told by Pinkerton: "While the President's airplane was approaching the field, a boy in a shot-up fighter was also approaching. He could have bailed out, but he was trying to save his plane and he did

I can tell you now one reason I think you've been having hard luck. I saw it in your faces last night. I can see it there now. You've been looking at a lot of air lately. You think you ought to have a rest. In short, you're sorry for yourselves. Now, I don't have a lot of patience with this 'what are we fighting for' stuff. We're in a war . . . a shooting war. We've *got* to fight . . . and some of us have got to die. I'm not trying to tell you not to be afraid. Fear is normal . . . but stop worrying about it, and about yourselves. Stop making plans. Forget about going home. Consider yourselves already dead. Once you accept that idea, it won't be so tough.
Now, if any man here can't buy that . . . if he rates himself as something special, with a special kind of hide to be saved, he'd better make up his mind about it right now, because I don't want him in this group!

(from *Twelve O'Clock High*, by Sy Bartlett and Bierne Lay, Jr.)

In this still from the 20th Century Fox film *Twelve O'Clock High*, Gregory Peck as General Frank Savage addresses the fictitious 918th Bomb Group. Both the book and the screenplay were written by Sy Bartlett and Beirne Lay, Jr.

save it, but in the process he cut the Sacred Cow (as we called the President's plane) out of the traffic pattern. Well, there was a big flap about that, and Eaker was ordered to reprimand the boy. I never saw the letter he wrote, but I was told it went like this: 'I must reprimand you for furthering the war effort by saving a valuable airplane and also your own life. By so doing you cost the Commander-in-chief an extra three minutes in the air. Such acts as this cannot be tolerated.' "

General James H. "Jimmy" Doolittle commanded the Eighth from January 6, 1944, until the German surrender, and was undoubtedly its most colorful leader. He was a small, keen-eyed man who liked to laugh, and, said General Eisenhower, "he was a dynamic bundle of energy."

A flight and air-gunnery instructor in World War I, Doolittle later became the first pilot to fly across the United States in less than a

day, and the first to take off and land an airplane solely by instruments. Flying in air races, he set new speed records while winning both the Thompson and Schneider trophies. In 1942 he led sixteen B-25 bombers from the deck of the carrier Hornet (though this was theoretically impossible) to make that famous first American raid on Tokyo. For this, he received a Congressional Medal of Honor and was made a General.

"General Doolittle ran the Eighth Air Force," wrote Ernie Pyle. "It was a grim, stupendous job, but he managed to keep the famous Doolittle sense of humor about it. [He said] he used to be six feet tall, but had worried himself down to his present height in the past five months."

General Curtis E. LeMay never led the Eighth, but his contribution to its success was enormous, nonetheless. LeMay was thirty-five years old when he came to the Eighth in 1942. A stocky, darkly handsome cigar chewer so terse and tough that he became known (though not to his face) as "Old Iron Ass," he came as a major commanding a group, and left in 1944 as a brigadier general appointed to head the 21st Bomber Command in the Pacific.

While with the Eighth, LeMay was a developer of the "combat box" formation without which daylight bombing would have become too costly to be continued, and he initiated the practice of bombing on signal from a lead ship instead of by individual sightings. Also, he was such a stickler for instrument training of pilots that ships under his command were apt to take off on missions when those under other commanders remained grounded because of weather.

The Eighth had many other leaders, great and small, who deserve to be listed here, and would have been had space permitted. But the ones who are listed are the ones who bore the most awesome responsibilities—who had to decide when and where a raid was to be made and who was to make it, and were forced thereby to play God by deciding who might live and who might die. It was a responsibility that weighed heavily on all of them, and their writings show it. But as General "Tooey" Spaatz once said, "You can't have a war and worry about that. What you have to worry about is whether or not you are winning."

left and far left: A 388th BG (H) insignia created by Walt Disney Productions for the Knettishall-based outfit. *bottom left:* 100th Bomb Group (H) headquarters at Thorpe-Abbotts. *below:* The fireplace in the living quarters of the commanding officer, 44th BG (H) at Shipdham.

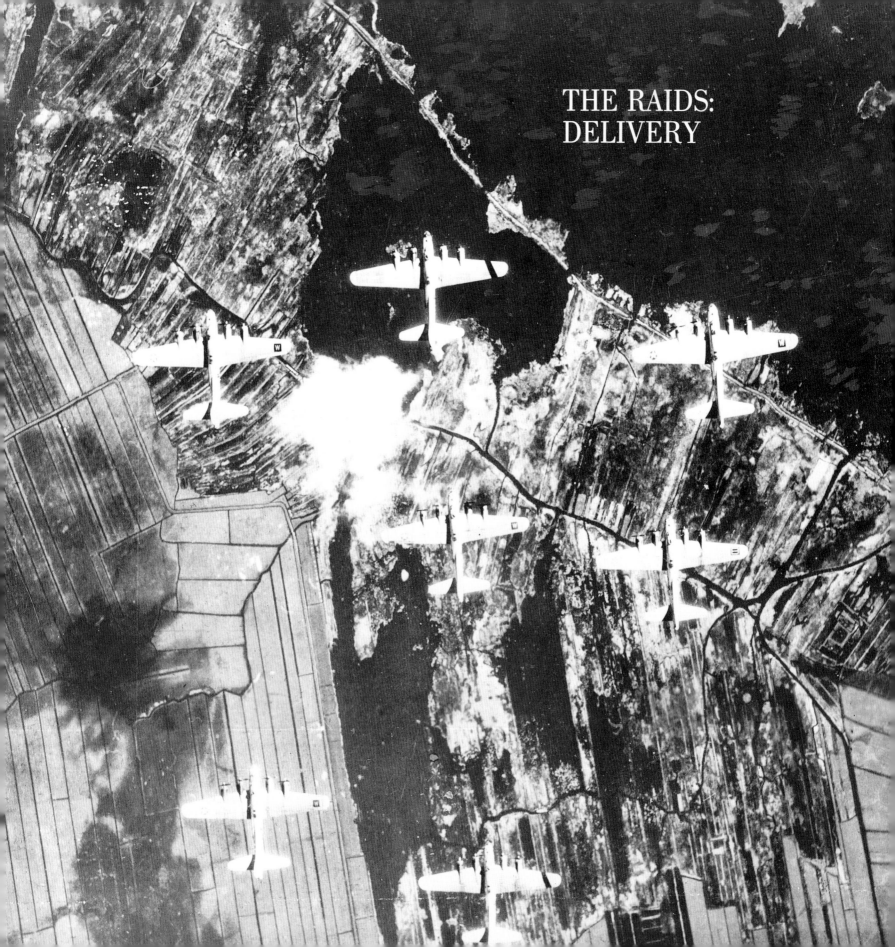

THE RAIDS:
DELIVERY

One of the hardest parts of a mission, at least as many combat veterans remember it now, was the idle time they spent at their airplanes while waiting for the green flare to go up. It allowed too much time for their fears to build, and for them to endure that peculiar combination of boredom and dread so well known to those who, after psychologically preparing themselves to face the hazards of combat, are forced to sit and wait.

Once they had begun their takeoff run, however, they were no longer bothered by boredom or excess thinking time. Their time was then fully occupied by the performing of one critical operation after another—of unforgiving operations whose punishment for failure was often death—and the first of these was the takeoff itself.

Taking an airplane off the ground and into the air is a process which, for obvious reasons, a pilot must perform properly the first time—and every time. This is not usually a matter of much concern, for usually a pilot attempts a takeoff only when the cards are so heavily stacked in his favor that a disaster is most unlikely and if it did occur would probably do so only because of his own carelessness. In the case of the bombers of the Eighth Air Force, however, the cards were stacked as much against the pilot as for him. One reason was the loads the bombers were required to carry, together with the length of the runways they carried them from. Another was the English weather.

A heavily laden airplane demands a great deal of runway on which to gain flying speed, and even then it will leave the ground only with sullen reluctance, and the B-17s and B-24s of the Eighth Air Force were heavily laden. Designed to take off and fly at a maximum gross weight of about thirty-three tons, they were sent out almost routinely at weights of up to thirty-six tons. At their various bases, however, the longest runway was rarely longer than 6,300 feet and the shortest was often no longer than 4,200 feet. And this combination of weights and runway lengths did indeed create, as someone put it, "nervous moments." Said pilot Lawrence Drew: "I'd have all the throttles wide open, then I'd just sit and stare at the white picket fence just beyond the end of the runway. Many times I'd feel that I'd just pulled the airplane off the ground with my own strength, then I'd feel sure my wheels were going to go right through that fence." And navigator W. W. Ford has told of the day when the airplane ahead of his did fail to get off the ground, and when his own then almost did the same: "We had a kind of mission we called 'the 2780 blues.' That was when your airplane had been loaded with 2780 gallons of gas, which was all it would hold, and with a full load of bombs on top of that, and on this particular day we had a '2780' to Berlin.

"The third airplane to go gained enough speed to partially lift off the ground ... then it stalled and came down, and its gear collapsed and the airplane went on down the runway on its belly. Shortly after that there was a big explosion and it looked like that whole end of the field had blown up. The rest of us were then instructed to go to the short runway, where with our full loads of gas and bombs we had to make a crosswind takeoff.

"We really sweated that one out ... but at the last minute the pilot bounced the wheels and got us into the air, and by then popping some

In the spring of 1944, the Allied strategic bombers were required for "Overlord," and the weight of attack on Germany itself was inevitably reduced. But by now we were the masters in the air. The bitterness of the struggle had thrown a greater strain on the Lüftwaffe than it was able to bear. By being forced to concentrate on building fighters, it had lost all power of strategic counter-attack by bombing back at us. Unbalanced and exhausted, it was henceforth unable to defend either itself or Germany from our grievous blows. For our air superiority, which by the end of 1944 was to become air supremacy, full tribute must be paid to the United States Eighth Air Force.

(from *Closing the Ring*, by Winston Churchill)

left: Fortresses of the 487th and 95th Bomb Groups en route to bomb an enemy target.

flap he gave us an extra goose that just got us over the trees at the end of the runway. . . .

"When we got back that evening we saw what the explosion had left . . . just a hole in the ground and two wings and a tail . . . but the crew had all managed to get out in time. . . ."

Hence, it is small wonder that one squadron leader once wrote, "Even in perfect weather I would be nervous [taking off] with this load." As a usual thing, however, the weather was far from perfect, and fog, low ceilings, and rain were more the rule than the exception. "Today there was another of those ankle-high ceilings," one pilot wrote, and in a June 10, 1944, letter pilot Keith Newhouse told his wife, Jean: "We've flown in weather when the birds beside the runway silently folded their wings over their eyes as we took off, and once a seagull even thumbed his nose at us. They're no fools. Wish we could say the same about ourselves."

Bad weather did not add much to the problems of getting the airplanes off the ground, but it added enormously to the problems of keeping them in the air once they were up. Under no-visibility conditions the human senses, not having been designed for blind flying, become unscrupulous liars. With all the power of human instinct they will insist to a pilot that his airplane is doing one thing when its instruments indicate clearly that it is doing something quite different. Theirs is a sirens' song that urges especially the more inexperienced pilot to believe it is his instruments and not his senses that are lying, that causes him to turn unconsciously to the course his mind rather than his compass says is correct, or to think he is flying straight and level when in fact he has begun the descending turn that if not

soon corrected will result in a nasty unplanned maneuver capable of tearing the wings off an airplane and known appropriately as "the graveyard spiral." But hard as it may have been sometimes for these relatively inexperienced and absurdly young pilots to believe their instruments instead of their instincts when flying blind, they faced an even greater blind-flying hazard in the crowded air. Whenever a mission took off in bad weather, its hundreds of aircraft, unseen by one another, were trying to occupy the same clouds at the same time, and any deviation by one from its assigned course, rate of climb, and airspeed was likely to put it into the path of another. "In an instrument assembly," said Donald Maffett, "you took off on a particular heading which you held for a certain number of minutes and seconds while climbing at a specified rate and speed. . . . The element of human error being what it is, it was almost impossible to hold exactly the specified rate of climb and heading for exactly the specified time. As a result it was not uncommon to suddenly find yourself in the propwash of an unseen airplane immediately in front of you. . . . We had numerous incidents of aircraft colliding with each other under these conditions."

Once the ships were off the ground, their pilots, copilots, and navigators immediately became embroiled in another critical operation—that of assembling them in the tight "combat box" formations they used when making raids. This, too, was difficult and dangerous. David Parry, 390th Bomb Group pilot, recently said, "What I can't remember is how the hell we were able to do it—to assemble in that terrible English weather without running into each other."

As it happened, they did not do it without occasionally running into each other, but they did it anyhow because it was necessary. The Eighth had learned early that aircraft in small or loosely-formed groups were sitting ducks for German fighters. Through trial and error it had also found that bombers flown in large, tight combat box formations could surround themselves with an envelope of defensive fire that by no means assured their survival but did vastly increase their chances for it. "You could, with a Wing, throw out maybe thirty tons of lead a minute," said Ray Wild. "But if you slid out 50 or 60 yards you didn't have that protection and the fighters would come down and hit you . . . so you always wanted the formation tight."

"When we left the [English] coast we were always in combat box formation," remembered Sidney Rapaport. "It was absolutely essential." W. W. Ford recalls that his commanding officer, Lt. Colonel James Wilson, "was real hard-nosed about his people flying in close formation, so, by

left: A USAAF navigation computer for true air speed, time and distance, and altitude correction.
below: A four-language phrase guide from an 8AF air crewman's escape kit.

NOT TO BE PRODUCED IN PUBLIC NOT TO BE PRODUCED IN PUBLIC NOT

LISTS OF PHRASES

FRENCH
DUTCH
GERMAN
SPANISH

GERMAN

ENGLISH	GERMAN	ENGLISH	GERMAN
One	Ein	Twenty	Zwanzig
Two	Zwei	Thirty	Dreissig
Three	Drei	Forty	Vierzig
Four	Vier	Fifty	Fünfzig
Five	Fünf	Sixty	Sechzig
Six	Sechs	Seventy	Siebzig
Seven	Sieben	Eighty	Achzig
Eight	Acht	Ninety	Neunzig
Nine	Neun	Hundred	Hundert
Ten	Zehn	Five Hundred	Fünf Hundert
Eleven	Elf	Thousand	Tausend
Twelve	Zwölf		
Thirteen	Dreizehn	Monday	Montag
Fourteen	Vierzehn	Tuesday	Dienstag
Fifteen	Fünfzehn	Wednesday	Mitwoch
Sixteen	Sechzehn	Thursday	Donnerstag
Seventeen	Siebzehn	Friday	Freitag
Eighteen	Achtzehn	Saturday	Samstag
Nineteen	Neunzehn	Sunday	Sonntag

ENGLISH	GERMAN
Minutes	Minuten
Hours	Stunden
Day	Tag
Night	Nacht
Week	Woche
Fortnight	Vierzehn Tage
Month	Monat
O'clock	Uhr
Thank you; please	Danke; Bitte
Yes; No	Ja; Nein
Good morning; Afternoon; Evening	Guten Morgen; Tag; Abend
Good night	Gute Nacht
Out of bounds; Forbidden	Verboten
To; From; Via	Nach; Von; Uber
Train; express; slow	Zug; Schnellzug; Personenzug
Third class	Dritte Klasse
God Bless	Grüss Gott
HEIL HITLER	Heil Hitler
I am in a hurry	Ich habe es eilig

There is no equivalent in German for "out of bounds". ".Verboten" (forbidden), would be used in most cases.

There is no German equivalent for "good afternoon". "Guten Tag" (good day) is used at any time of the day, and is much more common than any of the other forms.

ENGLISH
One
Two
Three
Four
Five
Six
Seven
Eight
Nine
Ten
Eleven
Twelve
Thirteen
Fourteen
Fifteen
Sixteen
Seventeen
Eighteen
Nineteen
Minutes
Hours
Day
Night

durn, you flew in close formation. He had a P-47 assigned to him, and he'd fly out to check on you. Any crew he found out of position got a royal chewing." While returning with a shot-up airplane and two wounded crewmen from a raid on Munich, pilot Dave Shelhamer of the 303rd Bomb Group at Molesworth received a practical lesson in the value of the formation. That night he wrote in his diary: "Being low on gas, we reduced power and began to trail back a little. This sure was a mistake because then we were hit by some ME 110s, which is the German twin-engine fighter. By giving the Seventeen all the throttle it would take we finally caught up with the formation. We received no additional holes in these attacks, but, gas or no gas, this boy is staying in the formation from now on."

Taking off at thirty-second intervals when the weather was clear and at one-minute intervals when it was not—and in either case with a longer interval between the last ship of one squadron and the first ship of the next—the aircraft would climb according to a preset flight pattern to the assigned assembly altitude. If at that altitude they were clear of clouds, they then would "home" on the radio beacon or "splasher" over which their particular group was to assemble. If at assembly altitude they found themselves in the clouds, they continued to climb until in the clear, then homed on the beacon. "The weather reports were real inaccurate," said Ray Wild, "So if they said you should break out of the clouds at fifteen hundred feet it might actually turn out to be eighteen thousand feet—and I recall one time when it *was*. When you broke out you did your circle, and the squadron and group leaders, wherever they

left: 92nd Bomb Group (H) B-17s high over Germany heading toward their target. *below:* Fortresses of the 8AF at high altitude over enemy-occupied territory leave highly visible contrails in their wake, alerting German flak crews to the American presence above.

above: German ME 109 fighters, a type often seen by 8AF aircrews on their raids. right: The 91st BG (H) "fort" called "Chow-hound" on a strike at the Erkner ball bearing works near Berlin, 8 March 1944.

were, would shoot off certain colored flares . . . and then you'd form squadrons first—lead squadron, high squadron, low squadron—then the squadrons would form into the group." As Frank Nelson remembers it: "The squadron would fly over the beacon in trail. Then the lead airplane would turn around and come back. As he did the other ships in that squadron would peel out and form on him. Then that squadron would go to a higher altitude and hold there while the next one formed. Pretty soon all squadrons would be formed and then assembled into group formation."

The building blocks of the combat boxes were "elements"—three ships formed into a tight vee. A squadron was usually made up of two elements, with the second element stationed about fifty feet (or even less) behind, above, and to one side of the first or "lead" element. The

exact arrangement of these squadrons in the group "box" depended on how many squadrons the group had in the air on that day. If there were three they were arranged in an echeloned vee, with a high squadron flying slightly above, behind, and to one side of the lead squadron, and a low squadron flying slightly below, behind, and to the other side of the lead. In the case of four squadrons, the fourth flew in the "slot"—a position a little below and behind the others—thus converting the vee into a diamond. Once a group was assembled, it homed at a pre-designated time and altitude on the radio beacon or "buncher" of its particular wing, and there took its assigned place in the wing formation. This formation, too, was a "box" and differed from that of the group only in that its high, low, lead, and slot positions were occupied by groups rather than squadrons. Finally, and also at predesignated times and altitudes, the assembled wings homed on yet another radio beacon —this one being a departure "buncher" located on the English coast.

On paper, at least, this system worked beautifully. When conducted exactly according to plan and schedule, the various wings arrived over the departure "buncher" at precisely the right times and places to bring the entire outbound armada together with the crisp precision of a formation by a college marching band. The way it worked in practice, however, was another matter. One problem was the congestion created by the necessity of assembling too many aircraft over too small an area. As Donald Maffett has pointed out, "We weren't the only group assembling at a particular time. Within a ten-mile radius there might be as many as five other groups

assembling also, and we had instances where one of our aircraft collided with one from another group." This was compounded, more often than not, by the contrails of crystallized vapor that at high altitudes streamed back from engine exhausts. "They look so beautiful from the ground," wrote one pilot, "But in the air, both in assembly and otherwise, they strike fear into everyone's heart. They appear behind the ships ahead looking so much like spun glass that you're afraid they will become entangled in your props and stop them. Then suddenly you're in them—in a blanketing fuzz that makes your heart pound like hell. Then the formation can be seen only occasionally through holes, at times you're flying totally blind, and you know that in one of those blind moments you may crash into a friend . . . so you squirm and pray." Because of these and other problems, as Keith Newhouse in 1944 wrote to his wife: "The layman cannot possibly imagine the thrills, narrow escapes and heartbreaking things that occur in assembly. The ships are so loaded that it is a physical effort to keep them in the air. As each smaller unit is formed it must join with a larger one on a schedule timed to the second. When the big units then start falling into line seconds still count, and if the timing is wrong whole formations suddenly begin sifting through each other. God-a-mighty what a turbulence it makes, and what a sickening feeling to see two big bombers tangle with each other and start falling earthward. If a man didn't have so much else to think about right then, it would take the heart out of him." And Bert Stiles, in his book, recalled that on his very first mission he was involved in just such a mix-up: "Our group got lined up in wing

formation, but someone was off somewhere. . . . Just as I was about to sit back and look around, we were driving through another wing on collision course, there were airplanes everywhere and we were flopping around in propwash."

Unquestionably, the assembling of the Eighth's bombers into their defensive combat formations was tedious, costly in time and fuel, and costly also in lives and aircraft. Interpolation of the Eighth's official records indicates that perhaps three hundred ships—about five percent of those it lost to all causes—were lost to in-flight accidents during assembly. The value of the resulting formations, however, was such that for every ship and life they cost, probably ten others were saved.

Once the departing bombers were clear of the English coast, their gunners tested their weapons, and even this was an expensive operation. A mere one-second burst from each of the guns in a medium-sized formation would throw out as much as three tons of lead to fall and sink to the bottom of the sea, and it has often been said that by the war's end the North Sea surely must have had a solid lead bottom.

In recalling his first combat mission, Elmer Bendiner, in *Fall of the Fortresses*, described this test firing as heard from his navigator's position in the airplane's nose: ". . . the tail guns chattered as if they were in another country. The belly turret provoked a slight tremor at my feet . . . the top turret, firing forward over the cockpit and nose, burst the air and left us gasping. [The bombardier's] guns shook the nose as a dentist's drill rattles one's head. And I joined the celebration with my own little rattler." The smell of the resulting gun smoke, Bendiner went

on to say, "was pungent.... On that virginal June morning it was an aroma as gaudy as a striped bow tie, zestful as the brine in a pickle barrel. I must have been supremely innocent to divorce it from the knowledge of death."

Bendiner was not alone in being innocent of the knowledge of death. To many if not most combat crewmen beginning their first raid, the war was not yet quite a real war in which one actually might be killed. Frank Nelson, for instance, has said of his first mission: "I was a very young guy with much to learn. When we crossed the European coast I was all enthused about finally getting to see Europe, so as well as navigating I was really looking around. I saw flashes from flak guns on the ground, then saw a big black puff appear on one side of us and another black puff on the other, and heard shrapnel pinging against the airplane. But none of this bothered me much; I was still too much of a tourist." Another who began his first mission as a "tourist" was 381st Bomb Group ball gunner Ken Stone. Upon learning they were to raid a German airfield just outside the French capital, "I took my binoculars along so I could see the sights of Paris." With this same innocent unreality, Bert Stiles first saw flak as, "pretty black puffs in a blue sky . . . harmless looking stuff." And he was to remember thinking when crossing into Germany a few minutes later: "The fields were just as green as England, greener than Illinois when we crossed it last. They used the same sun down there, and the same moon. But for some reason, the people down there were Nazis."

This innocence and unreality, however, rarely lasted through the first mission. Usually they came to an end right at the European coast—for until the last months of the war that was where German resistance began—and always the end was abrupt and shocking. In Frank Nelson's case it was ended by flak, and right after he had seen those first two bursts: "Sitting up there, looking around and really sort of enjoying myself, I leaned forward to get a better look at Europe. Just as I did, it sounded like someone had fired a forty-five pistol beside my ear. I looked around and saw a big hole in one side of my compartment and another big hole in the other. The piece of flak that made them had gone through exactly where my head had been a moment before. That, by golly, really impressed me." Bendiner's combat baptism came near the coast also, administered by both flak and enemy fighters: "Little black clouds materialized up ahead.... I felt the whoosh, and, as 'Tondelayo' reeled and plunged, I heard *ping, ping, ping*, like pebbles on a metal roof. I realized with a sense of shock that these were shrapnel fragments. . . .

"[Then] a squawk from someone, 'Fighters at nine o'clock!' . . . the fighters coming in were each an inch of silver against the blue. . . . The wings grew to two or three inches and touched off little sparklers. Then they were inches no longer but massive aircraft, flipping over, spitting, and sliding down out of my gunsights. . . .

"Cartridge shells littered the nose, and when I moved my feet I slipped on them. When I slipped I swore. When I swore I could feel sweat on my forehead and marvelled that a man could freeze and sweat simultaneously. . . ." Stone with his binoculars saw not the sights of Paris, but ". . . a B-17 from the wing behind us going down. I watched it all the way down and

Searching for danger. Nothing there. / And yet your breath will whistle and beat / As on you push the stagnant air / That breaks in rings about your feet

(from "The Bridge of Dread," by Edwin Muir)

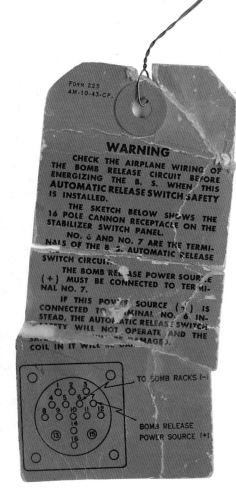

saw it hit the ground and explode. And when I saw that was when I really got scared." And Stiles received his introduction to the truth of aerial warfare through his radio: "I heard this guy call to the wing leader, 'We're going down. Our oxygen's gone. Can you get us some escort?' He was breathing like a horse. 'My navigator's shot to hell. I got to go down.' There was terror in his voice.

"Up there somewhere in that soft blue sky a navigator was dying. It was pretty hard to believe."

In an attempt to steer them away from the worst of the concentrations of flak guns with which the Germans had lined the European coast, the bombers were assigned on each mission "corridors" through which to fly in entering the Continent. But even though this may have saved them from some of it, it did not save them from enough. "As soon as you hit the coast of France, the first burst of flak would be right off your nose," said Ray Wild. "I don't know how the hell they knew where you were going to be, but they knew. . . ." W. W. Ford remembers a flak battery that greeted bombers approaching Holland: "He was located at the tip of the southern peninsula of the Zuyder Zee, and he was so deadly we called him 'Daniel Boone.' Once when we got in range of that guy he took three shots that put two airplanes on the ground and put holes in our tail and wings—all that with just three shots." And 56th Fighter Group pilot Robert S. Johnson has told of the coastal flak as seen from his perspective while escorting the bombers in a P-47: "The sky [around them] had come alive with savage energy . . . angry flame, sudden flashes from exploding shells . . . finally

the Fortresses were slogging through a mass of flame and smoke, driving through a rain of steel splinters." (From *Thunderbolt!* by Robert S. Johnson with Martin Caidin; Random House, New York, 1958.)

Just beyond the coastal flak, German fighters were waiting, ready to swarm up from one field after another in both the occupied countries and in Germany itself. Among these was one particularly well-remembered bunch— an elite group made up of Air Marshal Hermann Goering's personal squadrons. Based near the coast at Abbeville, and flying yellow-nosed FW190s, they were known as "The Abbeville Kids" or "The Yellow-nosed Kids," and by any name they were mean, aggressive, and trouble. Accordingly, it was at the coast that the bombers were joined by their "Little Friends," the fighter escorts sent to help them deal with the German fighters. In their briefings, Robert Johnson said in his book, the fighter pilots were told to "protect the bombers at all costs." During the last year of the war, the "Little Friends" were equipped with auxiliary fuel tanks that enabled them to accompany the bombers to all but the most distant targets. Before that they were able to do so only to about the German-Belgian border. Even that, however, was of tremendous help, and in recalling the war now, most bomber crew veterans are quick to say that without the help of their P-38, P-47, and P-51 fighter escorts, their daylight bombing of German military targets would have become too costly in lives and airplanes to have been continued.

In describing one such escort mission by the 56th Fighter Group, Johnson wrote: ". . . forty-eight Thunderbolts [P-47's] howling down

above: The warning tag which was attached to a Norden bombsight, the type used on 8AF bombers. *right:* Two wrecked German submarines at dockside in Hamburg following a massive Allied raid.

106

the grass runway into the air, forming quickly . . . climbing for altitude [to join] the 'Big Friends' [who] flew a staggered box formation, their guns unlimbered and poking into the slipstream.

"... Five miles from the European coast, six miles into space the squadron slid apart, Thunderbolts fanning out and moving into line-abreast positions, a giant swath of heavy fighters each some 100 yards apart. . . .

"Someone was on the radio. 'Fighters low at eleven o'clock. Climbing fast.' More voices . . . 'Two bandits, coming in level, twelve o'clock.' 'Look out for those four at five o'clock high.' The bomber crews, calling for help, announcing the arrival of Black-crossed Messerschmidts and Focke-Wulfs, the latter with yellow and red noses . . . the mark of the Abbeville Boys, Goering's finest. . . .

"One yellow-nosed Focke-Wulf tore through space not fifty yards in front of my plane, rolling slowly as he flashed by. I was so excited I forgot the rules of air gunnery and simply hammered a burst directly at the German instead of leading the target. . . . All I received for my pains was some camera footage of the Jerry as he dove. . . .

"It was my first aerial combat. . . ." (By the war's end Johnson had shot down twenty-eight German fighters, an Eighth Air Force record exceeded only by Francis "Gabby" Gabreski, also of the 56th FG, who shot down thirty-two.)

In the days before the Eighth's fighters had been equipped with long-range tanks, and so were not yet able to accompany the bombers more than a little way beyond the European coast, the German fighters often waited pru-

dently until they had gone before attacking the bombers. In speaking of the August 17, 1943, raid on Schweinfurt, for instance, ball-turret gunner Ken Stone recalled that: "Our fighter escort had to leave us near the Belgian border. Soon after that, enemy fighters—more than a hundred of them—came pouring out of the clouds." Even then, however, the Germans still were prudent and in their attacks used carefully preplanned maneuvers. This was because of their respect for the ten machine guns carried by every B-17 Fortress and B-24 Liberator—a respect so great that in the ready room of every Luftwaffe fighter unit there were charts showing the cones of fire of the bombers' guns, together with the probably least dangerous angles from which to approach them. Consequently, as Dave Shelhamer in June 1943 noted in his diary: "Jerry's favorite place of attack is the nose. A straight-in frontal attack gives him the best chance of scoring a hit without being hit himself. His favorite trick is to swing out to the side of the formation and get out in front of it a few thousand yards, and then come charging back head-on. When he comes in range he starts firing and rolling over on his back, shooting all the way. Then when he gets close he breaks away by doing a split-S out under the Fort." (A half-loop—thus, half of a letter "S"—which in this case would bring the fighter out right-side up below the bombers. And because the fighter pilot then would be on the same course as they, it would put him in position, with his greater speed, to again get ahead of them so as to make another attack.) Which was exactly how the August 17 attack described by Stone was made: "They lined up several thousand yards ahead of us in flights of fifteen flying abreast. The first flight came at us with guns blazing . . . then four more flights came through us. Our group's deputy leader fell out of formation with one engine blazing, and we saw the crew bailing out. Then three more ships fell out of our formation and parachutes billowed out of them also. But the Fortress gunners were deadly accurate, and enemy fighters were going down right and left. After what seemed like hours of fighting, the enemy fighters pulled away. Out of twenty ships in our group we had already lost four, and the mission had only just begun."

Although Stone did not mention it, his position in the ball-turret was a nerve-racking one during an attack. Cut off and isolated beneath the ship's belly, so small that a man did not so much occupy it as wear it, it required a man who was both great in courage and small in size. It was, said the 493rd Bomb Group's Larry Bird: ". . . An eerie position, so cramped you couldn't even take your parachute in with you. You'd crawl in it, close that damned door, then fasten the emergency strap around your back. You had a little window between the guns that you looked through, but your visibility was still so restricted that you had to depend on other crew members to call out the locations of the enemy fighters for you.

"If your plane was hit, you had to point your guns straight down, unhook the strap from around your back, unlatch the door, and pull yourself up out of the thing. Then you had to pick up your parachute and snap it on your harness before you could jump out. And if you had to get out of the plane in a hurry, that could be an awfully long procedure."

When enemy fighters came in from the front, rolling and shooting, said Donald Maffett: "Our evasive action was to turn the formation opposite to the way they rolled, which would throw their fire out of line with our formations. Because of their propeller torque the fighters had to roll to the left, so we would then turn to *our* left. That tended to throw their firepower off and was the only evasive action you *could* take when combatting a frontal attack. Your best protection, of course, lay in keeping the formation tight. There were not too many instances when they would attack a group that was in excellent formation—it had too much concentrated firepower."

Regardless of from where it was seen or how it was met, a fighter attack, said Sidney Rapaport: ". . . was a frightening, shattering experience . . . guns chattering like mad, and in the B-17, which had no soundproofing, they made one hell of a racket . . . Damn! . . . and cartridge cases flying all over the place. One of the things the Air Force gave me, I think, was the personal discipline that enables one to face that kind of situation."

But the feelings of the crews toward aerial combat may have been best and most succinctly summed up by a man riding with Ray Wild on a raid on Oschersleben: "He was," said Wild, "an awful nice guy named Nashold from, I think, Fargo, North Dakota, and was a new pilot taking his orientation ride by flying as my copilot.

"Well, a bullet came through the supposedly bullet-resistant plexiglass, stripped off his mask and cut a streak across his throat, then went on to lodge in my arm. He then passed out from lack of oxygen, and when the boys hooked

The Casablanca directive, issued to the British and American Bomber Commands in the United Kingdom on February 4, 1943, gave them their task in the following terms: Your primary object will be the progressive destruction of the German military, industrial, and economic system, and the undermining of the morale of the German people to a point where their capacity for armed resistance is fatally weakened. Within that general concept your primary objectives . . . will for the present be in the following priority: (a) German submarine yards. (b) The German aircraft industry. (c) Transportation. (d) Oil plants. (e) Other targets in enemy war industry.

(from *Closing the Ring*, by Winston Churchill)

to stay in formation. Finally had to feather #3 Engine (no gas) and break out of formation — Shot off distress flares and had spitfire escort until we hit the English coast. Made an emergency 3 engine landing at a strange field and the squadron sent a ship to pick us up — While checking up on battle damage we noticed the elevator cable, composed of six strands, had 3 shot away — This mission I was with another crew to get use to the formation etc. — Lovely time had by all — R.O. recuperating — Went to London on the 5th

---

him up to a portable oxygen set and brought him around, the first thing Nashold said was, 'There's gotta be an easier way to make a living.'"

Not only did the combat crews have to contend with the problems of enemy fighters and flak while making their forays over Europe, but also with the harsh environment of the altitudes at which they cruised. It might be summer on the ground, but it was always winter up where the bombers flew, and it was a winter made more frigid by the air that streamed past them as a self-generated wind equal to their indicated airspeed. In the case of the B-17s and B-24s this was a gale of a 150 miles an hour or more forcing icy draughts through every pinhole and crevice in the skins of those unheated craft, and swirling in great arctic gusts through the open windows where their waist guns were mounted. And in addition to being bitter cold, the air at those altitudes was too poor in oxygen to sustain human life and so low in pressure that any stray pockets of gas in a human digestive tract were likely to expand in ways both painful and embarrassing.

The crews' only defense against the cold was clothing—layers and layers of clothing topped off with fleece-lined leather flying jackets, trousers, and boots. They had also the Air Force blue "bunny suits" of electrically heated underwear which many wore but many others, for various reasons, did not. Those who did wear it, however, still wore all the other clothing as well. Otherwise they would suffer severe discomfort and probably severe frostbite if the suit's wiring should happen to short out or if its electrical supply should fail. Accordingly, those who flew in the bombers all flew so bundled up that they were, in one writer's words, "as fat as fall bears." Their movements were stiffly clothing-bound, and they could move only with difficulty through the passages and doors within their planes.

Almost as uncomfortable in its solution, and much more dangerous in its potential consequences, was the problem of oxygen. Tethering each crewman to his particular position was a rubber hose connected at one end to the airplane's oxygen system and at the other to a mask on his face. A dank, cold, rubber-smelling device, the mask felt, said one pilot, "like a clammy hand grasping your face." And, in a letter to his wife, Keith Newhouse once described it as: "a contraption that squeezes your nose, creases your face, hangs heavy with a rubber hose. . . . The condensation inside that instrument of torture drips down your neck to chill you and to freeze ice over your collar and on your flak vest." The danger of this oxygen system, as Newhouse then went on to say, was that the rubber connecting-hose was likely to "freeze entirely shut and stop the flow of the life-giving stuff." And the danger was compounded by the fact that oxygen starvation is a sneak-thief that gives its victims a sense of well being while at the same time robbing them first of the ability to think or react quickly, then of consciousness, and finally of life itself. For this reason, one member of every crew (usually the copilot or navigator) was given the duty of making frequent calls on the intercom to see, as navigator Charles Bosshardt put it, "if everyone was awake and alert." And in recalling that, Bosshardt went on to tell of the time when he, himself, was caught by oxygen starvation: "While I was working on my charts, Whitey, our bombardier, saw me slump unconscious over my table. Realizing what had happened, he managed to break up the ice in my hose and I roused up. Then, so he said, I went right back to writing like crazy without even realizing I'd been out." Tail gunner Paul Sink had a similar experience: "On the January 16, 1945 raid on Bitterfeld my oxygen froze up without my being aware of it. When Toggleer Larry Bird called out his next oxygen check, I didn't answer. The ball gunner and a waist gunner then came back and found me unconscious. They dragged me from the tail to the waist, where they hooked me up to a portable oxygen bottle and that brought me around all right."

Another hazard of the oxygen mask was the chance of vomiting while wearing it. This happened far less frequently than freeze-up, but men did occasionally become nauseated by airsickness or some other cause. When they did, they had to guard against unexpected vomiting while their masks were in place because this was likely to cause a fatal strangulation.

One man who invariably got airsick—although it never got him into trouble with his oxygen mask—was a 92nd Bomb Group gunner who flew in W. W. Ford's crew. "The poor soul wanted to fly more than anyone else in the crew," said Ford, "but he got airsick every time we left the ground. Never once did he not get sick, and he'd stay sick until he'd completely emptied his stomach. Then he'd be all right. So, we always took along a special box for this guy to empty his stomach in, and when he had done it we'd always then put the box in the bomb-bay.

In the back of my mind, while the pencil added and multiplied, I kept thinking, "You've been here only a short period of time, and you haven't had much experience flying in Europe, and no true combat experience yet. But you've got to imagine what the actual situation will be. You've got to figure out their precision fire." And then again: "Even though they are shooting at you, down there on the ground, they've got to lift a lot of rounds upstairs to get a hit on a target our size. They can only fire so many rounds in the time you're in their field of fire. Seems to me that the dispersion that they've got, with normal shell-fire . . . normal scattering, lack of accuracy, if that's what you want to call it, for that range. . . ."
Three hundred and seventy-two rounds. That was the way the answer came out.
Three hundred and seventy-two rounds, in order to hit a B-17 flying dead level, straight in. That was a lot of rounds, even for those busy batteries. I concluded that we could take this . . . thought it was worth a try. . . . Was.

(from *Mission With LeMay*, by General Curtis E. LeMay)

left: A portion of the October 9, 1943, entry in the diary of Ray Wild, pilot, 92nd BG.

"Well, of course when we opened the bomb-bay doors there'd go this gunner's dinner down on the head of some unsuspecting German down there. We always wondered if this caused some Germans to think we weren't fighting fair."

The problem of intestinal gas expansion at high altitude was controlled by diet—or was supposed to have been, at least. "The combat crews," said 390th Bomb Group pilot David Parry, "had a separate mess from the ground personnel. There were certain foods they weren't supposed to eat because they caused gas. Or, as colorfully explained by Paul Sink: "Tie off the neck of a balloon that has just a little air in it and take it up to altitude and it'll swell up bigger and bigger the higher you go until, if you go high enough, it'll explode. And that's why the ground personnel had their beans but we couldn't eat beans. God! Imagine how uncomfortable you'd feel."

But diet could not entirely solve the problem and, as was discovered one day by the 446th Bomb Group's Raymond Wilson while over Brunswick, its consequences could be very troublesome. Wilson was the radio operator in the lead ship of a squadron of B-24s that had just started its bombing run, when: "I knew I was in trouble. My stomach was about to blow! I called the Command Pilot [and] requested that our alternate lead take over communications. Then I contacted our waist gunners and asked that an empty ammunition case be placed where I could reach it. Next, I made preparations. . . . Oxygen was my first consideration . . . we were flying at 23,000 feet. The bomb-bay doors were open just below me and we were on our bomb-run to the target!

". . . I was holding my oxygen mask with my left hand and removing my flight suit with my right. . . . I disconnected my heated suit so I could get through three other layers of clothing and my 'long johns' so I could relieve my stomach in that ammo box. [I succeeded and] the action that followed was much like the blow-out of an auto tire.

"When I later told my story at interrogation some of the other fellows admitted having had the same problem but they had solved it in an easier way—into their clothes!"

Depending upon the bombers' path over the Continent they might or might not encounter heavy enemy resistance while en route to their target, but they were sure to encounter it over that target, especially if the target lay in Germany. In attempting to protect its strategic military and industrial centers, that nation, in the words of American fighter ace Robert S. Johnson, ". . . had become a bristling pit of anti-aircraft weapons . . . armed to the teeth with great guns that spewed torrents of steel, smoke and flame into the air. . . ." Most of these weapons were, of course, concentrated around the targets they were intended to protect, and this compounded their effectiveness because it was when they were approaching a target that the bombers were most vulnerable. To keep the formation lined up in such a way that its ships did not risk either colliding with each other or dropping bombs upon one another, and also to give the bombardiers the kind of stable course they needed for accurate aiming, the approach to the target was made by a straight and level run some twenty to fifty miles long. As described by Ray Wild: "First there's your Initial Point, or IP; then there's your Main Point of Impact, or MPI. The time between the two might be six or seven minutes—and in a bad headwind I've seen it take up to twenty-two minutes—where you fly straight and level.

"You flip on your automatic pilot, and the switch coupling it to the Norden bomb sight, and wherever your bombardier aims his bomb sight is where the plane flies. As pilot all you do is hold a constant airspeed and altitude (we went over the target in a B-17 at 150 mph indicated) and the bombardier controls all the rest."

Early in the war each bombardier aimed and dropped his bombs on his own initiative. It was not long, however, until the Eighth found that greater accuracy and tighter bomb patterns could be achieved by leaving the establishment of the bomb-run and the bomb aiming and dropping to highly qualified crews who were assigned to fly as group and squadron leaders. In the words of Frank Nelson, who flew as a lead navigator in the 487th Bomb Group: "The group lead crew performed all the navigation and timing for the arrival over the IP. Also, there was a lead crew for each squadron. Each squadron dropped its bombs when its lead ship dropped." "The group leader," said Sidney Rapaport, "would drop smoke streamers at the bombs-away point, and the rest of the group would then release its bombs at the same time. That way you got a pretty good bomb-saturation pattern." In recalling his impressions of this process, 390th Bomb Group waist gunner Robert Mygatt wrote: "The copilot called, 'Bomb-bay doors in the lead ship are opening!' I . . . looked about me at the other ships and their doors were slowly opening also.

"There is something grimly inexorable about . . . watching a formation of Forts running down on the target with all their doors yawning wide, as much as to say, 'Look out below! We're coming in, in spite of all you can do!' If there is any comfort to be felt on a bomb run, this is it." And on that particular run, the Germans had been doing plenty. "We were compelled to fly within range of perhaps three-hundred guns while holding a straight and level course," wrote Mygatt. "I felt like a sitting duck in a shooting gallery."

Which was always the case. The bombers, when on their long, straight bombing run, were always like ducks in a shooting gallery. Under other circumstances, flak gunners shooting at a ship at 25,000 feet, say, had to shoot at where they thought it would be twenty seconds later. But in the case of a bombing run, they *knew* where the ships were going to be. Accordingly, they simply chose a section or "box" of air through which the bombers would have to pass on their way to the target, and, with what was called a "box barrage," kept that section full of bursting shells. The barrage when seen from below looked like a cluster of polka-dots, but as seen edge-on by the bomber crews, it looked like a solid cloud—a cloud they grimly referred to as "iron cumulus"—and it was a frightening thing. "You could take no evasive action against a box barrage," said Ray Wild. "There was only one way to counteract it, and it began, 'Our Father who art in heaven. . . .' "

A B-24 in which 453rd Bomb Group copilot Bob Mallick was flying his final combat mission was hit in such a barrage over Kassel. In an arti-

And though we here fall down, / we have supplies to second our attempt, / if they miscarry, theirs shall second them, / and so success of mischief shall be born.

(from *Henry IV, Part Two*, by William Shakespeare)

113

The poignant misery of
dawn begins to grow . . . /
We only know war lasts,
and clouds sag stormy. /
Dawn massing in the
east her melancholy
army / Attacks once more
in ranks on shivering
ranks of gray, / But
nothing happens.

(from "Exposure," by
Wilfred Owen)

cle in the June, 1982, *Second Air Division Journal*, Mallick recalled the experience: "We turn off the IP, following the first groups toward the town. The [flak] is thumping pretty hot now . . . first to the right, then left ahead, then dead ahead with some red centers (*red centers mean down to earth trouble*) blooming and dying out . . . the skies are rapidly turning black with smoke puffs. . . . I'm waiting anxiously for the telltale smoke streamers to go out from the leaders to signify the drop zone. I want to tell [navigator-bombardier] Dave Parke to salvo the load and get the hell out of here! I do not like those red-centered bursts beside us that are beginning to ring and ding off the ship. . . .

"Smoke streamers are streaking down, pure white now—Bombs away time. As [Parke] kicks them out with the salvo switch we are hit and hit hard by three close bursts that we absorb with one hell of a lurch and sag. . . . We have to nose down and punch hell out of the left rudders. We are hurting somewhere!

"The instrument panel goes wild. It dawns on me that #4 engine has quit cold. . . . #1 engine is vibrating and detonating and running hot. . . . We sag downward and lose altitude and Doug turns slowly after the formation which is long gone. They look like gnats way out there fading swiftly away for home and I know instantly what 'lonesome' means. I can almost feel the ME 109's coming after us . . . to register a kill."

As it happened, Mallick's ship and crew managed with no casualties to make their way to a safe landing at an Allied emergency field in Belgium. Less fortunate, however, was the 401st Bomb Group's B-17 "Battlin' Betty" and her crew. While on a bomb-run over Stettin they took several hits so serious that the ship had to be abandoned. Ball-turret gunner John Hurd, who had been wounded in the buttocks when his turret was hit, later said: "It was very noisy when I left the ship, but after my chute opened the world became quiet. In fact, the bombardier, who was coming down near me, and I were able to talk to each other on the way down. And as we watched from our chutes, we saw my favorite B-17, "Battlin' Betty," hit and bury herself in a river.

"When I hit, I came to rest on my back and I struggled to keep my injured right butt out of the dirt. The bombardier, Al Autrey, landed right near me. Then a German officer showed up and herded us and two other crew members into a military vehicle. . . .

"A week later we arrived at POW camp Stalag 17-b. We rode three days in box cars to get there, which was pretty uncomfortable for me as I was not able to sit too well."

The moment they had released their bombs, the bombers headed for a nearby pre-agreed location called the Rally Point. There they pulled themselves back together in the best formation they could for running the gauntlet of fighters they could expect to find between themselves and home. And the fighters were sure to be there, but their tactics were likely to be different now. Earlier they had slashed savagely into the formation, trying to break it up and to keep it from reaching its target. Now, however, they were more apt to harass it like wolves harassing a herd of antelope, seeking more to pick off the slow, disorganized, or crippled than to attack the main body. Which meant, in turn, that at least some of the mission's crewmen could now enjoy a long-craved cigarette. "You were so damned busy making sure you hit the IP and the MPI on time, and with re-grouping," said Ray Wild, "and you wanted a cigarette so badly and worried about how soon you could have one." But even when the chance came, it was not easy to smoke while wearing an oxygen mask in air so thin a match would hardly burn. To do it, said Paul Sink: "You'd peel your mask off at one side, stick a cigarette in your mouth and light it—but you had to light it while the match was flaring because after it flared it'd go out, so your cigarette always tasted of sulphur." "You'd have to draw pretty often and pretty deep to even keep a cigarette going at altitude," remembered Robert White. "You'd take a drag, then put your mask back on and take in oxygen along with the smoke."

For those whose thoughts were of food rather than cigarettes, the process was complicated also, though not so much. As Charles Bosshardt recalled: "Since on a mission you'd miss the mid-day meal, they'd pack some candy and cookies for you. I remember lifting my mask off, putting a piece of candy in my mouth, then repositioning the mask. Somehow, this process always made me think of an elephant eating peanuts."

Regardless of the resistance the returning ships encountered over the Continent, they were sure to face a thicket of flak and fighters when approaching the European coast. But in the earlier days of the war this was also where they again were met by their Little Friends, the fighter escort. And whereas the escort could do nothing about the flak, they could and did do

something about the enemy fighters. In recalling his return from Schweinfurt as ball-turret gunner in the 381st Bomb Group's "Big Time Operator," Ken Stone said: "The fighters hit us again. Lt. Jarvis' plane already had one engine out; now its number three caught fire and its crewmembers waved goodbye to us as they dropped out of formation. There were chutes all over the sky—our white ones and enemy brown

above: The city of Duren, Germany, was visited by the Eighth in October 1943.

115

ones. It was thirty below zero but sweat was pouring off my face, I was positive we'd never see England again and I was praying to God, asking for courage to see this thing through.

"Then our fighter escort arrived and there were dogfights all over the sky, with Goering's Yellow-Nose Boys getting the worst of it." In his book, *Thunderbolt!*, escort pilot Robert Johnson described the time when, on November 13, 1943, his group ". . . picked up the Big Friends . . . just east of the Zuyder Zee. They were shot to hell. Many of the bombers lagged with smoking engines . . . crippled planes staggered along with gaping tears in their wings and fuselage. Every now and then a flare arced brightly, a pyrotechnic cry for an escort to shepherd a dying cripple."

For many of these cripples, arrival at the coast was decision time. To try to go on to England was to risk having to ditch in the North Sea—a dangerous prospect, especially in a B-24, which tended to break in two when striking the water. (4,361 Eighth Air Force crewmen ditched in the North Sea during the war. Only 1,538—or 35 percent—of these were rescued. The rescue percentage for B-17s was 38 percent and for B-24s 27 percent.) On the other hand, bailing out over Europe meant almost certain capture.

In recalling when he had to make such a decision, 390th Bomb Group pilot Robert White said: "We had two engines out and the third was acting up a little bit. We could crash-land in France and then try to evade capture. If we could make it over England we might have to crash land there, but we could probably make the base. But if we had to ditch . . . well the maximum time you could live in the water of the

North Sea in winter was fifteen minutes, so if we ditched we'd have to be rescued quick. Well, it was my opinion that we could stretch it out over the channel and get home, and that's what we did. It turned out to be the closest gamble I ever took—our last engine quit just as we rolled to the end of the runway."

Calvin Swaffer and his crew in "Memphis Blues" also tried to "stretch it" across the Channel, but with less success. Their ship had been badly crippled and ". . . seven FW 190s were trying to finish us off. We threw out everything we could to decrease our weight but we were still indicating only 95 mph and dropping at 500 feet per minute. We were at 4,000 feet when we crossed the French coast. When we were only a thousand feet above the water the seven FW's finally left us.

"We ditched and saw our B-17 sink within three minutes afterwards." Fortunately, Swaffer's ditching occurred in July and he and his crew survived their hour-and-a-half wait for rescue. In fact, said Swaffer, "We were told by RAF Air-Sea Rescue that we were the first B-17 crew to all be saved after ditching."

For those with fewer problems, there now remained only the matter of picking out their own home fields from the dozens of others crowded into the English countryside, and whereas this was not as simple as it might seem, there was one system favored above all others by navigators, and it rested on the fact that the shape of English forests never changed. "There's one sure way of finding your way home," said navigator W. W. Ford: "Fly your 'Gee' (radio navigation) line until you spot your particular set of woods. The forests were shown on our maps in green, and you could bet your life that each woods was gonna look exactly like it did on your map. From the air, every little English town looks just like the next one, but the woods were all different. Just west of Alconbury, for example, there was a wood shaped like an arrow. It pointed right down the runway, and when I was flying out of there that was always how I found my way home." When approaching the field, said Lawrence Drew, "If you had wounded aboard, the practice was to fire a double red flare, then other traffic would yield and let you land first, and right at the end of the runway you'd be met by ambulances." But sometimes, when there were many cripples desperately trying to get down while they still could, the system could become somewhat confused. Bert Stiles, for example, wrote of watching his returning group "... coming in four at a time on the approach, cutting each other out, floundering around in prop wash, dragging in low. . . .

A guy . . . in our squadron, who had lost his brakes in the flak, hadn't even started to slow down when he got to the end of the runway. He took out a fence and wound up two hundred yards down in some turnips. Nobody got hurt and the plane was all right, but he beat up a good many high-class turnips."

Then finally, when all the ships were home that were coming home and their crews were at last back on solid ground, the mood changed. Then, wrote Robert Mygatt, there were: "More cigarettes, much laughing and loud talk, flying clothes strewn about, machine-gun parts being carried out of the ship to be cleaned and put away, forms being filled in. . . . The thirty-odd B-17's which had carried us over the target and back already seemed to be sleeping. . . . As long shadows crept along the ground [the ships] rested quietly, as though storing up new energy for a repetition of the task tomorrow."

The rain slanted under the wing on a raw northeast wind. Of Cambridgeshire we had only an impression screened through the deluge-somber flatness, and mud; mud oozing up over the edge of the asphalt circle where we were parked; mud in the tread of the jeep, which rolled away on twin tracks of ocher, leaving us marooned; a vast plain, or lake, of mud stretching off toward a cluster of barely visible buildings.

(from *The War Lover*, by John Hersey)

THE GIRLS

"I walked the streets of Bedford with an English girl who lived with fear. . . . It was her fate which she shared with all Bedford, all England, all the world. We walked past [bombed out] fields of rubble and she would tell me who once had lived there." (Elmer Bendiner, in *Fall of the Fortresses*)

The uppermost thing in the minds of the combat crews and the ground personnel supporting them was the grim business of war. Next uppermost—as has always been true of young men, especially when gathered into armies—was girls. Their airplanes usually were named for girls and had pictures of girls painted on their noses, and their barracks were lined with pin-up photos of Hollywood "dreamboats" and, in Elmer Bendiner's words, "calendar art glorifying the female crotch." And in addition to these picture-girls there were, of course, real girls—the Girl Back Home, Red Cross Girls, and English Girls.

The girls in the airplane "nose-art" were never dressed for the cold altitudes where the airplanes flew. Some were scantily clad, more were nudes but coyly posed, and some were front-view nudes, bold and biologically complete.

The girls most popular in barracks pin-up photos were Betty Grable who had legs, Lana Turner who was the Sweater Girl, Dorothy Lamour who wore sarongs, Mae West, after whose bulging balcony an inflatable life-jacket had been named, and Rita Hayworth in a shot of her arising from bedcovers like Aphrodite from the ocean foam. The most desirable calendar art was the airbrush work of an artist named Petty, whose nudes were shown in poses and proportions as seductive on paper as they would have been grotesque in life, and were known collectively as the Petty Girl.

The place of honor among these pin-ups was occupied by shots of the Girl Back Home—a picture-girl whose one-time reality was maintained only through correspondence. Much time was spent in writing long and often torrid letters to her. Letters from her were the highlight of mail call. They were, that is, unless one of them happened to be a "Dear John"—telling the crestfallen recipient he had been replaced in her affections, and thus causing him to suffer days of black depression usually accompanied by a monumental drunk.

The Red Cross girls ran the base Aero Club, which, but for its lack of a bar, was to enlisted men what the officers' club was to officers. Also, in a van called a "clubmobile," the Red Cross girls took coffee and doughnuts to work crews around the base and to combat crews during mission debriefings. These girls usually were pretty and popular, and some, such as "Taddie" Spaatz at Polebrook, were daughters of high-ranking officers. They were difficult to date, causing some enlisted men to complain that Red Cross girls had eyes only for officers. The problem, however, was simply that they were so few among thousands of men. Accordingly, most dating by both enlisted men and officers was with English girls, who were not difficult to date at all.

"They are loose as a goose," wrote a Podington pilot in his diary, "and outspoken about what they will give you for gum or candy." He wrote that, however, after only six days in England, and had not yet learned that in percent-

Come, I'll be friends with thee, Jack; / thou art going to the wars, / and whether I shall ever see thee again / or no there is nobody cares.

(from *Henry IV, Part Two*, by William Shakespeare)

left: At Ridgewell, 381st BG air crewmen are met on their return from a mission to Germany by a member of the American Red Cross.

'And, General, how hold out our sweethearts, / Sworn loyal as doves?' / —'Many mourn; many think / It is not unattractive to prink / Them in sables for heroes. Some fickle and fleet hearts / Have found them new loves.'

(from "The Souls of the Slain," by Thomas Hardy)

far left: English girls watch as 8AF ground crewmen repair a B-24 engine.
top left, left and bottom: Lovely ladies on the walls of a mess hall kitchen at the 44th BG base, Shipdham.

Most near, most dear, most loved and most far, / Under the window where I often found her / sitting as huge as Asia, seismic with laughter, / Gin and chicken helpless in her Irish hand, / Irresistible as Rabelais, but most tender for / The lame dogs and hurt birds that surround her,— / She is a procession no one can follow after / But be like a little dog following a brass band. She will not glance up at the bomber, or condescend / to drop her gin and scuttle to a cellar, / But lean on the mahogany table like a mountain / Whom only faith can move, and so I send / O all my faith, and all my love to tell her / That she will move from mourning into morning.

(from "To My Mother," by George Barker)

122

ages of "loose as a goose," prim and proper, and somewhere in between, English girls were not too different from those in the States. The great influx of troops, though, had caused a sharp increase in English members of the "oldest profession." This "type of doll," wrote Bert Stiles, "can whisper her sales talk in a dozen languages . . . but she is at her best in the tongue of the Yanqui. She may be a hard-eyed bitch in the dawn, and she may put you away without pay for months, but when the mist is in your brain, and the war is yesterday and overhead and probably tomorrow, she is the princess of darkness."

As for the ordinary girls in the towns near the bases, they were "easy to meet" said Allan Healy. "You met them in the pubs [and at] our monthly dances."

At Molesworth, recalled Calvin Swaffer, "every second Saturday night we had a dance at our club. They would post signs in the local towns, inviting young ladies to attend. A truck would go and collect the ones coming, then we would meet it and each pick out one young lady to escort for the evening." And in speaking of Rackheath dances, Healy observed, "the base trucks brought the girls and took them home—most of them."

As recalled by many Eighth veterans now, one of the great rewards of these contacts was being invited by girls to their parents' homes where, in Healy's words, "you could forget for a while that you lived on an army base."

English girls seemed "peaked and pale," the Podington pilot said in his diary, adding that this was doubtless due to their austere wartime diet. Other wartime austerity, expressed in the English government slogan "Fashion is Ra-

tioned," caused them to lack good clothes. But, said Healy in his history of the 467th Bomb Group, "We learned not to judge them by their clothes . . . nor by beauty—drugstore or otherwise. Every day they seemed prettier, and there weren't only a few that one might marry—and did."

far left: Couples jitterbugging at a Red Cross party on the 353rd Fighter Group base at Raydon, 4 July 1945. *above:* At Molesworth, an American soldier entertains two children with a picture book at a Red Cross party for refugees on 10 October 1943.

Though I am old with wandering / Through hollow lands and hilly lands, / I will find out where she has gone, / And kiss her lips and take her hands; / And walk among long dappled grass, / And pluck till time and times are done / The silver apples of the moon, / The golden apples of the sun.

(from "The Song of Wandering Aengus," by W. B. Yeats)

above: Air crewmen rush to use a base telephone on their return from a raid over Germany. *above right:* 8AF WACs stationed at Middlesex decorate toys in their spare time. The toys were to be gifts for English orphans at Christmas, 1943. *right:* An Officers' Club dance at the 92nd BG base, Podington. *far right:* American Red Cross workers prepare coffee and doughnuts for airmen to enjoy following a combat mission.

FLAK

flak, n. [German *Flieger Abwehr Kanone* (anti-aircraft cannon).] 1. Explosive or exploding missiles fired from antiaircraft cannon. 2. Antiaircraft cannon, esp. in some attributive uses, as in flak battery, flak installation. 3. In intelligence usage: In sense 3, 'flak' as an attributive, includes not only those meanings in senses 1 and 2, but has been broadened to include also many forms of ground defense against aircraft: see flak intelligence, flak map.

Attrib. (in sense 1), as in flak barrage, burst, damage, umbrella, etc.

flak-happy, a. Suffering from combat fatigue caused esp. by flak. slang

flak jacket. A jacket or vest of heavy fabric containing metal plates, designed esp. for protection against flak. The usual type of flak jacket covers the chest, abdomen, back, and genitals, leaving the arms and legs free. Also called a "flak vest."

flak map. In intelligence usage, a map of a defended area showing the position and number of antiaircraft guns, surface-to-air launching sites, searchlights, radar installations, and other defense installations.

flak tower. A tower-like structure in which one or more antiaircraft automatic weapons are mounted.

(definitions from the *United States Air Force Dictionary*)

"The initial explosion caused us to go into a stall. We fell right about 2,000 feet on a vertical fall. Airplane out of control. And as we were pulling back up to altitude the second series [of explosions] started and that's when the bomb-bay

was hit in the number two aircraft. The whole thing started disappearing right in front of us as we were climbing up to it. Of course, the self-preservation thing takes hold and you just try to turn and get out of there quick as you can.

"Everything has gone wrong. Trying to figure out what it's going to take to save yourself, really... you're worrying about avoiding falling debris, avoiding the concussion, the fire, and by the time you get out of the mess and start looking around, you're into an area then where the German fighters are starting to close in on you because you're a single. So you start worrying about that and trying to figure out what that is, and you really don't have any kind of time to record what your feelings are. It's just genuine fear.

"When we recovered and pulled back up to altitude, Harold, my copilot, laughed and said, 'Don't say you never sweated in below-zero temperature.' It was 40 degrees below zero and the perspiration had rolled down over my eyes on the front of my oxygen mask. It was caked on the top of the mask a quarter of an inch thick. At 40 degrees below zero you can sweat."
Robert White
390th BG (H)

"Commonly the batteries would start tracking the lead aircraft in the first element of the first lead combat box. It is normal for enemy fighters or ack-ack gunners to try to knock down the leader of a formation. This pays off handsome dividends: it busts up the formation. The airplanes have to get back together in makeshift style when they've lost their leader. Obviously it

Most of the time when you are over enemy territory you have a funny feeling, particularly when you can see flak ... you know that it can hurt, but you look out there and it's fascinating because it comes up like a little armless dwarf. There's a round puff here and then there's usually two strings that come out of the bottom like legs ... and this thing will appear out of nothing. You don't see any shell; you don't hear anything. You just see this little puff of smoke and then shortly after, it sounds like somebody is throwing gravel all over the airplane. You're fascinated by it. You know that it can hurt you very badly, but you're fascinated by it ... you watch it. It's kind of like watching a snake.

(W. W. Ford, 92nd BG)

Until you see a burning wire shoot from the ground. As in a dream you'll wonder at that flower of fire, that weed caught in a burning beam.

(from "The Bridge of Dread," by Edwin Muir)

is an enormous advantage to split them up. The defensive firepower of the formation is confused for a time, and probably impaired throughout the mission."
(from *Mission With LeMay* by General Curtis LeMay)

"If there's anything an outfit hated to do, it was to take a three-hundred-sixty-degree turn for a second run on the target, because one Fort going around alone takes time enough, but with a formation you almost had to multiply that time by the number of ships, and you had to multiply the agony by plenty, too, because you'd thought the worst was almost over, and the fighters were still there, and the flak was still coming up, and it took forever. Oh, it was a nasty thing to have to do."
(from *The War Lover* by John Hersey)

"... Kept telling myself, just the way I told the men, that it was going to be a lot better to fly straight instead of zigging. We'd get through the area where they could shoot at us more rapidly, and the enemy would necessarily fire fewer rounds. All in all, we'd have a better chance of getting off with whole hides—people and airplanes alike."
(from *Mission With LeMay* by General Curtis LeMay)

"German flak was predominantly operated on two scales, the light flak positions and the heavy flak batteries. Light flak was provided primarily by 20mm. calibre machine guns—although 37mm. and 40mm. calibre guns were also

classed as 'light flak'—and seldom scored damaging hits above seven thousand feet; with its familiar green and yellow tracer shells it was used primarily as a defense against low-flying intruders which would otherwise be immune from flak defenses. The heavy flak batteries provided an often deadly defense against high-altitude bomber formations by using an A.A. version of the 88mm. which were the capital weapon of German artillery planning."
(from *The Destruction of Dresden* by David Irving)

"Oh Goddamn, that stuff ... well, actually I guess the times that I went, of course there was plenty of it there, but back in '42, '43, that's when it was bad. If you coulda walked on that stuff, you coulda WALKED on it. It was absolutely unbelievable, and those damned shells had altitude detonators and they'd punch a few of them ... maybe they'd be under you, and then they'd punch one of em ... maybe it would be above you, and about the fourth one they punched up ... was right in your damned window, man. GODDAMN, that was wicked stuff. One time I didn't go on a mission and the top turret gunner got killed ... oh, it had practically blowed the damned turret out of the airplane ... it was all just scrambled. I went up there and his upper teeth from about here around was stickin up in what was left of that damned turret. His teeth, gums and everything was blowed into that damned thing. But it's funny, you know ... you hate to see anybody die, but you get hardened to it, you know. Hell, you can go out there and pick up pieces of a body and put em in a plastic bag.

You don't think nothin about it. That's a helluva way to get, you know, but you get that way."
Ira Eakin
91st BG (H)

"The 918th proceeded on its bomb run. The bomb-bay doors opened. A red light appeared on the instrument panel. Up ahead, Savage watched ugly, black puffs of smoke appear level with the nose. Flak. Plenty of it. Enough to get out and walk on. But a lot less, he knew, than there would have been north of Hambrucken.

"A black burst mushroomed so close in front of the Lily that Savage could see the red heart of flame in the center of the smoke. Simultaneously there was a metallic crunch and he felt a jar, as a heavy fragment of steel punctured the nose compartment below. Over the interphone, he heard the single word from Roby—'Bombs . . .' But the word 'away' did not come. The red light blinked out. The B-17, relieved of its bomb load, surged upward.

"The navigator called frantically: 'Roby's hit bad! Let's get the hell out of here!' Savage moved the wheel into a left turn away from the target, looking down to see that Joe Cobb, on the inside of the turn, didn't overrun the formation. In the next second Savage was appalled to see a burst of flak catch Cobb directly in the tail, severing it. Cobb started straight down, but almost immediately the airplane exploded into a thousand fragments no bigger than a man's fist. Nor was there a trace of any chutes. Cobb's instant death registered on Savage's eyes, but not on his brain. He pressed his mike button. 'Able leader to Charlie two and Charlie three, tack on

behind able squadron!' he called sharply. The two survivors of Cobb's six-ship low squadron dropped back behind Savage.

"Calling on the bottom-most depths of his self-control, Savage set course for home. He sent Rexall below to check up on Roby. Then he looked back toward the target. Pillars of smoke rose from the vicinity of the Aiming Point at the ball-bearing plant. And above it, boring in through dense barrages of smoky flak, the other groups were raining down their bombs. The mission had succeeded."
(from *Twelve O'Clock High* by Beirne Lay, Jr. and Sy Bartlett)

"We didn't see any flash on the ground or anything . . . we just got hit. They got us with their first burst. We didn't even see any puffs of flak. They got us, the lead, with their first Goddarned burst. They knocked out two engines. Unbeknownst to us they got one of the landing gear, one of the tires and many holes. They must have got us under one wing. Obviously, we had to abort. You've always got a deputy and a follow-up lead, so we jerked it over to them. We made it back across the Channel and we ended up losing a third engine prior to landing. We made the base; we landed with one engine. We only had one gear partly down, and the other one was like a ruptured duck, so we landed one gear up and one partially down. We ended up making a belly landing. And we actually landed with just one engine. That gear gave away and of course, as soon as it gave away we dropped down on our belly. We had dropped our bombs in the Channel. We didn't make a complete 180, we made a

We are dying, we are dying, we are all of us dying / and nothing will stay the death-flood rising within us / and soon it will rise on the world, on the outside world.

(from "The Ship of Death," by D. H. Lawrence)

90 degree turn. Raised a lot of dust. We didn't land on the runway, we landed adjacent to it in the dirt. We didn't lose a person."
F. W. Nelson
487th BG (H)

"The 88s which were, I think, mostly used for flak, boy, they were tremendously accurate, just fabulous. They used two types. One was *predetermined*; the other was *barrage*. In barrage type, there'd be a flock of guns and they'd shoot at one spot in the sky and keep shooting at it. The other was predetermined aiming at planes. The most frightening one was the indeterminate one where they were shooting at a spot in the sky. You had to go through that spot when they weren't shooting. Emden, Kiel, Wilhelmshaven, Munich, Berlin . . . I think they did both at all five of those targets. But Schweinfurt was murder. I'm sure they shot barrage because they had so damned many guns. The German fighters stayed pretty much out of the flak, but on Schweinfurt they *did* come through the flak. It's one of the few times they flew in their own flak, but they were probably under orders. That indeterminate flak that was coming up, there was nothing you could do about it. This was something that was gonna happen. It was impersonal as hell."
Ray Wild
92nd BG (H)

"When you get on that initial point and start going in on that line, this is where their gunners are waiting for you. This is where the flak's gonna come up and stay right with you. They're tracking you and they're firing at you. You fly along over nothing and, all of a sudden, right off your wing big black puffs of smoke start appearing. Pow, pow, pow, pow, pow. And they'd stay right up there with you, and you wonder, 'well, by gosh, someone's tracking and they're doing a damned good job of it, too.'"
Larry Bird
493rd BG (H)

"We were sitting up there cool and silver and almost home, when the black puffs started coming up. The Germans had wheeled in a mobile battery and they had us zeroed. I could see the dull flashes right outside the window. The ship lurched and gagged and I could hear the stuff hitting the wings. Little slivers of glass splintered around the cockpit. The right wing bucked and I looked out there and saw smoke curling out of the oil cooler.

'Number four's on fire,' came over interphone, loud and scared.

'Just smoke,' Spaugh said coolly. 'Smoking bad, sir.' I looked down and we hadn't moved. We were standing still over France, and they were pouring it at us."
(from *Serenade to the Big Bird* by Bert Stiles)

"Flak has a terrible fascination. There is a five-ball burst, and the black smoke rolls out like a plume dancing in a heavy wind. Then it is caught in the slip stream and disappears. If it is close enough to hear, it is a rather subdued 'pooh.' The pieces sound like hail on the plane.

I have perceived much beauty / in the hoarse oaths that kept our courage / straight; heard music in the silentness / of duty; found peace where shell-storms / spouted reddest spate.

(from "Apologia Pro Poemate Meo," by Wilfred Owen)

left: Severe flak damage to this Kimbolton-based B-17 of the 379th BG (H) on 20 December 1943.

"But when it first starts it is generally low and ahead. Step by step it advances up. Then you find yourself saying, 'The next one is it. Can't miss this next time. This is it. Next one.' Well, so far, the next one hasn't done all it was expected to do. Perhaps there hasn't been a 'next one,' although we've had damage on the bomb doors. A fellow gets a detached air while watching those angry black puffs. Can't do a thing about them so you relax and observe, hypnotized by them. If I'm flying, I can't resist a corner of the eye glance to see how close they are."
Keith Newhouse
467th BG (H)

"I could hear him yelling, 'I've been hit. I've been hit.' He was standing there on the middle of the floor. He had his hands between his legs ... he was jumping up and down and yelling, 'I've been hit.' "
Larry Bird
493rd BG (H)

"Out there, we've talked quite friendly up to Death; sat down and eaten with him, cool and bland,—pardoned his spilling mess-tins in our hand. We've sniffed the green thick odour of his breath,—our eyes wept, but our courage didn't writhe. He's spat at us with bullets and he's coughed shrapnel. We chorused when he sang aloft; we whistled while he shaved us with his scythe.

"Oh, Death was never an enemy of ours! We laughed at him, we leagued with him, old chum. No soldier's paid to kick against his powers. We laughed, knowing that better men would come, and greater wars; when each proud fighter brags he wars on Death—for life; not men—for flags."
(from *The Next War* by Wilfred Owen)

"Now, passing beyond the coastline, our searching began in earnest. All we had seen up to this point had been a few black puffs of flak—the erratic, inaccurate antiaircraft firing we always seemed to catch at the rim of Europe, where the batteries either had had insufficient alert or were not of the quality of those ringing many of our targets."
(from *The War Lover* by John Hersey)

"I recall the first one that I flew. It was a relatively short mission into France. And as we went over the coast, I was so enthused about seeing Europe. It was the first time I'd ever flown over Europe and, boy, I was looking out the nose and navigating and what have you. And I saw these flashes down on the ground. And I said, 'There's a flak gun down there.' I could see the flashes. It looked like a three-battery job to me, and about that time there was a big black puff over here, and a big black puff over there. That didn't bother me too much. Then there were a few more black puffs and we got a little flak and I could hear it hit the aircraft. There wasn't any major damage on this first mission. I wasn't concerned. After that first mission we came back and talked about it. Some of the crew members would honestly build up in their own minds a fear of that flak. This is what we came up with as

And it rose up, a sullen stain / flawing the crystal firmament. / A wound! We felt the familiar pain / and knew the place to which we were sent.

(from "The Voyage," by Edwin Muir)

left: Flak positions are still evident on the roof of this large black building behind an amusement park–fairgrounds complex in the heart of contemporary Hamburg.

133

far as a term was concerned . . . they would get 'flak happy.' Everybody, I think, that flew over there hated the flak worse than the fighters. Flak you couldn't do anything about, particularly if you were on the IP going in on your run . . . you just went on in and you had to go through it. A pilot you could shoot back at. Flak, there was just something about it. So, the philosophy that I developed (and it's nothing unique; many people have developed the same philosophy, but it meant a lot to me) was: 'Well Frank, you've got 25 missions to fly over here. OK, you've got to do your job. That's your number one consideration. Now if it so happens you're going to get shot down or whatever the situation might be, so be it. But don't worry about it. Worrying about it is one of the worst things you can do.' So, I think every mission that I went on, I wasn't particularly worried about getting shot down, and believe me, I saw a lot of B-17s shot down, and real close to me too. I saw them blow up. But that's war. And you just have to keep your job as your number one consideration. There were some people who couldn't develop that philosophy. They were always worrying and as a result some of them had to be sent home or be grounded because they were nervous wrecks."
F. W. Nelson
487th BG (H)

From my mother's sleep I fell into the State, / and I hunched in its belly till my wet fur froze. / Six miles from earth, loosed from its dream of life, / I woke to black flak and the nightmare fighters. / When I died they washed me out of the turret with a hose.

(from "The Death of the Ball Turret Gunner," by Randall Jarrell)

"The noise is the soft flak. You can't hear it hit the airplane. I remember vividly on a raid . . . it wasn't Schweinfurt, it wasn't that rough on our crew, but it was terrible. We lost about half a dozen planes, and one of them was right in front

left: Fortresses of the 381st BG (Ridgewell) encounter heavy flak concentrations on a raid over Germany.

Over Berlin in March of '45 I saw an 88 come up and it sat there for maybe two or three seconds from the time it stopped rising, until it started dropping back down and then, just as it started dropping downward, it exploded. It was just sitting there in mid-air. I saw several shells coming up. Yeah, you could see them once in a while. Before they exploded, they were kind of hanging in the air . . . suspended.

(Larry Bird, 493rd BG)

of me in the formation, and he just absolutely exploded . . . just a big ball of debris and you could feel that debris hit your airplane, and that was a very unpleasant sensation."
David Parry
390th BG (H)

"A shell came up through the squadron navigator's table, through his map, past his nose, out the top, and burst about ten feet above the ship. A big chunk came ripping back through and smashed the pilot's knee, just clipped off the whole kneecap.

"The bombardier told us. 'We just went up and put a tourniquet on his leg. He didn't yell much. The co-pilot flew home okay.' "
(from *Serenade to the Big Bird* by Bert Stiles)

"The senses are not trustworthy. And the sky is treacherous with flak. The flak bursts about you and sometimes the fragments come tearing through your ship."
(from *Once There Was a War* by John Steinbeck)

"Some places flak could be pretty bad . . . pretty accurate. In and around Berlin . . . I think I went to Berlin about three times . . . the flak was pretty heavy. Of course, we would always have a flak chart. Our Intelligence would show us the route to take in and out of the city to minimize our exposure to flak. Sometimes I think they were just drawn up to encourage us a little bit. I don't think they were really too accurate."
Lawrence Drew
384th BG (H)

"When we came to a wide bay we saw the German smoke pots cloaking our target, Wilhelmshaven. Out of the smoke rose a storm of flak, rocking Tondelayo, sending fragments through its metal skin, biting into her delicate electric nerves."
(from *The Fall of Fortresses* by Elmer Bendiner)

"They all agree that what happened seemed to happen very slowly. The Fortress slowly nosed up and up until she tried to climb vertically and, of course, she couldn't do that. Then she slipped in slow motion, backing like a falling leaf, and she balanced for a while and then her nose edged over and she started, nose down, for the ground.

"The blue sky and the white clouds made a picture of it. The crew could see the gunner trying to get out and then he did, and his parachute fluffed open. And the ball turret gunner—they could see him flopping about. The bombardier and navigator blossomed out of the nose and the waist gunners followed them. Mary Ruth's crew yelling, 'Get out, you pilots.' The ship was far down when the ball-turret gunner cleared. They thought the skipper and the copilot were lost. They stayed with the ship too long and then the ship was so far down that they could hardly see it. It must have been almost to the ground when two little puffs of white, first one and then the second, shot out of her. And the crew yelled with relief. And then the ship hit the ground and exploded. Only the tail gunner and the ball-turret man had seen the end. They explained it over the intercom."
(from *Once There Was a War* by John Steinbeck)

AT EASE

Life on the bases was so busy that most of the men had little time to spend in daily recreation. This was especially true of the air crews, who, when not flying combat missions, were usually flying practice missions or attending training sessions. It was equally true for the mechanical crews, who usually were either preparing airplanes for a combat mission or patching them up after a mission. But for those who could find time, recreational facilities were available. For example, at Rackheath, said Allan Healy, there were softball games, a gymnasium with a basketball court, and "tennis was played on Sir Edward's court." Also, "bicycling became a major sport. English bikes were issued to many of the ground personnel and the fly-boys felt free to borrow. [This] got so bad that on one occasion all bicycles were called in by the MPs and their numbers checked and the original owners given back their wheels.

"A fair imitation of a movie theater was maintained on the base and we saw many old pictures and a few new ones. . . . USO shows came occasionally. . . .

"Large Nissen huts made up the Aero Club where enlisted men could enjoy a library, game tables, a snack bar, and the attentions of the Red Cross girls. The officers had their club . . . where the bar provided for most, and papers, magazines, checkers, bridge, or chess gave recreation to some. Here John Gile and Dick Grey pounded the pianos and the tinplated roof reverberated to 'It's a long rough road from Rackheath to Berlin,' and 'Rackheath Aggies.' Many of us had radios in our huts. We could hear the BBC . . . [and] often we listened to the Luxembourg station with its German propaganda."

preceding spread: Mail call at the 91st BG base, Bassingbourne. *above:* The simple pleasure of reading in the Special Services Library on base at Bassingbourn. *right:* After receiving permission from the farm owner, these men, attached to an air station in Norfolk, invade a turkey pen to select their annual Thanksgiving Day main course on 6 November 1943.

(Sam Burchell also remembers hearing those German broadcasts, and that within two hours of his group's arrival at its English base, "we heard a German announcer welcoming the 448th Bomb Group to Seething, and telling us where the good bars were and which girls had the clap.")

For those too busy to take much advantage of base facilities, on-base recreation consisted more of casual horseplay, poker when time allowed, and periodic parties. "People were forever tossing CO-2 cartridges into our stove," said Lawrence Drew. "You'd be backed up to it on a cold day, when all of a sudden it would just blow up and hot coals would fly all over the place and scare everybody."

"We played poker," said Max Pinkerton, "and it would get expensive because we weren't used to English money. The pound note was really a five-dollar bill, but it said 'One' on it, and when you bet a pound, in your mind you were betting a dollar. A pot could get to two–three hundred dollars without anybody realizing it, and when you were making $150 a month plus flight pay, that was a *lot* of money.

"Fortunately we didn't have much time for poker," Pinkerton continued, "and our best base recreation was parties. Every so often we were given a 'guaranteed stand-down' for a couple of days, and then we'd have a big spread of food and, of course, drink. We'd send buses to Peterborough for young ladies who'd care to come, and the buses would come back filled.

"Our squadron, the 511th, always prepared for these parties with a 'combat briefing.' If the party was to start, say, at seven in the evening we might begin the briefing at one in the

afternoon. We roasted everybody, and the drinks flowed free, and I remember at one of them I fell out of the window. We did it real formally with one guy acting as the CO and another as the Intelligence Officer. We had maps, and discussed how to attack this party, and said real solemnly, like they always did in a real briefing, "Of course, we must expect losses." That's still a catch-phrase in my family now. When we're planning for some lively event, we say, "Of course, we must expect losses."

Some "at ease" time, of course, was spent in neighboring towns. From Rackheath, wrote Healy, "A liberty run of trucks went to Norwich every night, parked at the Cattle Market, and brought home those who had gone to the flicks, the pubs, or their girls. The Red Cross clubs in Norwich were excellent, the Maddermarket Players gave good theater, the Lido, Blackfriars, or Samson and Hercules had dances."

At some point well along in their tours, when they were beginning to get "flak happy," combat crew members were given a week's R&R (Rest and Recuperation) at an Air Force rest home or "Flak Shack." And this, as a rule, was an unforgettable experience. "On our week of R&R," said Sidney Rapaport, we went to a hotel in Southport, on the coast near Liverpool—a marvelous Victorian edifice with chimneys, and staffed by the Red Cross. We had a whole group of activities, great cuisine, and a dance every night, and all the women from Southport came in. A joyous experience, that R&R, a time when you got almost no sleep at all but it was worth it."

Then, there was London—magic word, magic town, mecca for all the Eighth. "Every

left: Interior of the 381st BG Officers' Club at Ridgewell. *above:* Part of a fairy tale-like mural on a large hut wall at the 95th BG base, Horham.

five missions, you got a three-day pass," said Pinkerton, "and what you did was head for London. Those were memorable trips and a thousand stories could be told about 'em—quite a few not printable."

"That three-day pass was a marvelous thing." Rapaport recalled. "We'd catch the train at Bury St. Edmunds. The cars were old-fashioned English carriages with compartments with doors. I'd walk down the line until I saw a compartment with a WAF or an army girl alone in it, and I'd choose that one.

"You never had to worry about hotel accommodations because we had officers' clubs in some of the swankiest parts of London, but you always somehow wound up sleeping somewhere else anyhow."

After base life, London was to each man whatever he wanted it to be. Westminster Abbey and the Tower and Buckingham Palace, a luxury hotel, a pub, a Piccadilly Commando, the theater—whatever a man was seeking.

"One went to the theater at six-thirty and saw the Lunts or a musical comedy," wrote Healy. "Most somehow found girls and sat in pubs or went to 'bottle clubs.' You saw the incredible gaiety and corruption that was Piccadilly in the wartime blackout."

While Calvin Swaffer was in London, "My CO called asking me to go with him to meet some dignitaries. Well! They turned out to be the King and Queen, who wanted to meet a Yank who piloted a Flying Fortress. We had tea and visited for ten or fifteen minutes. I'll never forget that moment."

Bert Stiles and his pilot first had three double-scotches in their hotel room, "Then we

left: Incredibly orderly, the Post Exchange of the Deenethorpe-based 401st Bomb Group.

top: Football in off-duty hours at Kimbolton. *above:* Taking full advantage of the only occasional sunshine at Mount Farm. *right:* A 381st BG barbershop.

above: Crew members of the 91st BG B-17 "Our Gang" check in at the American Red Cross Club in London for a well-deserved 48-hour leave. *above right:* The Kings College Chapel, a familiar meeting place for the American airmen stationed in Cambridgshire. *right:* The London red doubledecker.

The troubles of our proud and angry dust / Are from eternity, and shall not fail. / Bear them we can, and if we can we must. / Shoulder the sky, my lad, and drink your ale.

(from "The Chestnut Casts His Flambeaux," by A. E. Housman)

above left: The ever-present British lion adorns this London townhouse entry. *above right:* A quiet street in Norwich, a "liberty" town frequented by Second Air Division personnel. *left:* St. Paul's, a true survivor.

149

left: When 8AF crews earned a one-week respite from flying combat, they were often sent to "rest homes" such as this one at Salisbury for seven days of complete rest and relaxation, or so read the prescription.
below: The great AAF band of Major Glenn Miller entertained the men of many 8AF bases in WW2.

You see, my good wenches, how men of merit / are sought after; the undeserver may sleep, / when the man of action is called on. / Farewell, good wenches. If I be not sent / away post, I will see you again ere I go.

(from *Henry IV, Part Two*, by William Shakespeare)

above right: The Swan in Lavenham where men of the 487th and 94th Bomb Groups gathered to refly a day's mission and develop a tolerance for the tepid brew called "bitter." *right:* An ancient pub sign at Parham near Framlingham, a 390th BG watering spot. *far right:* London sits shrouded in a heavy watercolor sky. It was a wonderful "liberty town."

were ready to wander. I lost Sam in the first place. . . . I tied up with an RAF bomb-aimer in the Ritz, and we had a Free Frenchman with us for a while in the Savoy, and a fairy tried to join us at the Dorchester. We drank scotch . . . and gin and rum and Pimms and port. . . ."

Next day he met a girl and, "We had chow in a little Russian place . . . and we drank nut-brown ale until closing time in a quiet pub. . . . We threw darts with some Royal Engineers and lost three times in a row." Then after taking the girl home and returning to his hotel, Stiles "stood outside for a moment and listened to the city, London under the moon. Tomorrow it might be Berlin under the sun.

"Somehow I didn't care. . . . For a while I'd been away from it."

Not all who went to London in 1944, however, did get away from the war. In that year it often followed them in the form of German V-1 and V-2 flying bombs which in 1944 cost London more than 30,000 casualties, and the evenings they had expected to spend in pubs or theaters they often wound up spending in shelters. Ira Eakin vividly recalls the V-2 rocket that struck a crowded night club just after he and a crewmate had left it to return to their room in the nearby Rainbow Corner Red Cross Club.

"We'd just gone to bed when the damn thing hit, and our floor buckled and bounced. I threw on my pants and shoes, and Abe was so excited he put both legs down one leg of his pants, and there he was—couldn't get 'em on *or* off. I said, 'Let's get to hell out of here before the building caves in!,' and he said, 'Fuck ol' Rover, Eakin! I'm a-comin', but first I gotta get my legs outta my damn pants!' "

above left: Film star Leslie Howard, honored guest at an Eighth Air Force party at Watford, signed autographs to give English girls and American soldiers. *above right:* Bing Crosby and members of his troupe entertained personnel of 2nd Base Air Depot, near Lancashire in September 1944. *right:* Joe Louis and Billy Conn with the troops of BAD 2 on 6 July 1944. *far right:* On that same day at another 8AF base in England, Princess Elizabeth met the crew of "Rose of York."

PRISONER OF WAR

WESTERN UNION

1201

LB305W (TWO) 46 GOVT=PXXWMUB WASHINGTON DC 30 551P=

DEC 30 PM 6 17

MRS CECELIA MCCARREN=

            10 PARROTT ST (LYNN MASS)=

THE SECRETARY OF WAR DESIRES ME TO EXPRESS HIS DEEP REGRET

THAT YOUR SON STAFF SERGEANT WILLIAM R MCCARREN HAS BEEN

REPORTED MISSING IN ACTION SINCE TWENTY DECEMBER IN EUROPEAN

AREA PERIOD IF FURTHER DETAILS OR OTHER INFORMATION ARE

RECEIVED YOU WILL BE PROMPTLY NOTIFIED PERIOD=

        ULIO THE ADJUTANT GENERAL.

The Eighth Air Force was readying another strike in the "precision daylight bombing" of Hitler's Third Reich. The raids had been increasing in intensity for a year. The target was the shore installations and underseaboat pens at Bremen. It was to be a "maximum effort" with over 900 British and American fighters serving as escort for 2,000 bombers. Our crew of ten took little experience (and considerable apprehension) with us as we left the briefing by truck to the B-17 assigned for the day's operation.

It was to be a very long mission for us.

A chilling fog hung over the base. It was December 1943 and, like a gray theater curtain, a heavy mist was lifting to the accompanying roar of 8,000 engines. Ships were scattered over the great bases; "dispersed"—to make mass destruction difficult for an enemy raider. The spare assigned to us appeared more like a sick pigeon than an attacking eagle. Patched and battered-looking, it was parked in the furthest revetment. We busied ourselves in the area of our responsibility. I reported the intercommunication outlets were equipped with low-altitude microphones for what was to be a high-altitude mission. This condition would make it necessary to remove oxygen masks before "pressing to talk" rather than using the high-level choker type mikes to pick up throat vibrations. Talking without oxygen for a moment was not dangerous . . . the resulting delay could very well be.

The pilot was anxious to go along with the group (or embarrassed to abort). He chose to ignore the problem. Strike one?

We were behind the others because of the switch in aircraft, and armorers hurried to load the bomb bay with incendiaries. Though small these little candles from hell raised havoc when dropped on an area already blasted by high explosives. They defied ordinary fire-fighting equipment. We checked our guns; mine was the fifty-caliber machine gun mounted in the open hatch above the radio section. Parachutes were next along with oxygen lines, heated suits, transmitters and receivers, flare gun and code books. Worriers worked harder than others, I reasoned . . . but maybe . . . lived longer?

The takeoff was a respite—but not from our practice of "sweating out" the performance of the pilot. We "sweated out" everything he did . . . formation flying or landings. We knew the pilots were only a year away from their desks or hot rods and everything about flying was new to them (sudden death would also be new to us). The gasoline and bomb-laden hulk seemed to hesitate as it taxied to the top of the runway before it lumbered down and just (shakily) cleared the trees at the end. (Why are there always trees where you don't need them?)

Looked around when we were airborne. The sky was a heaving hornets' nest of 17s and the box-like B-24s. Each ship had a crew of fully-armed (and partly-trained) men. The armada oozed power . . . probably 20,000 men organized last-minute details as they jockeyed for position over the Island Kingdom. This "forming" sought the alignment that would have the planes in the best arrangement for protection against flak or interceptors. We seemed finally to be heading in a particular direction. Because of the constant position of nearby aircraft, it was as though we were standing still in the sky. After gaining altitude, the cold made "contrails" out of condensation pouring back from the heated

above: William R.
McCarran, 1943. *right:*
McCarran again in 1982.

exhausts. These showed a forward motion as nothing else could.

It was freezing and the 17 vibrated like all hell. (Two conditions that accent each other, when people are nervous and when people are thinking of killing—or being killed.) The equipment was as ready as it ever would be . . . but were the anxious people? Had time to think of history and how we were now a part of it. Dunno why, but the Mongol invasions of Eastern Europe came to mind. I wondered if kids would read of our exploits as we had read of those ancient savages. We were supposedly "civilized," yet we had enough destruction with us to do in hours what it would have taken Kublai Khan and his hordes years to "accomplish."

Wondered why we were here. Were the Germans as bad as the necessary lies of war would have us believe? I remembered the aftermath of WW I when both sides admitted the ruses used to fire the flames of patriotism. Von Luckner, the "Sea Wolf," and Richoften, "The Red Baron," were heroic warriors to the schoolboys of the Twenties. Here in WW II the "Flying Circus" was storybook stuff and Erwin Rommel was already the legendary "Desert Fox."

"Fighters," someone yelled . . . off came the oxygen mask to ask "where?" . . . "they are ours," came the reply. My pulse slowed when I recognized the escort cavorting in the distance. . . . Their speed and maneuverability were reassuring. (I'm a guy who needed all the reassurance available.)

Over the Frisian Islands a token amount of flak popped up . . . but it seemed distant and harmless giving us (me?) a false sense of invincibility. The engineer-gunner called the pilot's at-

tention to a faulty supercharger, a condition bad enough to slow the ship should a burst of speed be needed for evasive action. Again, as captain, the pilot chose to ignore something that could prove disastrous. Whether or not this determined later events, those of us at the middle and rear of the plane would never know. It failed, however, to raise our now bewildered morale.

Strike two?

"Blat." I was certain a bullet had slammed past my ear and out the other side of the radio shack. I was equally sure that one of Reich Marshal Goering's most skilled people had singled me out for a special target. (Odd—people cautioned us never to underestimate the enemy. . . . I never expected anyone but the most formidable of opponents.) The shot must have been from one of our aircraft . . . one of the gunners "testing" without "aiming." There were no enemy airplanes in sight.

Not yet!

It wasn't long (enough) until flares dropped by the lead plane indicated the beginning of the run over the target. We began the approach. The bomb bay doors opened O.K. They were never to close.

"Whooof" came the flak to "Whack" all around us. The plane rocked with explosions and rattled with flying metal. The bursts were close. They were black and threatening but drifted off like puffs of innocent white clouds. Our plane must have been one of the first to prove the accuracy of gunners—five miles below.

"Bombs away" came over the intercom and down went the incendiaries from a bay already afire. (I remember thinking it strange to see aluminum burning.) "Bomb Bay Doors Closed" came the order—this from the front of our staggering and flaming 17. (These messages were delayed because of the microphone problem.) There were more hits and more explosions. The confusion began. . . .

Strike three?

It took time to inform the pilot that the doors were jammed. The instructions came back, "Close them by hand." It was my assignment and I went for the crank clipped to the partition between the radio room and the bomb bay. Before moving I had to connect my oxygen to a walk-around bottle. The communication foul-up continued. The top turret gunner (engineer) came back through the walkway. He had neglected to use the emergency (oxygen) system and passed out in the fire-filled bay. He had to be revived and led back to the relative safety of his gun position.

Because of the brake-like action of the open bays, we were falling behind the protection of the formation and were being clobbered by fighters (ME 210s). I couldn't budge the doors with the crank and returned to the radio room. (I was still strangely fascinated by the sight of metal burning.) I didn't fully comprehend the danger when I saw an unexploded 20mm shell beneath the transmitter. I just stared at it. . . . It blew and the force threw me face down into the opposite corner. I was stunned. Couldn't get up until the thought came—"my mother would be sad if I stay here." I got to my feet, and, following another series of hits, decided to leave. There was then no contact with the front of the aircraft. I had no orders. I knew any place had to be an improvement and figured, if fire could

melt aluminum, it could certainly burn my ass.

I lurched back through the smoking and shuddering wreck. The waist gunners were sprawled near the guns. The ball gunner was up and out of his turret. Their faces were a weird greenish color. Indicating my intention to the others, I kicked open the escape hatch. I saw them lined up behind and pushed out into space. I went nowhere! I hung suspended by a broken cable while fire from the inboard engine crackled around me . . . "Whew." One of the waist gunners, although badly wounded, managed to help me up and back in, where we loosened the wire (that was nearly my skewer). He was tremendous . . . and I was lucky he was there.

I pushed out again this time free . . . to what seemed the quiet of an arctic waste. We had been told that to escape continuing action we should delay pulling the release cord. I dropped as far as I dared before doing so. There was no sensation of going down; and, when the chute opened, it was as if my umbrella and I went up from wherever we were at the time. I heard, afterwards, that those in the front of the plane had left before us. The waist gunners reported the ship exploded seconds after they left. Those in front survived and were taken prisoner with the exception of the copilot. He was killed in his seat at the time of the original problem with the bomb bay.

There were other parachutes in the sky. Some were darker than the white one over me and looked like lighter-than-air toadstools. Guessed them to be those of the enemy. "Enemy"—I had forgotten everything except staying alive. The enemy became real when a

FOOD PARCELS

ONE PER WEEK PER MAN

RED CROSS

BRITISH			AMERICAN			CANADIAN		
Condensed Milk	1	can	Powdered Milk-16oz.	1	can	Powdered Milk	1	can
Meat Roll	1	can	Spam	1	can	Spam	1	can
Meat & Vegetable	1	can	Corned Beef	1	can	Corned Beef	1	can
Vegetable or Bacon	1	can	Liver Paste	1	can	Salmon	1	can
Sardines	1	can	Salmon	1	can	Cheese-8 0z.	1	can
Cheese-4 oz.	1	can	Cheese	1	can	Butter-16 oz.	1	can
Margarine or Butter	1	8oz.	Margarine-16 oz.	1	can	Biscuits-soda	1	box
Biscuits	1	pkg.	Biscuits--K-Ration			Coffee-ground-8 oz.	1	bag
Eggs-Dry	1	can	Nescafe Coffee-4 oz.	1	can	Jam	1	can
Oatmeal	1	can	Jam or Orange Pres.	1	can	Prunes-8 oz.	1	box
Cocoa	1	can	Prunes or Raisins	1	can	Raisins-8 oz.	1	box
Tea-2 oz.	1	box	Sugar-8oz.	1	box	Sugar-8 oz.	1	bag
Dried Fruit or Pudding	1	can	Chocolate-4oz.	2	bars	Chocolate-5 oz.	1	bar
Sugar-4 oz.	1	box	Soap	2	bars	Soap	1	bar
Chocolate	1	bar	Cigarettes	5	pks.			
Soap	1	bar						

REICH ISSUE

WEEKLY RATION

Army Bread-1 loaf	2100 grams		Soup-Oatmeal, Barley or Pea	3 times
Vegetables-Potatoes	400 grams		Cheese	46 grams
Other Seasonal	?		Sugar	175 grams
Jam	175 grams		Mare	215 grams
Meat			Salt	
Flour---on occasion				

Messerschmitt 109 roared past. The pilot waved. (I was glad he didn't shoot . . . heard all kinds of stories.) He banked . . . made another pass, and was gone. I wondered if it was really me . . . drifting in the bluest of skies, watching an airplane . . . an airplane with the markings of the German Luftwaffe on its fuselage. He must have been reporting my location. I wondered then (and many times since) how "they" ever got strangers to shoot one another.

It was heartening to see land when old worrier me half expected to see the icy waters of the North Sea. (Wasn't positive why the 109 had let me alone.)

There was a covering of snow, a village way over, and a church steeple. I figured the church was gonna get me one way or another until I saw the tree rushing towards me. I remembered instructions on how to guide the contraption and pulled on the lines to steer it one way or the other. Didn't alter my course an inch. I noticed I still had the rip cord and threw it away. Then, kerrunch . . . rippp . . . crash . . . there was the would-be hero . . . upside down in a tree . . . in Europe yet!

There was no one in sight, and I struggled to free myself. The chutes were difficult under normal circumstances; but I was upside down and my weight put too much pressure on the straps of the harness. I was helpless. I realized I had been working with only one hand and removed the glove from my left hand. The wrist and hand were bleeding badly. I didn't remember getting hit . . . it must have been fragments from the 20mm shell. Still did not hurt. I had also sustained a puncture wound on my thigh. This stopped bleeding on its own with no real damage to the bone or leg muscles.

Gave up on the harness and took a possum's eye view of the area. People were approaching. They had shotguns and pitchforks (which looked ungood from any angle). Some of them wore wooden shoes, and I thought, "this must be Holland" (wasn't thinking too clearly). They stopped a short distance away and asked, "pistola?" I did have a .45 when in the plane, but now its holster was empty (dunno what happened to it). I replied, "no pistol" and two teenagers were sent to release me. They noticed the blood and the crowd came closer. It took the excited young men a while to release me. A young soldier joined the group as I got to the ground. Until then, there was only the very young or the very old. A lady asked where the planes had struck; her family was in Bremen and she was concerned for them. I gave no answer. (They still had the guns and pitchforks, but at no time did they threaten to use them.) They pointed the direction they wanted me to go—so what else? . . . I went. Captured by women and children yet!

I was led to a farmhouse where the family, after cutting the sleeve of my suit, splinted and wrapped my arm. The bones of the wrist and hand were shattered but the bleeding had stopped. They tore either a pillowcase or a sheet for a bandage. Each window in the kitchen was filled with a curious German face. The lady of the house showed a picture of a young man in a German army uniform. She cried. (I felt like it when I thought about my own mother.) They gave me water and offered cookies. The young boys had gathered the parachute from the tree and brought it into the farmhouse. I hoped they would be able to keep it for the care they had shown me.

A pompous older man entered, and I couldn't believe it when he actually clicked his heels and shot out his arm in the Nazi salute. "Just like the movies," I thought. Even more when he said, "Heil Hitler." It was my introduction to the uniformed insanity of National Socialism. He asked questions of the people. He took charge and ordered me out of the house and onto the road. He pointed a small gun at my back (looked like a water pistol), and the two-man parade went down the street. The small man in a natty uniform and me in my bunny-like heated suit (with its cord dragging in the snow). I had a burned helmet and floppy oversized flying boots. From the reaction, it seemed my captor was no more popular than his prisoner.

We walked a mile to the next hamlet where I was searched (in a one-room schoolhouse) by members of the "Volkstürm" (home guard). When they discovered the escape kit we all carried in a leg pocket . . . one would have thought they had Eisenhower. They "ach'd" and "so'd" over each article: a map, sulpha drugs, some concentrated food, and a small amount of German money. From there it was to a jailhouse fire station nearby, and I heard a lock click behind me for the first time.

I had a chance to think about what was happening to me. I hoped my parents wouldn't be too shocked when they received the "missing in action" telegram from the Secretary of War. We had been told that would happen to us in the event of capture and had been briefed on the approximate location of the camps. This—provided we were in the hands of the military. I

was not . . . as yet. It was a local policeman standing guard outside.

The strangeness of the situation wore off. I thought of the basics. I thought of survival. The place was unheated and there was a bucket for a toilet. Perhaps I was the only one who cared . . . the only one who would be "looking out" for me. Confronted with a future where my decisions could make the difference in getting home or not, I went through a personality change that was to last a year and a half. Where I had always been an easy-going, shy, let-the-other-guy-do-it person, I became a doer and a schemer (who took risks when holding back would have lessened my calculated chances of getting home in one piece). I am a born coward (from a long line thereof), but for my time in Germany I played the role of a bolder person than I had been before (or since).

I thought of the movies (again) when a German soldier clanged the cell door open and hustled me into the back of a panel truck. I thought the ball gunner and the tail gunner were dead. They were laid out on the floor (it was only because the roof was so low they could not ride in a sitting position). The tail gunner had a badly broken leg while the ball turret man had only a broken nose. Followed by a staff car of sorts, the truck chugged through the blacked-out countryside and picked up three more prisoners captured in the area. We were driven to a Kriegsmarine (Naval) hospital where everything possible was done to repair our wounds. The more seriously hurt were attended to immediately, while I waited with the tail gunner (he of the broken nose). I did get a fright when a doctor, after checking my arm, drew a purple line about four inches above the wrist bone. I guessed wrongly regarding his intention. I protested. I used sophomore French and a bit of graduate obscenity. He should have been angry, but he patiently explained that he was locating the area where he needed X-rays. I cooperated for my own embarrassed benefit. The bones were set and the wounds dressed. They used only a compress on my leg but put an elbow-length cast on the arm.

We wondered if the waist gunners would live or die. They had lost a lot of blood and were given transfusions while the doctors worked on their terribly injured legs. German guns had inflicted damage in defense of the Fatherland. Their medical skill repaired the wounds, and German blood was used to aid the recovery of the attackers. It was all very strange . . . and confusing.

We were kept overnight, and in the morning three of us were shipped out. The ball gunner (we guessed) was sent to a staging camp for POWs in the south of Germany. I was sent, along with another prisoner, to a Lazerette (prison hospital) near the town of Sandbostel. Strapped on stretchers we were carried into a one-story brick building by two (quite small) Yugoslavs. There were no beds, and a discussion took place on how to get this well-nourished American to a place in the far corner of the room. (I still weighed close to 200 and the little Yugos were exhausted!) I explained that I had only a bad arm and could walk. Everyone laughed, except the stretcher bearers who had red faces (and hernias?).

There were *Kriegsgefangenen* (prisoners of war) from almost every nation in Europe. Poles, French, Belgians, Yugoslavs, and British. There were some Americans and Canadians. Most were ground troops caught up in the Blitzkrieg (lightning war); others had been captured in the desert by the Afrika Korps of Rommel.

The food at Sandbostel was adequate (to say the most) and the medical service as good as could be supplied by a Yugoslav doctor (major) who had very little equipment. Our waist gunners joined us a week later. They were bed cases. Both (we heard) were later "repatriated" (sent home, under neutral supervision, in no condition to fight again and requiring constant medical attention). We were careful (most of the time) when discussing our ill-fated mission.

Germany and the United States were signers of the Geneva Convention Agreement regarding the humane treatment of prisoners of war. So were most countries in the European theater . . . but not Russia. Those captured on the Eastern front were treated as animals by both sides. The Russians at Sandbostel were kept, with no housing, in holes dug in the frozen ground. Burial details saw burlapped corpses carried past the fences every morning.

There were several Americans and three Britishers in our room. I was the only one who could move around. One American (read about him later in a *Reader's Digest* article) had survived after coming down 24,000 feet in the shot-off tail of a B-17. His head injuries made him a very strange roommate. Nightmares sent him into wild screaming delirium. He would fling anything movable into the blacked-out room. Another had suffered ripped muscles and a severely twisted pelvic girdle when his parachute snapped open. He had failed to properly tighten

smile, and the numbing laces / Are cut from my wrists with praise. When I woke the rabbit was gnawing / His great, slow, ragged bites / From the wood of the wired-in hutches, / And dusk had greyed the white / Leghorns hunched on the roosts of their run. / The train mourned below / For the captives—a thinning echo. . . . / It all comes back to me now.

(from "Prisoners / Stalag Luft," by Randall Jarrell)

Dear All — Dec 25 1943

Just a few lines to let you Know that I'm a Prisoner of War I certainly get around don't I? I am feeling fine and that is the truth. The mail will be slow, so please dont do any worrying over me as I'm out of the war now and will be very much OK The only worry I can possibly have is that this situation does cause you folks any bother So, Ma, eat well and stay strong. Pa, look after things as I'm sure you can. and I Know

the rest will remain the same good crowd. I'm sure now of coming home some day so lets hope this mess is over soon You can write but not too often — More later from the same guy — Bill

the leg harness. A third American was in a sitting position when flak tore into his rear. A Britisher, on a night mission, landed (as I did) in a tree. In the darkness, he had felt for the ground with his foot . . . thought he had it . . . and (with the quick release of the English chute) dropped to the ground twenty feet below. His back was badly damaged. He would never walk again. . . .

Spent my first Christmas as a prisoner. Things could have been worse. Days brought bug bites and some laughs. A gunner from Philadelphia supplied most of the laughs. (I believe lice were the leading contributors in the bite department.) He told of dragging himself (broken leg and all) out of a barn when he saw a "goddam big thing with horns." Said there were very few cows in the "tenderloin" section of Philly.

The railroad center of Hamburg was to the southeast, and our first experience under our own air raids was enlightening (and frightening). Night attacks found me at the boarded-up windows describing what I could see to those unable to move from their straw-covered sections of the floor.

The first of February came and three of us were told we were to leave Sandbostel. We were not told our destination but just that we were to "board a train at Hamburg." We rode an empty boxcar into the marshalling yards there and hiked to the battered railroad station. The great city was nearly level, and 18,000 had been killed during recent night attacks by British aircraft (this according to the stories we heard). At the station the crowds were hostile (who could blame them?). Despite my Yugo jacket, wooden shoes, and baggy trousers we were recognized as

"Luftbandits" (allied airmen). I even wore an Italian cap (which the previous owner had no use for; there was a bullet hole above the right ear). The people didn't harm us, but it would have been understandable if they had. Boarding a special train, in the company of nurses, we saw a contingent of burned kids, blind kids, kids missing arms and legs. . . .

That this scene was also taking place in London and Rotterdam didn't seem to make it right.

I wondered how German fliers would be received in an American city (say Boston) had they been captured following such destructive raids. The discipline and regimentation of the German populace paid off for us at such times. Some spit and called "schwein," but no one touched us. Our young guard led us to a coach heading northeast and a most uncomfortable scene had been "sweated out."

We arrived at Wismar, Mecklenburg, after many hours of sidings changes and reroutings made necessary on the railroads of a country engaged in total war. The guard left and two Luftwaffe corporals took over. They were surly and taciturn . . . gave the impression that here, at last, we would learn the brutal side of the Teuton character. We were driven to an imposing Luftwaffe hospital on the shore of the Baltic. It was most modern. Fifteen-foot pictures of Hitler and Goering hung in the marble rotunda. I never could figure why they took us to such a place, though they seemed to a have a logical explanation for every move.

We were suspicious and watchful. The corporals told us that we were to be quartered (hoped it didn't mean cut in four pieces) with Russki commissars. We were sent into an immaculate ward where we heard what we supposed was a greeting in Russian from patients already there. One spoke terrible English and apologized for it. I, speaking for the three, replied (very slowly) that he did much better in English than I could hope to ever do in Russian. When this brought laughter from patients and guards, we realized we'd been had. The "Russkis" were Americans from Milwaukee, Toledo, and Miami . . . plus two British noncoms. They had arranged the charade with the guards when they heard of our arrival. What a "horror camp" that was. The POWs introduced us to the guard force (such as it was) as though they too were from Brooklyn or points west. We all thought (for sure) this was a phony setup to get information. If it was, it was the most elaborate (and wasteful—we knew nothing anyway) game ever. The Allied prisoners had been there over a year, and all were recovering from the most serious of injuries. They had learned to know the guards (also recovering from wounds) and all were greatly interested in each other's stories and attitudes. Until I left the place thirty days later, I was amazed at the concerned care we received. I still am.

I was given a toothbrush and a towel and enjoyed my first bath since leaving England. I used a borrowed dull razor to remove my six-week-old beard (could'a used a package of band-aids for an aftershave). Two of us Sandbostel grads had scabies, a skin infection that develops from flea bites (not phlebitis) and accumulated body filth. The problem nearly cost us the use of the clean and mattressed beds. However, after bathing we were given a salve for the sores

left: Bill McCarran's first letter home from the camp in Germany.

165

around our midsections and were okayed for the bed department. The itching and rash subsided after a week of soap and warm water. It was much more comfortable than Sandbostel.

The night and day air raid alerts were the only bad part of the stay at Wismar. The small port, though never a target, was directly beneath the route taken by the RAF into Berlin and that used by the Americans into Eastern Germany and Poland. When the sirens would wail, all work stopped and the weary personnel would lead, carry, or wheel every patient to the bunkers (bomb shelters) in the basement below. If the ships came within range the antiaircraft batteries of the town would open up. They did not take us to the bunkers ... the guards explained that, should there be a chance hit, it would complicate an already tense situation. We remained in our room on the top where we could watch any action. The biggest thing in the area was the hospital so we were in very little danger. The daylight missions bothered only the weary staff, but the nights, to me anyway, held a special terror. My imagination was as big as the whole night sky. I learned to "listen" to the chase of the bombers by the speedy nightfighters of the Lüftwaffe. A British wireless (radio) operator taught me to recognize the different sounds. He had been on many such missions and knew the synchronized drone of the Lancasters and the uneven pulse of the German interceptors. This guy lived for one reason (he said). He wanted to "get" Air Marshal Tedder of the Royal Air Force. His contention was that Tedder actually listed the selected cities and the time of attack for the German High Command. Doing this, he (Tedder) boasted, made it possible for the RAF

to destroy the fighters when they came up. The Germans did lose planes because of this strategy (?) but were able to move their mobile 88s (flak guns) into position where they took a terrible toll. All the while Tedder kept the target locations secret from even his wing commanders until briefing. The now crippled Britisher reckoned that Sir Arthur owed him one hand, one leg, and the sight of his right eye.

(Later that year we found that the Americans were doing the same thing. They dropped leaflets announcing the cities and when they were scheduled for obliteration.) Why the hush-hush security? It really was the craziest of wars. Are any of them rational?

Saw Germans bringing rosary beads with them into the shelters. I told the guards that we sometimes had bishops blessing the aircraft before a mission. I doubt very much if God approved of either side.

The routine went on and on and on. After every alert the staff dragged the patients (and themselves) back to the wards. To keep them busy attack bombers roared in and out at low level simply to harass the populace.

We received the same food as the German patients: Breakfast—a roll and ersatz coffee; Lunch—black bread and a vegetable; Supper—black bread and soup. Sundays, same thing but a small piece of meat with the vegetable. Red Cross parcels arrived. We now had better rations than the Germans, plus cigarettes which had our guards working for us. They supplied beer for a few smokes. There was some resentment from the doctors and nurses, but the American nature is generous. We supplied the sicker patients with smokes and tobacco; hungry oldsters were also given some. The German officers frowned on such fraternization but never moved to stop it . . . neither did they stoop to use what amounted to Yankee largesse.

I pestered the Milwaukee gunner into drilling me on basic German. He spoke very well, and I worked on it constantly (figuring it might be of use later on). It was.

The British claimed an unwritten code said that a POW should not attempt escape while receiving medical treatment. I doubt if any of us seriously considered getting safely out of that country of passes, identification points, and sharp-eyed military, state, and local police. Allied armies were still in southern Italy while the Soviets (the Germans always referred to them as "Bolsheviks") were battling in the marshes of eastern Poland.

The guard detail was made up of convalescing German wounded. A more screwball organization has never existed in any army, at any place, at any time. All corporals, they argued daily over who was in charge and wrestled on occasion trying to decide who was to bring the attendance report to the office. I talked mostly to a young guard from Nuremburg.

He personally disliked Hitler, hated Churchill, considered FDR an unknown; but, above all, he feared and despised Stalin. A few times the whole room got into discussions. The Limeys, Germans, and Americans argued points that would have interested the home folks. Once in a while I would take the side of a neutral (Eire) to complicate matters. I knew the more sensitive smarted a bit when their leaders were subjected to ridicule (doubt if anyone cared that much for the leaders, but defending them became a personal thing).

The Germans could never understand why we fought on the same side as a Josef Stalin; it seemed our only counter was to question their unholy alliance with the Japanese. The guards had all been to the Eastern front and their stories told of hardships and cold from Stalingrad to the outskirts of Moscow. They described the dogged forward push of the Red Army over piles of its own dead . . . of Russkis—outgunned, outmanned, and outmaneuvered—still coming on, until the Germans ran out of ammunition (or the energy to use it). Germans couldn't equal such fanaticism and were steadily losing ground. Allied bombings in central and eastern Germany were preventing supplies and replacements from reaching the hard-pressed and retreating Nazis (without the British and American pounding, German armies might still be deep in Russia).

We were not supposed to leave the room, but the rule was never enforced; until the guy from Milwaukee and myself (after meeting a new nurse in the hall) agreed to show her where the "unspeakable pig dogs" and "air bandits" were held. (I kept my kindergarten Deutsche to a few "schweinhunds" and "ach sos.") She whispered that those in the room looked much like ordinary people (just before a brisk German officer ordered us back to the room). She was embarrassed . . . and we were concerned about further restrictions because of our foolishness.

We were forbidden to associate with the nurses (another unenforced rule). We helped them reroll bandages. If it was aiding their war effort to help with bandages that were to be used for us as well as them, we were guilty of fur-

above: John Hurd at his base, Deenethorpe, in 1944, and again on the day he was shot down and taken prisoner in Germany.

While flying near Hannover, Germany, (April 11, 1944) and still heading toward the target, my squadron was hit hard by flak. We lost four B-17s from this action. There were many. . .

thering the cause of the Third Reich. These *schwestern* (nurses) were a pleasant though fatalistic group. They said that all would be dead, "*alles todt*," and no one would win the war. That part of Germany was occupied by the Bolsheviks.

In the light of a global war in progress, several ridiculous things happened (some of which seem worthy of recalling). I was given a stamp collection by the Nuremberg guard. The postmarks were from German army field posts all over Europe. Places like Stalingrad and Kiev ... temporary places that would never again be under German control. One corporal acted as barber for cigarettes. I amused the group by using a comb to imitate (you know who).

The comb was short and black and held flat beneath the nose with the left hand. The right arm was extended forward (slightly up) with the palm of the hand down. One guard imitated Churchill's "Ve vil fight zem on ze beaches" and Roosevelt's "Eleanor and I boz hate Var." In that cuckoo room, everyone laughed. I taught them the words to the "Beer Barrel Polka" and "You are mine Zunshine." I learned the words to Brahms' "Lullaby" (in Deutsche). We even had a going-away party, of sorts, for one of the guards who was leaving for the Eastern front (how they hated that eventuality). This guy had limped more than usual before taking his fit-for-duty physical, and the others had kidded him for being a faker (he wouldn't admit this; neither would any one volunteer to replace him on the shipment roster).

When the cast was removed from my arm, I was declared ready for travel. Two others were to be with me, and although not told our destination, we guessed correctly that it was Dulag Luft, near Frankfurt-am-Main. With two guards (one from the force at Wismar) we headed south. It was a good opportunity to observe a country at war and to study its people. It seemed that a lot of the women had a "pinched face look," a hurt expression with an extra furrow in their brows. Thought it was the result of the constant threat from the skies or worry should the country be overrun by the dreaded "Bolsheviks." The stations and the countryside were filled with slave labor ... "captured peoples," some in their fifth year of imprisonment. The sight of these unfortunates and the realization of how many there were in Germany and its satellites eliminated any doubts about National Socialism as seen at Wismar. There was no difference in the slavery practiced in our own South before the War Between the States except the color of those held in bondage. Each had been taken from his home by the right of might and each made subject to the whims of a people who considered themselves superior. Whether it was kind and humane treatment, as I have seen, or brutally cruel (I saw a uniformed man beating another man over the head with a piece of lumber), this system had to be eliminated. With the disclosures (after the war) of the terrible treatment given Jews, political prisoners, Jehovah's Witnesses, and the Gypsies, it was amazing that we knew nothing of this. We did hear "quiet rumors." They were the most concealed crimes in the history of man's inhumanity to man. I could not believe people could do such things. There had been frenzied slaughters all through history. This was done methodically—by a people considered cultured and intelligent, who respected their parents and raised the most disciplined of children. But they did it!

We rode alternately with troops going on furlough or returning to battle. Others were being sent to hospitals or rest camps to recover from wounds received in the battle that would determine if Hitler was to rule the destinies of Europe and the world. The military people were indifferent. The country was filled with prisoners of every description. Civilians showed more interest; perhaps because we had two guards for three men.

I thought of how we were witnessing history from front-row seats. (I hoped not "box" seats!)

The train clacked along the Valley of the Rhine . . . picture-book stuff. Little towns, brick and orderly (fireplace wood stacked just so at the rear of every home). Castles, always on a hill, housed the descendants of feudal barons. It appeared that in "the old order" the "big men" insisted on being above the more common folk, in fact as well as in social position. Hitler built his "Eagle's Nest" on the highest peak at Berchtesgaden while espousing a "new order." Nothing changes.

At Cologne we saw the great cathedral, undamaged in a city destroyed. In Frankfurt-am-Main the same scene of destruction greeted us. The railroad station was in shambles. Its small paned domed-glass roof was a jagged and distorted mess. Water and gas mains pointed uselessly skyward and broken sewer mains fed a million rats. Repairs were being made by slaves (under the gun). Still I was impressed by a people continuing a daily routine. They took their straw baskets to what was left of the marketplace and perhaps got a ration of bread from the boarded-front bakery, and, hopefully, a bottle of beer or wine before returning to their apartment. Pounded mercilessly from above, some sections looked like cut-a-way models of toy towns . . . rooms of furniture were exposed to public view and awaited the return of tenants now dead. Bathtubs were no longer hidden and doors opened to nowhere. Pictures hung on wall-papered walls now suddenly outside walls . . . endless stairways went up . . . or down . . . it no longer mattered.

The people were mostly old and tired. The children were off to the safety of the country . . . a lot of the young men were in uniform (or dead). Young women manufactured the tools of war.

We walked the cobblestoned streets after riding part way in a trolley car. It was our first close look at a heavily populated city . . . a city being systematically destroyed. However, the heavy cobblestones and those structures still standing gave the place a sense of historic permanence. The staging camp at Dulag Luft was a series of single-storied barracks in the center of Frankfurt. Next to it stood the office buildings of the I. G. Farben conglomerate. Somehow these had remained undamaged in the middle of saturation bombardment. The prison camp had been hit the week before, and British and American prisoners had been killed.

Inside the barbed-wire enclosure we were stripped, given our emptied outer garments, and led immediately to what is called "solitary confinement." I hated that because I feared it. It was supposed to frighten prisoners into divulging military secrets. According to the Ge-

flak bursts around our ship, "Battlin' Betty." From my ball turret position I was able to watch under the wings for fires. Immediately the number three and four engines started smoking and shortly after, my ball turret was hit and I was injured in the right buttock. Our bombs were salvoed to guard against an explosion as one of . . .

neva Convention "reasonable limits" were set for this subtle torture. . . .

How "reasonable" men determined twenty-eight days was a "reasonable time" for people to be kept from human company convinced me that stupidity was something practiced by statesmen in times of peace as well as in times of war. The Germans wanted information concerning new weapons, Allied strategy, location of bases, and numbers used (stuff like that). If I had been kept in that little room for twenty-eight days I would have told them anything I knew . . . maybe stories of my grandmother's girlhood affairs.

I always had (and still do) an unreasonable fear of being trapped in a small place.

There was a polite knock on the door and a major (from intelligence?) came in for interrogation. . . . He knew a lot about me (all I knew about him was that he was smart enough not to be freezing his ass on the Eastern front). He knew the group I was with! He knew when we had arrived in England; he knew where we had trained in the States. We had been told that the Germans had a clearinghouse for all State-side newspapers in Lisbon. They clipped anything pertaining to air crews. "Sgt. Jones received his gunner's wings at Wendover Field" or "Lt. Smith, while his parents watched, graduated from flight training at Lackland." They would add this trivia to solid intelligence and convince some prisoners that it was senseless not to talk. They were interested in navigators and pilots mostly . . . they went through the motions with us possibly to verify something that might have been a rumor. He threatened to "throw away the key" (I prayed he was talking through his fancy braided cap) if I stayed with the "name, rank, and serial number." Our G-2 advice was they would extend your stay . . . not shorten it . . if you talked. He wanted to know if flak or fighters got us . . . I stayed with the name, rank . . . etc. He said I was "stupid."

Again we were lucky . . . anything would have been better than that terrible six-by-four room. They needed the space for the hundreds of fliers knocked down in the first daylight raid on Berlin (March 6, 1944). We were released like a thousand Yanks coming on to the parade ground.

I breathed easier . . and got right back to where I was before the interview . . . (using nerve I never had before or since). I demanded the return of the stamp collection I picked up at Wismar. The German in the "check room" ignored me while I screamed of my rights under the Geneva Convention. It did me no good . . . and also cost me a cigarette. A gunner from Portsmouth, N.H., witnessed my performance (to him I was speaking fluent German) so he refused my request for a cigarette. He was security-minded, being fresh from the Berlin raid. All he saw was a strangely attired character yelling at a German. He figured I was a plant . . . and spread the word. I was avoided like a leper for a while . . . (one who didn't smoke).

From the solitary barracks we were taken to the main camp . . . a shower, shaving kits, and new clothing. The supplies were 90 percent American and were distributed by a staff of prison personnel. I wore my first pair of shoes since leaving England (wondered who had the shoes I had left under my bunk). When a crew failed to return from a mission other crews kept their shoes. . . . I had accumulated about a dozen pairs. I wasn't sorry to heave the wooden clodhoppers into the pile . . . along with the Yugoslav jacket . . . and the Italian cap (the one . . . with the hole above the ear).

Officers and enlisted personnel quizzed us "long termers" on what to expect from the enemy. Couldn't tell them too much (from lack of knowledge) and we too were security-conscious. . . . Some Allied personnel had gone over to the Germans . . . (getting information for favors and privileges). We were given Red Cross parcels and had plenty to eat . . . and plenty of cigarettes.

The Yanks laughed with appreciation (and surprise) when a German sergeant, resplendent in the dress finery of the Luftwaffe, roared orders in Army English, such as: "Line up you bums . . . Where did you take basic? Atlantic City?" or "If you bums hadda been taught by us how to use parachutes, you mighta had fewer broken hooves." He had been going through this routine for a long time and became a first-class standup comic.

We remained there for two days while they arranged transportation to an outlying permanent camp. We were not sorry to leave. Frankfurt was near the top of the list of cities to be destroyed (the list dropped on leaflets from Allied aircraft). We knew the 8th Air Force knew Dulag Luft's location, but we also knew the accuracy of "precision bombing." The lead bombardier was usually the best and the others followed him (provided they weren't in trouble). If a plane needed to jettison bombs to lighten the load . . . the deadly cargo would go down with no warning that "there could be a camp below for American prisoners." I know I went, with no regrets, to the boxcars and a trip in a northeasterly direction. We passed undamaged cities . . . a strange sight. We saw vast fields and empty space that gave the lie to the Nazi plea for "Lebensraum" (living room).

There were twenty-five to a car . . twelve men on either side and one in the middle with the guards and the pot-bellied stove . . . I remained as close to the door as possible. I wanted to know where we were and where we were heading. The doors were kept open a crack to handle the smoke the small chimney couldn't. The train stopped now and then for fuel or water . . . We were allowed outside at such times to relieve ourselves. Many times it was in full view of civilians. If they were not embarrassed, I certainly wasn't.

Knew very few people in the area.

On the outskirts of Berlin, in the marshalling yards, we sweated out a night raid on the Reich capital. We were not even close to being hit, but my fear of the unknown always placed the drone of the British bomber directly overhead. The fearless (or foolish) watched the searchlights and the flashes from the crack in the door. The rest tried to crawl into the straw-covered floor.

Moving again, we went up and into the Polish Corridor, where the initial assault by German tanks began the shooting part of WW II. We passed the former Free City of Danzig, and the Kriegies had little to say as the train swung off to the south. We were told we were going to Heydekrug, East Prussia, but we were headed in a direction that would take us closer to the Russian front. Ever-present rumor factories had us

our B-17s blew up. "Battlin' Betty" finally came clear of the flak and we were slowing down and losing altitude. I was then asked to leave the ball turret and have the radio operator look at my injury. He was not able to do anything as I had too many clothes on. About this time the pilot . . .

burying German dead or digging trenches for the retreating Nazis. We were never sure of anything and were relieved when the train again headed northeast.

We saw trains loaded with human misery on our way. Near Königsburg we stopped across the tracks from a freight loaded with Russian women and children. There were no fires in those cars and barbed wire prevented any relief or respite from the cruel confinement. They had been snatched from their homeland by a vicious and spiteful retreating invader. They would be used as forced labor on factories and farms. Those that survived the train ride would. . . .

We were kept in comparative ease and comfort even though we had destroyed German cities and German families. They fought two separate wars—the Western front was "gentlemanly," the Eastern, two dogs in a pit.

Nothing sensational greeted us at Stalag 6 at Heydekrug. The Germans carried out the processing with typical thoroughness and great attention to detail.

It seemed that the Germans enjoyed detail. Guess it made them forget the whole picture. We were searched, deloused, examined by a doctor, and photographed. We were issued *Kriesgefangenen* "dog tags" and given straw mattresses. We were confident on that day—March 15—that in weeks, a month at the most, we would be free. Logic said no nation could stand such pressure on all fronts—the pitiless bombing, and the lack of supply. Some of us were liberated more than a year later. Some never made it.

Stalag 6 at Heydekrug was divided into three parts: the *Vorlager*, where the guards were

quartered and the official buildings stood, the British compound with its 1,500 English, Australian, and Canadians, and our *lager*, where with our arrival the total was brought to 500 (the Germans left plenty of room for expansion). All the prisoners were noncommissioned officers. Officers were held at other camps. Although we had a few made of brick, the barracks were mostly wooden. There was suction-cup mud everywhere. Wars create mud, I thought. They used land for camps that seemed more suited for crops.

I heard a familiar voice on my first afternoon there in East Prussia. I had wallowed through the muck to the washroom and toilets at the far end of the compound when someone said, "why don't you take your own advice?" Sitting on the end seat of rough and splintery wooden you-know-whats was my friend from Sioux Falls and Keesler Field. I had warned him that "aerial gunnery is only for idiots." "You can't fall off the ground," I reasoned, "and, on top of that, the Germans have radar operated flak guns and great pilots." "Run out of schools?" he asked, as he reached absentmindedly for nonexistent tissue.

He had been shot down two months after I was. We talked and wondered over the crazy coincidence that landed us in Mississippi in 1942 and here in March 1944.

When spring came to that part of the world, things looked better at Stalag 6. The war was going well for our side, the mud had dried, and food improved. Softball, tag football, and basketball leagues were formed in our section; the British had their soccer and boxing. Contests were fiercely competitive with food and cigarettes wagered on the results. I was an official at first. It was a shade less dangerous than flying combat in a ball-turret. I played some after the hand and wrist improved.

Escape was really only a topic of conversation. Where to go? How to get there? . . . and, what can I contribute if I should get back? We were expendable and believed the war to be nearing its inevitable end. "Why risk a shot in the ear when it would be all over in a coupla weeks?" That was the general opinion. However, we were told it was our duty to attempt escape (to keep more men occupied in holding us captive).

There were few escapes. I believe everyone was either recaptured or killed. When we had men beyond the fences, we would do our best to take the daily count. Men would slip out of the barracks after answering roll call and be counted at the next barrack. If the *posterns* (guards) were satisfied, it would give the people outside more time to leave the area. When the *appel* (count) was incorrect they used a "sheep count" out in the compound. All POWs passed single file between two lines of counting guards. It was comical to see their elaborate system beaten . . . but it was risky for those who darted from line to line.

The big rumor . . . (the main topic of conversation) was the impending invasion . . . We heard everything imaginable . . . some of the stories were even started by bored Kriegies to make life interesting. We got solid information from the British side of the camp every now and again. . . . They had worked on a "ferret" (one of the inside guards) who, unarmed, moved in and around the area poking and probing,

looking for information and signs of escape attempts. . . . They (the British) with cigarettes and chocolate gifts had this unfortunate in a position where exposure could have meant his head . . . They demanded (and got) enough parts to build a small radio receiver. They listened to the British Broadcasting Company and would pass the news across the fences between the compounds. With someone watching the door we would hear the BBC's version of how the war was going. Although they made the most extensive searches possible, the Germans, aware that we were getting the latest, never found the set.

We were thrilled on June 6 when the Allies came ashore at Normandy, and we closely followed the progress of the Red Army toward our sector. My plans were always keyed on the same objective: getting home. I attended a class in beginner German being given by an American of German extraction. I gave up cigarettes when I realized that some would exchange food for them.

The biggest single sporting event was a boxing match with a Yank who claimed great experience in the ring. He was a beautiful physical specimen . . all tanned and beautifully muscled (he weighed about 160). This guy had chin whiskers and we called him the "Bearded Marvel." His opponent was about 150 pounds . . . and a tall and quite pale Englishman. I forget his name but he "looked-like-a-cinch" from across the fence. Thousands of smokes and many candy bars were wagered and the match (with permission of the Germans) was to be held on the Fourth of July. The British claimed it was Guy Fawkes Day or Empire Day . . . anyway it was gonna be another war.

gave the order to bail out. I now hooked on my chest-type parachute and placed my GI shoes inside my chute harness. We were over flat country and somewhere east of Hannover. I looked out of the bomb-bay and decided to jump out the waist door. We were somewhere . . .

173

The ring was set up at the end of our compound (the tower guards had the best seats). Both sides of the wire were packed with excited Kriegies. There were no preliminary events . . . just the main go. Our tiger was the first into the ring . . . (boy was he ever rugged!). Being sporting people, we felt a little sorry for the skinny white-livered looking guy. Our guy came out bobbing and weaving like in movies we had seen of Dempsey. Their guy stiff-legged forward in an old John L. Sullivan pose. Their guy swung a short chop to the whiskers. Our guy went down for the count of a hundred.

It was a sad day for our betters, but they took it well—though hardly anyone talked to the "Marvel" when they revived him.

He shaved the next day.

The sound of Russian guns got closer, and we really believed we would be liberated.

The Germans said nothing; but orders came to be ready for a march. We did the best we could to prepare. A few hid under the toilets when we were ordered to the road. This proved foolhardy because trained dogs smelled them out when the Germans checked. (Anyone could have smelled those guys.) . . . Three or four hid in the rafters of the washrooms . . . or so we heard . . . Never did find out what happened to them. Heard (later) the area stayed under German control for four months.

We hiked into the small town of Heydekrug where we boarded a waiting train to the German-held port of Memel (Lithuania). It was good weather and a trip by ship posed a novelty more wondered at than feared. The port was filled with German armor and activity . . . The Russians were close. They must have considered us mighty important to hold us prisoners with manpower that could have been used to stem the Red advance. Don't know why we figured on bunks aboard the ship . . . but we did . . . there were nearly 2,000 of us. . . . The ship waiting was a coal boat of sorts . . . My group was one of the last to board . . . and we dutifully followed a long single line. . . . When the guard asked me to remove my small pack, I was in no particular hurry . . . I inquired in my Sunday Deutsch as to the direction to go from where I was . . . this question, for some reason, loosed the wrath of a real monster. He cursed and shoved me down a long rusty ladder into the hold below . . . my little pack bounced off my head as I descended. The hold was crowded and stifling . . . no room to lie down or sit . . . men just stood. I looked for my belongings while the German above swore and spat at me . . . amazement was followed by frustrated anger . . . I cursed the bastard right back . . . this gained me nothing but more spit so back into the crowd I let myself be pushed. The ship, the *Mauserin*, was much larger than it appeared from the dock, but it was never meant for such a passenger list. The hold was in two sections, separated by a drive shaft running full length. It was an all-steel and filthy coal bin. Christ, was it ever hot! Don't know the exact number crowded into it . . . (but I'll bet the record still stands). . . . It seemed the whole Allied army was jostled about as the ship pulled away and headed down the mine-laden Baltic . . . it was impossible to reach the food and other supplies. Men were standing like packed cigarettes. The last down were higher than the rest because they were standing on the first supplies thrown in . . . they could not move. . . . When we realized this was all the space we were to have, a bit of planning made a small line possible to ascend the ladder for sanitary reasons. . . . The guard allowed one at a time to come up to relieve himself . . . it was July . . . there were too many people to make it . . . nature took its course as time (and the Kriegies) went. Unlucky were the ones who wore leggings. Anyone with a weak stomach was really a rotten egg . . . A few water buckets were lowered . . . (everyone was thirsty) . . . a weakness in the American character showed in this predicament. . . . The Yanks, accustomed to everything all their lives, just couldn't believe they could ever be so uncomfortable and so goddam thirsty. . . . The bunch near the ladder grabbed what water there was and made no attempt to share . . . once satisfied they were loud in their insistence that the water be shared equally by one and all. . . . Maybe I felt this way because I was off and away and had no chance for a drink . . . but I've seen similar situations where British troops carried out the division of scarce supplies in a fair and orderly manner. In general, the continental troops faced up to reality more than we emotionally charged Yanks. We were aboard the *Mauserin* about thirty-six hours and everyone thought we might run afoul of one of the British mines and that some of the Limeys in the hold with us had personally dropped from the skies. . . .

This fact cheered no one. One of our men, after getting to the top of the ladder, ran to the side and dove into the water. . . . Some said we were close enough to Sweden and he had a chance . . . I dunno just where we were . . . the guards opened up with machine pistols . . . hope he made it . . . (but I doubt it). . . . It was a be-

draggled group the ship carried into the naval base near Stettin beyond the island of Schweinemunde. Crappy but happy we were hustled off the floating pigsty. Daylight looked good but solid ground looked better. But, dammit, events followed each other too quickly. We had no time to enjoy the fact that we were out of the soot-filled hold. Sirens wailed and the flak guns of the harbor opened up just as we'd been hustled into the ever-present boxcars. We were handcuffed in two's behind barbed wire enclosures in the 40 and 8s . . . (it really said 40 men or eight horses in French). It was our first experience in handcuffs. This did not overcome my anxiety concerning the raid. . . .

When the "all clear" sounded (the bombers were going deep into Germany—not nearby), the train left the harbor area and the *Mauserin*. We demanded the removal of the cuffs as contrary to all agreements. It did no good. They reasoned that, restricted this way, we required fewer guards . . . they were badly needed elsewhere and on into the province of Pomerania went Billy in the boxcar. Near a town called Kiefheide we pulled off onto a spur track and stopped for the night. Some of the more mechanical-minded showed us how to remove the shackles. Alone, it couldn't be done—but another person could snap the spring release. We put them back during a night check.

Next morning I awoke to the sound of loud commands to get us on the road. Someone was screaming . . . "murderers of women and children," "bonus bombers of hospitals," and "pig dogs in the pay of the Jews." The voice sounded wild . . . insane . . . I warned my partner in cuffs that we had better be ready for anything. I un-

between the 15 and 18 thousand foot altitude. The two waist gunners and I were waiting to jump when I heard a loud crash noise and the ship started to rock to the left and knocked us against the left side. I thought to myself, "It's now or never," so I gave a big push and all three of us went out the door. It was very noisy as I left the ship, and shortly after, I pulled the rip cord. The chute opened . . .

derstood the gist of the shouting. The door slammed open and guards (with bayonets affixed) pulled and shoved us out. We were lined up before the livid face of a raving *Hauptman* (captain). He was standing on the rear seat of a jeep-like vehicle ranting (incoherently at times) over our responsibility for the destruction of German cities. He addressed himself to the regular guards and to a detachment of young Kriegsmarines (naval cadets). Survival was still dominant in my mind . . . fear was close . . . but it was behind my desire to get home again.

They also had dogs. . . .

We had our belongings on our backs or under our arms . . . still manacled, hungry, and out of condition; we were no match for the Kriegsmarines. . . . They averaged sixteen years, and the orders were to "run, run, run" (from that mad bastard captain). Run we did; with the cadets jabbing at our buttocks with bayonets and vicious dogs snapping at lagging heels. . . .

Packs were dropped . . . Kriegies fell over them and stumbled into other men . . . (only to be jabbed in the rear by the kids). . . . The "Beast," as we named him, was riding alongside shouting encouragement to the guards until we hoped the son-of-a-bitch would die of frenzy. It was good my partner could run . . . cause, though I sure respected the point of a bayonet, I lived in mortal fear of canine teeth. Neither of us was hurt as we steamed into view of the prison camp. There were many wounded and nearly all had dropped their food and cigarettes along the mile-long uphill run . . .

Picard (the captain) seemed satisfied that we had lost our belongings and had been taught who was "boss."

Before this experience, most believed being held by a country fighting for its life was just a matter of sweating out its inevitable defeat, then packing up for home. We knew now . . . getting home would take some doing. . . .

Pushed into the *Vorlager* (front section) we were forced to lie on the ground by a threat that if we stood we would be fired on. From this disadvantage point, we could see the rest of the Yanks charging up the road on the short end of the same treatment. English and Canadians were next and, if anything, received worse jabs from the bayonets and the butt ends of German rifles.

We thought this was the end for some of us, but most were so mad there was little time for the fear that follows logic and reasoning. Again the captain began his threats. He ordered all handcuffs removed by the guards. The Americans infuriated him when they removed the shackles before the guards could do it. They threw the cuffs to the ground. This show of disdain led the lobster-faced one to order the guards to open fire. A minor revolt took place among the guards . . . good thing the young Kriegsmarines had left . . . I'm sure (to them) an order was an order. The major commanding the camp overheard the shooting order and had it countermanded . . . Whew!!

When things quieted down . . . (some of the guards let us know they also thought the "Beast" had gone too far), we were herded to buildings where we were searched. There we met the second worst character in Nazidom . . . a guy we nicknamed the "Iron Cross." He was a sergeant and had received the medal in World War I. His pleasure was belting people. Another known as "Big Stoop" would also hit Kriegies with little provocation. Deloused (we needed it), we were taken into the main section of the camp and "B" *lager*. This Stalag (No. 4) was divided in an A B C arrangement. Americans, already there, had been prisoners since May and June. According to their stories (and gaunt faces) they'd undergone a near starvation diet. They said the food situation had improved only a week before. Once again we were fortunate. The barracks were full and, when the last of us were brought in from the *Vorlager*, we were assigned to small huts (doghouses we called them). They were about six feet wide and fifteen feet long. Ten men lived in each. It wasn't as bad as it reads. Although there was no room for furniture ... (had any been available), they were better, I thought, than the barracks. They had the advantage of open windows; not boarded up at night as were those in the barracks (no lights to be blacked out).... During those summer nights we had plenty of clean air in our "*hundhaus*" while barracks Kriegies lived with the sweat (and worse) of a hundred itching bodies. We could see the sky at night and watch the "ferrets" as they snooped about the compound with their dogs.

The "tower boys" were always there but were generally ignored by the POWs. Days were spent walking around the perimeter or playing games, the feeling of being watched never entered the mind. Except for avoiding the warning wire, the rifles in the tower were of little interest.

The "warning wire" was not a wire, but a small strip of wood running fifteen feet inside the barbed-wire outer fence. We had been told that anyone going beyond this point would be fired on. It was understood that that person was trying to escape. Tower *posterns* were expert riflemen and proved it on occasion. At Heydekrug, a Kriegie left his barracks early ... he thought the ferrets had unlocked the door. It had remained unlocked during the night. He walked to the washroom and was on his way back when a single shot killed him. True, there was a rule about being out ahead of time, but this was an honest mistake and the man had made no move toward any fence. The *postern* must have been anxious to kill or to show his superiors how good he was at following orders.

Here at Stalag 4, a Yank chased a ball beyond the wire ... he should have signaled and obtained permission ... shots from two towers whistled between his legs in the few seconds it took him to dive back to safety. A British airman, "around the bend" (as they put it), rushed the fence ... he was dead in seconds. Another rule (one about using the door instead of the window when leaving the barracks) was respected more after a prisoner had been shot for disregarding it. Stories such as these paint a picture of continuous cowering under the guns ... but they were scattered incidents. Much of the time was spent playing football or softball, with reading and cards for the less active.

The food at Kiefeheide was pretty good, and in October when some of us were moved to barracks in a newly-constructed "C" lager, things were OK there on the plains of Pomerania. Allies were deep into France and heading for German soil. The Russians advanced in the east while in the south the German position in the mountains of Italy had become precarious. Bombardment from the air continued relentlessly.

and the world was quiet. About this time I heard some machine gun fire and I looked around but did not see anything. I looked down and there was a river/canal directly beneath me. I wondered if I would land in the water. I looked up and the bombardier was very close to the top of my chute canopy, so we talked to each other on the way down. My favorite B-17, "Battlin' Betty," with 25 missions completed, buried itself in the river or canal as I watched from my parachute. I drifted away from the water and as I neared the ground it...

The "OK KID" (an English language paper printed for the POWs) gave accurate stories of the locale of the fighting as well as stories straight from Herr Goebbels' propaganda presses.

In "C" lager I was in a barrack with the people I came to know best as a POW. My friend from Long Island was there, an Italian from near Altoona, Pa., a former pro athlete (who later became a big league umpire), a stocky kid from Cambridge (a guy who had played a lot of hockey in civilian life) . . . we called him "Little Man"—Little Man was Irish. Another was a Jewish college student from Pittsburgh . . . baked a cake for me for my first anniversary in Germany. . . . Another Jewish kid from Brooklyn . . . my bridge partner . . . (drove him up walls with my absent-minded moves). . . . An older guy called "Gramps" was a fisherman from the state of Washington. . . . Two characters from Portland, Maine, and a real young kid from Webster, Mass., were the rest.

We sure talked in that room . . . arguments aplenty . . . but no real fights . . . sports, politics, religion . . . everything was discussed during the day and into the pitch black night. We had our petty disputes, and (like in families) some didn't speak for a while. They were a good bunch.

We divided the food by using two decks of cards . . . each man had a card and the second deal was for the portions. It was fair . . . (though some always seemed to get the smaller potatoes). Once we cut cards for a single potato that arrived in the daily allotment of soup. Remember one time our Pennsylvania Italian and myself (strong-stomached we) got double portions. We'd seen small carcasses hung near the main kitchen . . . (looked too small for sheep and too big for rabbits) . . . when the meat appeared in the potato soup, all we had to do was bark a couple of times—Gramps and Little Man pushed their bowls to us. . . .

Around December 20 . . . when we had the anniversary cake . . . we were again considering liberation. We always were.

We analyzed the problems of the Germans.

American and British forces were storming the "Fatherland" in pincer movements north from Italy and the Riviera and across France from Paris to Aachen . . . Russians were coming out of the Pripet Marshes driving toward Berlin. Other Red armies were fanning out from the southeast towards Vienna.

Then the news that stunned. The great German counterattack (by forces under Von Rundstedt) . . . was headed toward Antwerp to split the armies of the invasion and literally throw the Allies into the Atlantic. In the beginning both guards and the Kriegies took the reports as more of Dr. Goebbels' hors-. . . . BBC gave their accounts and the Kriegies were discouraged.

The final result of the war was never doubted, but the continuance of this battle of attrition, maybe for another year, was disheartening. The Allies held at places like Bastogne and the war was won (no more offensive war by the Germans). It was to be a while before the moustached paper-hanger threw in the sponge and swallowed a cyanide pill. . . .

Christmas came for my second time in Kriegie-land and it was a good day for all. Parcels arrived from the Red Cross . . . we had entertainment. A group put on a show complete with costumes . . . a band played YMCA instruments. There was a lot of talent in Stalag 4. We had mass, and other groups had services. An Irish priest was there. When given his choice, he had chosen to go along with the prisoners taken at Tobruk . . . that was a long time back.

Again rumors surrounded us because, during January, we heard the sound of guns as we had in Heydekrug. "They" said it was impossible to take us in any direction. However, from the activity, those of us from Heydekrug believed we would travel again, despite the fact that more prisoners were arriving in C lager, and the sound of small arms fire could be heard in the distance. We who had been so close before went about preparing to march. . . .

The order came on February 6, 1945, and we were less than enthused to leave the warm barracks for the open road. There were plenty of Red Cross parcels in the *Vorlager*. Each man was given two. These were heavy and we were told the schedule called for a minimum of fifteen miles a day. I found by tying the ankle part of extra trousers, filling them with supplies, and securing the waist, they could be worn (bandolier fashion) over our shoulders and under the other arm. It could be easily shifted and used as a pillow when needed . . . great compared to some of the elaborate packs devised by some.

The angry face of *Hauptman* Picard greeted our column as it swung down the road he had run us up before. He said nothing, and I, for one, liked it that way. Didn't want any of his treatment and, it appeared, no one wished to goad him into action. I know we all cringed a bit thinking of what a forced march under his command would be like. Our guards were middle-aged infantry, or younger men unfit for duty at the fronts. There were a few Lüftwaffe officers and noncoms along from the staff at Keifheide. The POWs plodding along the icy road were supposedly the more able-bodied of the bunch. The sick and injured left a day early to travel by train. With them had gone some who were in good condition, but who faked illness to save wear and tear on the feet.

We had only gone a mile or two when the roadside took on the look of a retreating army. The more heavily burdened threw away food, extra clothing, and keepsakes. Our escort traveled light with loaded wagons of supplies bringing up the rear. . . .

Guess we walked twenty miles the first day and stayed overnight in a barn . . . (the first of many). They would order the prisoners through the big doors . . . and that was it for the night.

Didn't take too long before the men found certain parts of the barns more advantageous than others. Lofts were comfortable, but in the darkness it was a job to crawl over ladders (and loudly protesting fellow inmates) to reach the door. Permission had to be obtained to relieve yourself outside. The best spot was along the wall on the ground floor, away from any path to the doors. The less considerate had little use for asking permission to go. It was also a good idea to be under the solid flooring above. No one looked up .. even when praying!!!

Laughed one night. The barn was small, the number in it large. A conscientious guy (with cramps) was heard working and groaning his way to the door. We followed his path by the curses of sleepy stepped-on guys. When he reached the door, he cried meekly, "*Postern*" . . .

came up with a rush. I hit the ground and finally came to rest on my back. I struggled for several moments getting to my feet as I wanted to keep my injured right buttock out of the dirt. The bombardier landed nearby and I walked over to him. He started to look at my butt and tear a bandage from his chute, and I started to put my shoes on when a German officer came up to us and motioned for us, and two other crewmen, to walk over to the military vehicle (an open touring car) nearby and get in.

(John L. Hurd, 401st BG [H])

To all Prisoners of War!

The escape from prison camps is no longer a sport!

Germany has always kept to the Hague Convention and only punished recaptured prisoners of war with minor disciplinary punishment.

Germany will still maintain these principles of international law.

But England has besides fighting at the front in an honest manner instituted an illegal warfare in non combat zones in the form of gangster commandos, terror bandits and sabotage troops even up to the frontiers of Germany.

They say in a captured secret and confidential English military pamphlet,

THE HANDBOOK
OF MODERN IRREGULAR
WARFARE:

". . . the days when we could practise the rules of sportsmanship are over. For the time being, every soldier must be a potential gangster and must be prepared to adopt their methods whenever necessary."

"The sphere of operations should always include the enemy's own country, any occupied territory, and in certain circumstances, such neutral countries as he is using as a source of supply."

England has with these instructions opened up a non military form of gangster war!

Germany is determined to safeguard her homeland, and especially her war industry and provisional centres for the fighting fronts. Therefore it has become necessary to create strictly forbidden zones, called death zones, in which all unauthorised trespassers will be immediately shot on sight.

Escaping prisoners of war, entering such death zones, will certainly lose their lives. They are therefore in constant danger of being mistaken for enemy agents or sabotage groups.

Urgent warning is given against making future escapes!

In plain English: Stay in the camp where you will be safe! Breaking out of it is now a damned dangerous act.

The chances of preserving your life are almost nil!

All police and military guards have been given the most strict orders to shoot on sight all suspected persons.

Escaping from prison camps has ceased to be a sport!

(the guy was hurting). If he stepped out into the night without permission, he would be shot. Again the *"Postern"* ... this time with more volume—and more desperation. Another quick *"Postern"* was followed by curses calling the slow-answering guard everything but *"Postern."*

"Next mornings" weren't too good . . . legs and feet go along well when loosened and moving . . given a chance to stiffen overnight in the unheated barns, it was murder to get them going after a cup of ersatz coffee and a piece of black bread.

Our scarlet-visaged captain was seen at infrequent intervals. He was, I believe, coordinating columns. After a week of this we were fairly well beat and covered less distance each day. We must have walked in circles cause it took a week to reach Schwenemunde where we had left the *Mauserin.*

The night before taking the ferry over to the island (a short trip across a harbor) we slept in a forest. There was an air raid and freezing rain soaked us. Fingers were so cold that trousers couldn't be loosened.

It had to be our worst night in Germany. . . .

Food supplies were exhausted and water difficult to obtain. The guards were slowing down as we trudged the miles across the island of Schwenemunde. We were becoming independent and often left the column to trade soap for bread and water with farm or village people (over the protest of our escort). My beginners' Deutsch stood me well in these transactions. I did as much business as any of the traders. Once a hungry-looking German woman gave me a whole loaf of bread as we passed. She refused my offer of soap or cigarettes.

We spied piles of kohlrabies in fields under manure and proceeded to raid this supply of food. The guards warned us that eating them raw would produce unwanted results. We ignored them and stuffed ourselves. The cramps and dysentery hit a short time later. The laughs of the wise guys who had refrained from eating the turnip-like vegetable were short-lived (most had been eating snow to quench their thirst). Everyone was in trouble and good locations behind fences and trees were at a premium.

The wagons to the rear were loaded with men unable (or refusing) to walk . . . barns were closer together . . . columns were all over the island and those who reached the end first were kept in the same barn while stragglers were assembled.

We crossed a long bridge near Anklam and walked in the direction of Berlin. Rumor factories had the Germans ringing the beleaguered city with POWs in an effort to halt the bombings. This course was no good. But we went only as far as the town of Zehdenick when we turned northwest. Dysentery and malnutrition slowed the column down so badly that the sicker ones were put in a separate or invalid group. My pal and I went along with them.

By this time the guard force was made up of old, disinterested men . . . they watched only when they had to. The lack of vigilance led some of us to sneak from the barn to forage around the countryside and in the village nearby. Led on by food others brought back . . . two of us tried in daylight. Got only a few yards into the field when we were challenged by the "Hans

Oop" of a seventy-year-old *postern*. It was like something out of Mack Sennett, but the old guy had a gun (that, with some effort, might go off). We accompanied him back to the barn. For a long time, we'd see him going over the details of his "capture" with some other old timer on the listening end.

We were fortunate to have with us one of the best-known POWs in Germany—Dixie Dean, an Englishman who, during five years of imprisonment, established himself as a leader of Allied prisoners. We heard about him before leaving England. The Germans respected him and did his bidding (on occasion). His manner was tactful, yet forceful. He knew things about the Geneva Convention the authors were unaware of (or so the stories went). A diplomatic person, he had gained the confidence of Nazi officials by suggesting they would receive better treatment should Germany lose the war. He demanded care for the sick, and they got the best available. . . . The German Medical Corps gave us powdered charcoal to stop the "runs" and it worked. He insisted on more bread. We got it. By promising a good word for the baron, Dean lived in the big house where he had access to a radio receiver. He kept us informed on the progress of the war.

The front came closer. Roads were jammed with refugees . . . seemed like the whole miserable population of Europe dragged itself past the road in back of the farm.

Orders came to march, and off we went on the crowded, muddy, embattled roads to the south. Just one day on the road and we were loaded on to the now despised boxcars . . . no 40 and 8 this time . . must have been nearly eighty

jammed in. The doors were locked and, once more, we were jostled about the harassed railroads of a dying Reich. The nearness of the front and the known presence of speedy attack bombers (objective railroads) added to our discomfort. Nearly all of us had some dysentery and there were few tiled bathrooms available. Three days of crap, sweat, and growling passed.

Next stop . . . Fallingbostel, where we got off and into a camp containing POWs from every nation battling the Germans. Here was evidence that, forgetting politics and the human element, one had to marvel at a people that, for the second time in the modern era, stood off the rest of the world in the roughest game of all. They were beaten, yes, but it took the combined manpower and production of nearly every nation on earth.

The food at Fallingbostel was practically nil, with the Germans in the same situation. It was a lackadaisical staff there. With nothing to eat . . . roll calls were but a formality . . . they weren't even close. We waited for the end . . . Germans wondering what was to become of their families and their homes. The POWs couldn't understand such resistance in a cause now lost. . . .

Allied planes ranged freely over the cities, blasting anything standing . . . low-flying attack bombers and pursuit planes strafed anything that moved. I believed then, as I do now, that unconditional surrender was a foolish ultimatum. No argument that they must destroy a nation to do in a paperhanger (and a few friends) could change my opinion.

Hordes of POWs arrived at the camp as ever-moving swarms of refugees flowed past the gate. It was evident the position was to be abandoned. An order came (for all those able) to march again. My friend and I parted company for the first time since our meeting at Heydekrug. I refused to go, figuring the roads were no place to be and that I'd be better off in camp—didn't intend to be a part of any last-ditch stand. I demanded to see the Kommandant when the guards ordered me into the column. They threatened but did nothing when I turned my back . . . I returned to the barracks. The only guards left when the column departed were too old to care or unable to do anything. We stayed while the German Army in retreat passed the fence. They were beaten.

For want of gas, trucks were towed by commandeered horses. British shells whistled overhead, and the Germans threw back token rounds from armored vehicles and tanks. There was no major action in the area close to the camp. Again our luck had held out . . . but it bothered me—horses against aircraft?

We slept that night, but not much. . . .

At 5:00 AM we were awakened by fire from a field near the camp. We heard the 88s from a stalled German panzer and fire from (we found out later) light tanks of Montgomery's British Army Corps. For a skirmish there had to be two sides. Everyone able climbed the barrack roof in time to see the panzer and an armored vehicle take off over a meadow in retreat.

We cheered . . . it was our first view (other than of aircraft) of Allied armor. Shortly after, a tank from the original "Desert Rats" pulled up in front of the main gate. We were free. There was no time for a guy, conditioned to scheming, to enjoy the moment. Although a lot of hand-shaking and shouting was going on, everyone figured angles. Being a POW, a guy was on his own. "OK, the British were there," . . . and . . . "the guards had surrendered their guns" . . . "should we take the British officers' advice to hang on?" "Don't leave the camp" . . . "Wait for transportation back to France." Some Kriegies remembered when, in Italy, they had been freed only to be scooped up again after a counterattack. They were here a couple of years later . . . some left immediately . . . others stayed . . . while some took off to look around . . . I decided to do both. With another POW, I went into town planning a return to camp. The town was a madhouse. POWs looted a giant warehouse of everything portable . . . food, clothing, and luxuries (probably once stolen by the Germans when they overran France and the Low Countries). White flags hung from windows and scenes of disorder met our eyes .. Yugos driving wagons loaded with looted material . . . Italians drunk and singing . . . French slapping former "masters" (in payment for past indignities) . . . Russkis dying from the aftermath of stuffing hunger-shrunken stomachs. Talked to a Frenchman who claimed to have murdered a family at a nearby farm. . . . "They had held me and used me like an animal for years." He invited us into the house where the bodies were still warm . . . we made excuses. The British shot a Russian for rape and killed two more for the safety of everyone. They had gone mad with their freedom. The blank faces of the townspeople contrasted with the excited (and drunken) faces of the newly liberated POWs. There in the battered town of Fallingbostel we were looking at the end of an empire and the "Reich that was

The fate we share as prisoners / Is drab and often grim / Existing on such scanty fare / As Reich bread, spuds and klim
Beds and books and little else / To fill time's flapping sail / She makes or loses headway / All depending on the mail
Oh drab the days slow to pass / Within this barbed wire fence / Where all the joys of living / Are still in the future tense
So here's to happy days ahead / When you and I are free / To look back on this interlude / And call it history

(from "Clipped Wings," by J. B. Boyle)

to rule for a thousand years."

We went back to the camp where trucks were ready to take us to the rear. The rush to get on disgusted the efficient Britishers who soon abandoned their "system" in favor of the American idea of "jump aboard while there is room."

Names and numbers made little difference . . . the road to the airfield where planes waited to take us out was lined with the fresh graves of those killed. The only difference was the type of helmet near each grave. Near the evacuation airport there was a camp where they separated the able from the sick or injured. The airfield, once the pride of the Luftwaffe, was swarming with military personnel and correspondents. Eisenhower and Montgomery were there and were questioning some of the newly released . . . I didn't get close enough to talk, but got a good look at the famous generals. Heard atrocity stories—those doing the talking had never been subjected to them. Correspondents took it all in but Ike was paying little attention . . . although acknowledging the greetings. No doubt his thoughts were with those of his men still ranging deeper into the vitals of the enemy.

The trip to Belgium in a transport gave an aerial view of the carnage of destruction that was Germany in April 1945 . . . small towns that had borne the twin furies of ground action and aerial bombing were pitiful sights . . . cities were either untouched or simply blasted and burned out shells.

The sense of being airborne again was overshadowed by the scenes of chaos below. The plane landed in Brussels, where we were put up in a hotel (after being deloused, bathed, and clothed).

From Brussels it was on to Namur, Belgium . . . by boxcar . . . what else? This time, however, there were only eight or ten of us . . . more delousing and more credit and more Schnapps and more champagne. . . .

Put on a regular train to Le Havre . . . we passed Paris and the Eiffel Tower . . . wished now I had stopped to see it. They had no records of who we were and some of the men took their time getting back.

I stayed on determined to get home.

Met my Freeport chum again at Camp Lucky Strike (a processing station near Le Havre for liberated Yank POWs). When he left Fallingbostel, the British caught up with his column within twenty-four hours. The guards tried to hurry them along but they had taken their time, and all were liberated.

I didn't return to the States with him. He was processed with a later group. We were fed very well there and given a chance to write home. The weight came back quickly. I was around 130 at Fallingbostel but it was a fairly healthy-looking bunch that was driven (about fifteen days later) to the S.S. *Washington* for the trip back to New York (via Southampton).

The harbor was filled with invasion debris . . . sunken and capsized shipping. Newly arrived American troops and war-weary French civilians gathered to see us off.

Bill McCarran

Bill McCarran was part of a B-17 crew assigned to the 379th Bomb Group (H) at Kimbolton. We are extremely grateful to him for permitting us to publish the story he lived and wrote.

WESTERN UNION

A. N. WILLIAMS
PRESIDENT

1201

CLASS OF SERVICE

This is a full-rate Telegram or Cablegram unless its deferred character is indicated by a suitable symbol above or preceding the address.

DL=Day Letter
NL=Night Letter
LC=Deferred Cable
NLT=Cable Night Letter
Ship Radiogram

158P

The filing time shown in the date line on telegrams and day letters is STANDARD TIME at point of origin. Time of receipt is STANDARD TIME at point of destination

BD155 23 GOVT=WUX WASHINGTON DC 3 131P

MRS CECELIA MCCARREN= 1945 MAY 3 PM 2 04

10 PARROTT ST

THE SECRETARY OF WAR DESIRES ME TO INFORM YOU THAT YOUR SON S/SGT WILLIAM R MCCARREN RETURNED TO MILITARY CONTROL 16 APR 45=

J A ULIO THE ADJUTANT GENERAL.

16 45.

THE RAIDS:
RESULTS

During its 1,008 days in action against the enemy, the Eighth Air Force burned a billion gallons of gasoline, fired ninety-nine million rounds of machine gun ammunition, and expended 732,000 tons of bombs. It lost 5,982 bombers, 3,000 fighter planes, and 146 other aircraft, and more than 46,000 of its men were killed, wounded, or captured by the enemy.

These are but some of the costs of the Eighth's operations in World War II and they are impressive. They are, however, only statistical costs, and to the men who flew the missions the cost was not statistical but personal and painful. It was not measured in gallons or rounds or tons, but in ships of friends that did not come home, in broken bodies removed from broken airplanes and taken to the base hospital or morgue, as the case might be, and in a personal feeling of dread that grew heavier with each completed mssion. In his *Serenade to the Big Bird*, Bert Stiles wrote: "One flak shell had burst just ouside the waist window. The waist gunner wore a flak suit and flak helmet, but they didn't help him much. . . .

"I climbed in with the medico, and, in getting through the door, I put my hand in a gob of blood and brains that had splattered back that way. I took one look at the body and then climbed out again, careful this time where I put my hands.

"I felt no nausea, just a sense of shock, just a kind of deadness inside. . . .

"I didn't know the guy . . . [He] could have come from anywhere, Seattle or Wichita or the valley of the Three Forks of the Wolf. Maybe the guy was a quiet one who taught a Sunday school class . . . maybe a drunk. But now he was man-

left: These air crews are being interrogated by group Intelligence officers shortly after returning from the 8 March 1944 raid on Berlin. In front is the crew of the B-17 "Idiot's Delight." In the background is the crew of "Tremblin' Gremlin." *above:* The sergeant at right waits to sign for his wallet upon returning from a raid over Leipzig on 20 February 1944.

In our new planes, with
our new crews, we
bombed / The ranges by
the desert or the shore, /
Fired at towed targets,
waited for our scores— /
And turned into
replacements and woke
up / One morning, over
England, operational. / It
wasn't different: but if
we died / It was not an
accident but a mistake /
(But an easy one for
anyone to make). / We
read our mail and
counted up our
missions— / In bombers
named for girls, we
burned / The cities we
had learned about in
school— / Till our lives
wore out; our bodies lay
among / The people we
had killed and never
seen. / When we lasted
long enough they gave
us medals; / When we
died they said, "Our
casualties were low." /
They said, "Here are the
maps"; we burned
the cities.

It was not dying—no,
not ever dying; / But the
night I died I dreamed
that I was dead, / And
the cities said to me:
"Why are you dying? /
We are satisfied, if you
are; but why did I die?"

(from "Losses," by
Randall Jarrell)

gled and smashed . . . no good to anyone."

In recalling a raid in which all ships in his squadron but his own had been blasted from the air in a chain of explosions begun by a flak burst in the bomb bay of one of them, Robert White said: "What bothered us most of all was seeing the clean-out crew gathering up the gear of the fellows who had gone down that day—who were no longer with us and because of the concussions of those explosions the odds were that they had been killed. Most had been in the barracks with us from four to eight months, and seeing the clean-out crew getting their stuff together for shipment back to the States gave you a sinking feeling in your stomach, and you felt like getting a barrel of whiskey and just crawling into it." And Elmer Bendiner, remembering the first Schweinfurt raid, wrote in *Fall of the Fortresses*: "Did we win? Did we lose? Did we really see those planes burning on the ground? Did this one fall, and that one fart black smoke from his engines? Whose chute opened? Whose did not? Questions turned in the hollow mind bereft of thought, like an awl in wormwood, biting into nothingness, the nothingness of spent men at last asleep."

Did we win or did we lose? There Bendiner touched on the key question of the entire bombing effort over Europe. Of the 732,000 tons of bombs expended by the Eighth, 691,000 were delivered to their targets—the remainder having been either jettisoned by ships in trouble or carried by ships shot down before reaching their targets. But did that 691,000 tons sufficiently damage the Nazi war machine to justify the price of its delivery in matériel and men? Not only was this question debated then, but to some

extent, at least, it is still being debated today, with some people claiming that the Allied bombing of Europe proved in the end only to be a costly and even barbaric exercise in futility. It seems strange that it should continue to be debated today, when both Allied and German records are fully available and show beyond doubt the contribution of the bombing to the final victory. It is not odd that it should have been debated at the time, however, for at the time dependable information on bombing results was hard to come by.

The first results information came from debriefing sessions held by Intelligence officers with the flight crews immediately after they had landed from a mission. As recalled by Larry Bird: "They'd pick you up in a truck and haul you to this little building, and you'd go in and sit down at one of the long tables inside. Somebody'd say, 'OK, they're opening the bar, so go and get your drink,' and everyone was given a glass of whiskey—a small glass, a double shot. Then you'd all sit there chattering about what we saw and you saw, and so forth."

Every air crew was interrogated as a group by the group Intelligence officer. The mission was reported by each crew member from his own perspective. Discrepancies were identified by the interrogators as they probed for information about the German reaction to the raid. Efforts were made in the conversations to determine if the Luftwaffe was trying any new tactical wrinkles in its response to the Americans' attack. Questions were asked about the accuracy of the USAAF premission predictions about flak and fighter response. Immediate analysis of the Flash Reports (tabulations of the

In Hamburg today this tower is nearly all that remains of the Church of St. Nicholai, destroyed along with much of that city in the concentrated British and American attacks of July 1943. The ruin of St. Nicholai has been preserved as a striking midtown reminder of the tragedy of war. *overleaf:* The wreck of a crash-landed 91st BG B-17 at its Bassingbourn base. Off-runway emergency landings were common occurrences on the fields of the Eighth.

raw data from the interrogations) was then done by the Headquarters staff.

But this system, even though it helped mission planners to keep abreast of German defensive developments, was not too helpful in revealing the actual accomplishments of a mission. While in the heat of action and plowing through flak, it was hard for men to be accurate and dispassionate observers—a fact apparent in every debriefing. "I'd hear what some of the other guys were saying," recalled Keith Newhouse, "and wonder if we'd been on the same mission." As remembered by Paul Sink: "You'd been on oxygen for six or seven hours, you were tired, so stiff you could hardly stand up, and still half-frozen from having been so damned cold. Then they'd give you your shots of whiskey, and by the time you got into the interrogation, hell!, you didn't know yourself what you'd seen." To which Larry Bird, taking part in the same conversation, responded: "Right! they'd ask what we'd seen, and, my God!, everybody saw something different. Everyone was excited and all trying to talk at once and yelling, 'Oh no! That's not how it was!' How Intelligence could ever decipher any hard facts out of all that confusion I'll never know, but I guess they could somehow."

While the crewmen were being interrogated, the film from their automatic bomb-bay cameras was being developed, and it told a more definitive story. The notion that Allied bombing was damaging Germany's war effort, declared a noted American economist after making a postwar study of the German wartime economy, was "perhaps the greatest miscalculation of the war." And one of the reasons he gave for this

supposed ineffectiveness was the bombing's inaccuracy. In the air operations of World War II, he wrote, nothing "was subject to such assault as open agricultural land." But the record of the bomb-bay cameras, where the Eighth Air Force is concerned, at least, gives decisive evidence to the contrary. During the first half of 1943, it is true, the men of the Eighth managed to place only 14 percent of their bombs within 1,000 feet (or about two-and-a-half city blocks) of the target-center or MPI, and placed only 32 percent within 2,000 feet. Over the next two years, however, they gradually brought those percentages up to 44 percent and 73 percent respectively; and during the entire war, according to the photographic record, they placed 37 percent

far left: The result of a relatively successful belly-in on the runway of an 8AF base, 5 March 1944. *above:* Burning furiously, this "fort" of Ridgewell's 381st BG nearly made it home to its field after having been severely damaged on a raid into Germany.

Many years after WW2, oddments like these have been found near the long-abandoned hardstands on the disused fields of the Eighth.

195

of their bombs within 1,000 feet, and 64 percent within 2,000 feet, of the centers of their targets. And when you consider that trying to drop bombs into a 2,000-foot circle while speeding past at an altitude of 25,000 feet in a bomber under fire was much like trying to drop grains of rice into a teacup while riding past on a bicycle under fire, that was a very good record indeed.

The bomb-bay cameras, together with those of photo-reconnaissance planes, did an excellent job of recording bombing accuracy, but they were not very effective in revealing its effect on the German war effort as a whole. For that information, the military analysts of the time had to depend mostly on spy reports, hunch, and hope. Now, however, we have the complete records to guide us, and it is on some of those records that those who claim the bombing to have been ineffective base their claims. They point out, for example, that Germany's average monthly production of tanks and self-propelled guns rose from 136 in 1940 to 1,583 in 1944, and that over the same period her monthly aircraft output rose from 854 to 3,300. "In the face of these figures," they ask, "how could anyone possibly claim that the German war-making ability was damaged by Allied bombing?"

Those who ask that question, however, are overlooking another most obvious question not overlooked by British historian and authority on Nazi Germany, Dr. R. J. Overy. The question is: What would Germany's military production and military power have become had there been no Allied bombing? In his recent book, *The Air War 1939–1945*, Dr. Overy has given his answer. "The important consequence of the [British and American] bombing," he wrote, "was not that it failed to stem the increase in arms production, but that it prevented the increase from being very considerably greater." And in addition, Dr. Overy pointed out, the bombing offensive caused a great deal of German manpower and production to be tied up in detecting and defending against the bombers, and thus to be "destroyed" insofar as any offensive use was concerned. This, according to Germany's own figures, included 30 percent of her gun production, 20 percent of ammunition production, 50

left: Elation and relief in the faces of the crew of "Jersey Jinx" on their safe return to base after a raid. *below:* At least as common a postmission reaction for crews was the extreme fatigue that resulted from the physical and emotional strain, a very long and uncomfortable ride, extended use of oxygen, and exposure to air and ground attack.

percent of her electronics manufacturing, 33 percent of her optical industry, and two million of her soldiers and civilians.

Then, too, it did the Germans little good to produce machines they had no fuel to operate and, according to Luftwaffe Generalmajor Albrecht von Massow: "The [bombing] attacks on German oil production, begun in 1944, was the largest factor of all in reducing German war potential." Neither did it do them any good to produce military goods they could not then transport to the point of need, and, in the words of another German general: "The [aerial] attacks on the German transport system, coordinated with serious losses in the fuel industry, had a paralyzing effect."

But the greatest contribution, in fact the vital contribution, made by the Allied bombers and their fighter escorts to the defeat of Germany was their destruction of the German Luftwaffe. By destroying the Luftwaffe's production plants and fuel sources, destroying its airplanes both on the ground and in the air, and decimating its force of trained pilots, they stripped away Hitler's aerial umbrella and left German oil, transport, manufacturing, and military facilities nakedly exposed to Allied aerial bombardment. And once that had been accomplished, the end was quick in coming. The inveterate diarist of the Third Reich, Dr. Joseph Goebbels, for instance, wrote in March of 1945: "Our Luftwaffe has gone totally to the dogs. . . .

"The Americans now overfly German territory practically unresisted . . . [and] the damage done to our armaments potential is quite beyond repair. . . . petrol available to the Lüftwaffe has fallen from 193,000 tons to 8,000. What use

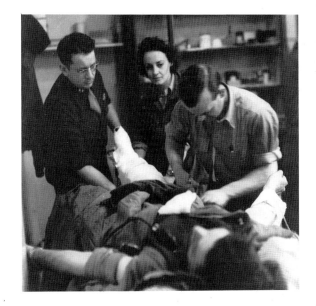

far left: Emergency aid is given to this wounded Ridgewell-based air crewman in the airplane during a raid on 20 February 1944. left: Medical attention is given to the injuries of a crew member who was wounded during a 401st BG mission over Schweinfurt in April 1944. below: Wounded airmen of the 401st BG convalesce in their base hospital at Deenethorpe, Northamptonshire, in July 1944.

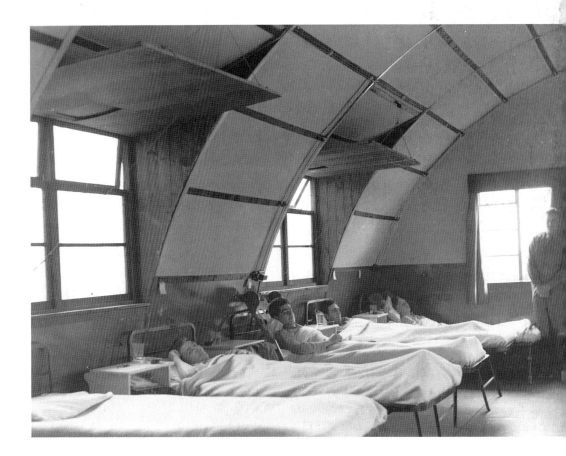

is all this output of fighters when we have not even the petrol or crews to put them in action?

"The air war is still the great tale of woe. . . . The situation becomes daily more intolerable and we have no means of defending ourselves against this catastrophe."

Two months after Dr. Goebbels wrote those words Germany was finished and the war was over. Then dozens of other German leaders gave their reasons for the German defeat and the remarks of the few who are quoted below echo the views of almost all. "Germany lost the war the day it was started," said German Finance Minister Dr. Hjalmar Schacht, "Your bombers destroyed German production." Generalmajor Herhudt Von Ruden voiced the opinions of most German commanders when he said the Allied invasion of Europe "would have been impossible without strategic bombing." And Field Marshals Albert Kesselring and Karl von Runstedt, generally acknowledged to have been two of the Third Reich's most astute and competent military leaders, were in agreement that, in Kesselring's words, "Allied air power was the greatest single reason for the German defeat."

In commenting on the contribution of the American air forces to that defeat, Lüftwaffe general Karl Bodenschatz said: "I am very much impressed by the accuracy of American daylight bombing, which really concentrated on military targets and factories, to the exclusion of others." And the chief of the Lüftwaffe, Reichsmarshal Hermann Goering, just before his suicide in 1945, summed up his remarks on the war by declaring: "Without the United States Air Force the war would still be going on . . . [and] not on German soil."

And you are past. / Remember then, / Fix deep within your dreaming head / Year, hour or endless moment when / You reached and crossed the Bridge of Dread.

(from "The Bridge of Dread," by Edwin Muir)

left: So very glad to be safely back from a raid, these 390th BG airmen enjoy the Red Cross-furnished coffee and doughnuts at an ARC Clubmobile on their Framlingham base in October 1943. *overleaf:* The J-type hangar still standing at the 305th BG base, Chelveston.

ONE LAST LOOK

... our tribute of respect and admiration to the officers and men who fought and died in this fearful battle of the air, the like of which had never before been known, or even with any precision imagined. The moral tests to which the crew of a bomber were subjected reached the limits of human valour and sacrifice. Here chance was carried to its most extreme and violent degree above all else.

(from *Closing the Ring*, by Winston Churchill)

The 305th Bomb Group of the 8th AF, Chelveston, England, reunion will be held September 9–12, 1982, in Orlando Fla.

Members of the 91st Bomb Group will return to their former duty station at Bassingbourn, England . . . on April 29–May 12, 1983.

Excerpts from the Air Force Association magazine, Air Force.

Nearly forty years have passed since the armadas of the Eighth last flew over Europe, but among their veterans memories of those days are still fresh and esprit de corps still endures. Each of the old divisions and groups has its own association that periodically holds reunions—usually in the United States; but almost every group has held at least one reunion among its old neighbors and near its old base in England.

On returning to England the veterans usually find their old bases covered with grass, or converted to tilled fields, housing developments, or industrial parks, and only a few hay-filled Nissen huts indicate they were ever there at all. At some of the old bases, however, airplanes do still fly. Seething now serves as a base for gliders, and Lavenham, where many wartime buildings still stand and the old control tower is a private home, occasionally has its old runways used by crop dusters. Shipdham's tower has become a lonely ruin used as a roost for passing birds—and perhaps a home for ghosts—but its old runways and two hangars remain. Halesworth has become a turkey farm and so have Attlebridge and Wendling. At Rackheath the tower remains, but it is hard to find, for now it is only one of many buildings in a busy industrial park.

But the returning veteran who finds his old base gone entirely will often find it is remembered by some sort of a memorial to the Americans who died while in service there. The memorial may be in the form of a sculpture, an engraved stone, a column, a church window of stained glass, or just a simple plaque. It may be located on the site of the base or in a nearby town. It may have been established by the veterans of the group or by their one-time English neighbors.

One of the most notable memorials is the Second Air Division Memorial Library, located in the Norwich Central Library and underwritten by the division's survivors "in memory of our fallen comrades." It is a handsome, airy room stocked with books and Eighth Air Force memorabilia, and in each of its fourteen bays there is a plaque commemorating one of the division's fourteen groups.

Except among themselves, the veterans of the Eighth don't talk much about their war any more. They were not heroes, they will tell you, but just a bunch of fellows trying to do a job they had been sent to do. Nor were they zealots burning with the fires of a holy cause.

But if the men of the Eighth did not treat their mission as an ideological crusade, neither did they treat it as a vendetta. This was not due to their virtue but to the nature of their combat. A ground trooper, for instance, sees the enemy trying to kill him, and that enemy becomes a person to be hated. Free-Polish pilots who saw Nazis kill their people and shatter their cities, said Bert Stiles, "wanted to kill every German in the world. But with me it was different. . . ." And indeed it was different. To the men of the Eighth it was a curiously impersonal war. They never saw the gunner who fired the flak, and if they saw the pilot of the enemy fighter, it was only as a speed-blurred shadow. Thus their attackers seemed not to be hostile men, but hostile hardware, and their conversations still show it. They speak of hating the flak and the fighters, but rarely do they mention the flak's gunners or the fighters' pilots.

By the same token, since the Eighth's pinpoint bombing was designed to destroy Hitler's war machinery, its crews saw their targets, also, as hardware rather than people. "You knew the people were down there," Frank Nelson said, "but you couldn't think about that. You had to feel you were bombing *things*, not people."

They were most likely to think of people as being under their bombs when battle damage or other circumstances forced them to drop their bombs elsewhere than on the target. A number of air-crew veterans' feelings were summarized by the B-24 pilot whose jettisoned bombs "fell on a peaceful village where I could see wash on the clothesline. They burst in a line right down the main street, and I still feel bad about that today."

But the general attitude toward bombing was that stated by Elmer Bendiner. "We were not unconcerned with the hells we left behind us. The hells were perceived, however, only as pillars of smoke, not as human anguish. . . ."

In either case, Eighth veterans know today what they could not have known then—that any human anguish their bombing caused was nothing compared to the anguish it helped to relieve. They could not have known, of course, how Hollander Arie Brakel, when he heard their formations rumbling overhead, would turn to his daughter and say, "Listen, Helene. That is angel music!" But they know now why he would have said that. And they know now why other Hollanders, late in the war, had risked Nazi retribution to plant tulips in the form of an American flag accompanied by the words, "Thanks Boys."

"The sight of it," said Larry Bird, "would bring tears to your eyes."

Elmer Bendiner knew then that he and his "Tondelayo" crewmates did not go down in flames over Kassel only because none of the eleven enemy shells found in "Tondelayo's" gas tanks that evening had exploded. Because Intelligence was protecting an unknown saboteur at a German-occupied ammunition factory, he did not know why they did not explode. Now he does. Ten of those shells were entirely empty and the eleventh contained only a slip of paper. Scrawled on it in Czech were the words, "This is all we can do for you now."

The Eighth veterans know these things now because they know now how bad conditions in Hitler's Europe really were. They know now that there was a Buchenwald and a Belsen and a Dachau, and that there would have been more of them—and not just in Europe—had Hitler not been stopped. And they know from the words of Germany's own military leaders just how much they, as members of the United States Army Air Force, contributed to stopping him.

Veterans of those days in the Eighth, looking back today and summarizing their memories, almost all agree with Frank Nelson:

"I wouldn't want to go through it again—too many sad things happened—but I'm glad I did go through it. It was a necessary job, I think we did it well, and I will always feel satisfaction in having been a part of it."

THE 384th BOMBARDMENT GROUP (H) OF THE U.S. 8th AIR FORCE FLEW FROM THIS AIRFIELD. 1943-1945.

LEST WE FORGET

PERPETUAL MEMORY OF
THESE VALIANT AMERICAN
OF THE 457th BOMB
DURING WORLD
THEIR LIVES THAT

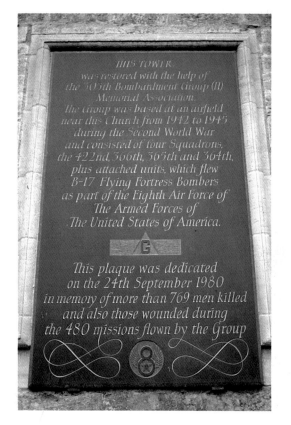

THIS TOWER
was restored with the help of
the 305th Bombardment Group (H)
Memorial Association.
The Group was based at an airfield
near this Church from 1942 to 1945
during the Second World War
and consisted of four Squadrons,
the 422nd, 366th, 365th and 364th,
plus attached units, which flew
B-17 Flying Fortress Bombers
as part of the Eighth Air Force of
The Armed Forces of
The United States of America.

G

This plaque was dedicated
on the 24th September 1980
in memory of more than 769 men killed
and also those wounded during
the 480 missions flown by the Group

IN MEMORY OF
THE
351ST BOMBARDMENT
GROUP (HEAVY).
EIGHTH UNITED STATES ARMY
AIR FORCE.
311 GROUP COMBAT BOMBING MISSIONS
WERE FLOWN FROM THIS AIRFIELD OVER
OCCUPIED EUROPE BETWEEN 1943-1945.
175 B-17 FLYING FORTRESSES AND THEIR
CREWS WERE LOST. 303 ENEMY AIRCRAFT
WERE DESTROYED IN AERIAL COMBAT.

509TH SQ.   510TH SQ.

508TH SQ.   351ST B.G. (H)   511TH SQ.

1943   1945

top row from left: 384th BG memorial at Grafton-Underwood; a "Fort" being restored by the Imperial War Museum at Duxford; memorials to the Glatton, Great Dunmow, and Wendling-based Bomb Groups; the U.S. airman statue in the American cemetery at Maddingley near Cambridge. *bottom row from left:* Memorials to the 305th BG at Chelveston, the 351st BG at Polebrook and the 34th BG at Mendlesham.

DEVELOPMENT, EDITING,
PRINCIPAL PHOTOGRAPHY AND
DESIGN BY PHILIP KAPLAN

TEXT BY REX ALAN SMITH

PICTURE CREDITS

Photographs by Philip Kaplan are credited: PK

Jacket front and back: PK. 2/3: PK.

PROLOGUE 8/9:U.S.Air Force. 10:PK. 10/11:PK. 13:U.S.Air Force. 14:PK. 16/17:PK.

THE AIR CREWS 18/19:U.S.Air Force. 21:U.S.Air Force. 22:Mrs.Ray Wild. 24:U.S.Air Force. 25:PK. 27:Harold Haft. 29:Ken Stone,-29:PK. 30/31:U.S.Air Force. 32/33:U.S.Air Force.

THE BASES 34:PK. 35:PK. 36:PK. 38/39:PK. 40/41:PK. 42:PK. 43:PK. 44:PK. 45:PK. 46/47:PK. 49:PK.

IN QUARTERS 50/51:U.S.Air Force. 52:PK. 53:PK. 54:U.S.Air Force. 54/55:U.S.Air Force. 56:PK, except top right and center right, Jon Goldenbaum (2). 57:PK. 59:Columbia Pictures. 60:PK. 60/61:PK.

THE RAIDS:PREPARATION 62:U.S.Air Force. 64:PK. 65:U.S.Air Force. 67:U.S.Air Force. 68:PK. 69:PK. 70:Military Antiques Museum-Santa Monica. 71:U.S.Air Force. 73:U.S.Air Force. 74/75:U.S.Air Force.

THE VILLAGES 76:PK. 76/77:PK. 79:U.S.Air Force. 80/81:PK. 81:PK.

THE AIRCRAFT 84:U.S.Air Force. 86/87:PK. 88:U.S.Air Force.

THE LEADERS 90/91:PK. 92/93:Twentieth Century Fox Pictures. 94:top left-U.S.Air Force, top right-Walt Disney Productions, bottom-Jon Goldenbaum. 95:PK.

THE RAIDS:DELIVERY 96:U.S.Air Force. 98:Military Antiques Museum-Santa Monica. 99:Ken Stone. 100/101:U.S.Air Force. 101:U.S.Air Force. 102:U.S.Air Force. 103:U.S.Air Force. 104/105:U.S.Air Force. 106:PK. 107:U.S.Air Force. 108:Military Antiques Museum-Santa Monica. 109:Military Antiques Museum-Santa Monica. 110:Mrs. Ray Wild. 111:Ken Stone. 112:U.S.Air Force.

THE GIRLS 118:U.S.Air Force. 119:U.S.Air Force. 120:PK. 122:U.S.Air Force. 123:U.S.Air Force. 124:U.S.Air Force. 125:U.S.Air Force.

FLAK 126:E. Butler. 131:U.S.Air Force. 132:PK. 134/135:Ken Stone. 137:U.S.Air Force.

AT EASE 138/139:U.S.Air Force. 140:U.S.Air Force. 141:U.S.Air Force. 142:U.S.Air Force. 143:PK. 144/145:U.S.Air Force. 146:U.S.Air Force. 146/147:U.S.Air Force. 148:PK, except top left, U.S.Air Force. 149:PK. 150/151:U.S.Air Force. 151:U.S.Air Force. 152:PK. 153:PK. 154:U.S.Air Force. 155:U.S.Air Force.

PRISONER OF WAR 156:William McCarran. 158:William Mc-Carran. 159:William McCarran. 160:Quentin Bland. 164:William McCarran. 167:John Hurd. 171:Quentin Bland. 174/175:William McCarran. 180:Quentin Bland. 183:William McCarran. 185:William McCarran.

THE RAIDS:RESULTS 186/187:U.S.Air Force. 187:U.S.Air Force. 188:Military Antiques Museum-Santa Monica. 189:PK. 190/191:U.S.Air Force. 192:U.S.Air Force. 193:U.S.Air Force. 194:PK. 195:PK. 196:U.S.Air Force. 197:U.S.Air Force. 198:U.S.Air Force. 199:U.S.Air Force. 200/201:U.S.Air Force.

ONE LAST LOOK 202/203:PK. 205:U.S.Air Force. 206:PK. 207:PK.

ACKNOWLEDGMENTS

We thank the many Eighth Air Force veterans whose enthusiastic participation in our research has made this book possible. We are grateful to the English farmers, landowners and caretakers for their cooperation in allowing us access to their properties for our photography and exploration of the disused Eighth Air Force fields.

We are particularly grateful to the following people whose contributions and assistance in the areas of book and article reference materials, additional photographs, personal interviews, the loan of personal memorabilia, research and other forms of assistance have aided enormously in the preparation of this book: Robert E. Abrams, Beth and David Alston, John T. Appleby, Dana Bell, Elmer Bendiner, Cecelia Bessette, Larry Bird, Quentin Bland, Charles Bosshardt, Sam Burchell, Richard Bye, Martin Caidin, Chicago Tribune Syndicate, James H. Doolittle, Lawrence Drew, Ira Eakin, Jacob T. Elias, W. W. Ford, Roger Freeman, Ernest K. Gann, Jon Goldenbaum, Harold Haft, Allan Healy, John Hersey, John Hurd, Randolph Jacobs, Richard Johnston, Robert S. Johnson, Claire Kaplan, Joseph Kaplan, Neal Kaplan, Myron Keilman, Cleon T. Knapp, Will Lundy, William McCarran, Donald Maffett, Bob Mallick, Glenn R. Matson, A. D. McAllister, Jr., John A. Miller, Jim Murrey, Robert Mygatt, Keith Newhouse, Frank W. Nelson, David Parry, Max Pinkerton, Sidney Rapaport, Walton Rawls, Paige Rense, Peter Rix, Andy Rooney, Neil Shakery, Dave Shelhamer, Susan Simpson, Paul Sink, Norman Smart, Wanda Smith, Mark Stannard, Bert Stiles, Ken Stone, Lloyd Stovall, Eric Suter, Calvin Swaffer, John B. Thomas, Jr., Robert White, Ray Wild, Ray Wild, Jr., Ruth Wild, Raymond Wilson.

Our intent was not to provide comprehensive coverage of the Eighth, but rather to show and tell about many aspects of real life in its heavy bomb groups in that time. As these aspects were relatively similar from group to group, we felt that the use of a representative selection of groups and fields would appropriately serve our purpose. Clearly, no attempt was made to include coverage of Eighth Fighter Command or the other notable 8AF organizations, as we agreed that a narrower focus than say, the Eighth Air Force as a whole, was essential to our requirement. —the authors

SELECTED BIBLIOGRAPHY

After The Battle Magazine and the Royal Air Force Museum, reference material on the Attlebridge airfield site.
Appleby, John T. *Suffolk Summer.* Ipswich: East Anglia Magazine, 1948.

Bailey, Ronald H. *The Air War in Europe*. Alexandria: Time-Life Books, 1981.

Bendiner, Elmer. *The Fall of Fortresses*. London: Pan Books, 1982.

Birdsall, Steve. *Log of the Liberators*. New York: Doubleday & Co., 1973.

Blue, Allan G. *B-24 Liberator*. New York: Charles Scribner's Sons, 1977.

Bowman, Martin. *Fields of Little America*. Norwich: Wensum Books (Norwich), 1977.

Caidin, Martin. *Black Thursday*. New York: E. P. Dutton & Co., 1960.

Churchill, Winston S. *Closing The Ring*. Boston: Houghton Mifflin Co., 1950.

Churchill, Winston S. *The Grand Alliance*. Boston: Houghton Mifflin Co., 1950.

Craven, Wesley Frank, and Cate, James Lea. *The Army Air Forces in World War II, Volumes 1–7*. Chicago: University of Chicago Press, 1948.

Davis, Kenneth S. *Experience of War*. New York: Doubleday & Co., 1965.

Editors of Time-Life Books, The. *The Luftwaffe*. Alexandria: Time-Life Books, 1982.

Eisenhower, Dwight D. *Crusade In Europe*. New York: Doubleday & Co., 1948.

Frankland, Noble. *The Bombing Offensive Against Germany*. London: Faber and Faber, 1965.

Freeman, Roger A. *Airfields of the Eighth*. London: Battle of Britain Prints International, 1978.

Freeman, Roger A. *The Mighty Eighth*. London: Macdonald & Co., 1970.

Freeman, Roger A. *Mighty Eighth War Diary*. London: Jane's Publishing Co., 1981.

Galland, Adolf. *The First And The Last*. New York: Ballantine Books, 1954.

Gann, Ernest K. *Fate Is The Hunter*. New York: Simon & Schuster, 1961.

Gibson, Michael L. *Aviation in Northamptonshire*. Northampton: Northamptonshire Libraries, 1982.

Gurney, Major Gene. *The War in the Air, World War II*. Bonanza Books, 1972.

Healy, Allan. *The 467th Bombardment Group*. Privately printed, 1947.

Heflin, Woodford Agee. *The United States Air Force Dictionary*. Princeton: D. Van Nostrand Company.

Hersey, John. *The War Lover*. New York: Alfred A. Knopf, 1959.

Impact—Volumes 1–8. New York: James Parton & Co., 1980.

Irving, David. *The Destruction of Dresden*. London: William Kimber & Co., 1963.

Jablonski, Edward. *Airwar*. New York: Doubleday & Co., 1971.

Jablonski, Edward. *Flying Fortress*. New York: Doubleday & Co., 1965.

Jablonski, Edward. *America in the Air War*. Alexandria: Time-Life Books, 1982.

Johnson, Robert S. with Caidin, Martin. *Thunderbolt*. New York: Ballantine Books, 1958.

Lay, Beirne Jr., and Bartlett, Sy. *12 O'Clock High*. New York: Ballantine Books, 1948.

LeMay, General Curtis E., and Kantor, MacKinlay. *Mission with LeMay*. New York: Doubleday & Co., 1965.

Logan, Ian, and Nield, Henry. *Classy Chassy*. New York: A & W Visual Library, 1977.

Manchester, William. *Goodbye Darkness*. Boston: Little, Brown & Co., 1979.

Maurer, Maurer. *Air Force Combat Units of WW 2*. New York: Franklin Watts, 1961.

McCarran, William. Letters and private papers. Unpublished.

McCrary, John R. (Tex), and Scherman, David E. *First of the Many*. New York: Simon and Schuster, 1944.

Munson, Kenneth. *The Blandford Book Of Warplanes*. Poole: Blandford Press.

Nalty, Bernard, and Berger, Carl. *The Man Who Bombed The Reich*. New York: Elsevier-Dutton, 1978.

Newhouse, James K. Letters and private papers. Unpublished.

Overy, R. J. *The Air War 1939–1945*. New York: Stein & Day, 1981.

Peaslee, Budd J. *Heritage of Valor*. Philadelphia: J. B. Lippincott Co., 1963.

Pyle, Ernie. *Brave Men*. New York: Grosset & Dunlap, 1943.

Redding, Major John M., and Leyshon, Captain Harold I. *Skyways to Berlin*. Indianapolis: Bobbs-Merrill Co., 1943.

Rust, Ken C. *Eighth Air Force Story*. Temple City, Ca.: A Historical Aviation Album Publication, 1978.

Scutts, Jerry. *USAAF Heavy Bomber Units—ETO & MTO 1942–45*. New York: Sky Books Press, 1977.

Sears, Stephen W. *Air War Against Hitler's Germany*. New York: American Heritage Publishing Co., 1964.

Second Air Division Association Journal. Various issues. Ipswich.

Shirer, William L. *The Rise and Fall of the Third Reich*. New York: Simon and Schuster, 1960.

Simmons, Kenneth W. *Kriegie*. New York: Thomas Nelson & Sons, 1960.

Slater, Harry F. *The Big Square A—A History of the 94th Bomb Group (H), 1942–1945*. 1980.

Sloan, John S. *The Route As Briefed*. Cleveland: Argus Press, 1946.

Speer, Albert. *Inside The Third Reich*. New York: The Macmillan Co., 1970.

Steinbeck, John. *Once There Was A War*. New York: Bantam Books, 1958.

Stiles, Bert. *Serenade to the Big Bird*. New York: W. W. Norton & Co., 1952.

Sunderman, James F. *World War II in the Air*. New York: Franklin Watts, 1963.

Sweetman, John. *Schweinfurt: Disaster in the Skies*. New York: Ballantine Books, 1971.

Target: Germany. New York: Simon and Schuster, 1943.

Taylor, A.J.P. *English History 1914–1945*. New York: Oxford University Press, 1965.

34th Bomb Group (H) 1941–45. Nashville: Reprinted by the Battery Press, 1981.

Thomas, Lowell, and Jablonski, Edward. *Doolittle—A Biography*. New York: Doubleday & Co., 1969.

Turner, Richard E. *Big Friend, Little Friend*. New York: Doubleday & Co., 1969.

Verrier, Anthony. *The Bomber Offensive*. New York: Macmillan & Co., 1968.

Wild, Raymond W. Letters and private papers. Unpublished.

Woolnough, John H. *The 8th Air Force Album*. Hollywood, Florida: The 8th Air Force News, 1978.

Woolnough, John H. *The 8th Air Force Yearbook*. Hollywood, Florida: The 8th Air Force News, 1981.

Woolnough, John H. *8th Air Force News—Journal of the 8th Air Force Historical Society*. Hollywood, Florida: 1976–1983.

A PARTIAL SUMMARY OF EIGHTH AIR FORCE OPERATIONS EUROPEAN THEATER 17 AUGUST 1942 TO 8 MAY 1945

The Eighth Air Force was activated at Savannah, Georgia, 28 January 1942. In February, a small detachment of officers arrived in England to make initial arrangements for the housing and basing of groups to follow, and by June, 1942, aircraft, crews and ground personnel had begun to arrive in the U.K. On 17 August 1942, the first operational mission in its own aircraft was carried out by the Eighth Air Force . . . the first of 459 days on which heavy bombers struck at enemy targets.

In World War 2 the Eighth Air Force was commanded by a total of five officers from the date of its activation. They were Brigadier General (then Colonel) Asa M. Duncan from 28 January 1942 to 4 May 1942; General (then Major General) Carl A. Spaatz from 5 May 1942 to 30 November 1942; Lieutenant General Ira C. Eaker from 1 December 1942 to 5 January 1944; Lieutenant General James H. Doolittle from 6 January 1944 to 9 May 1945 and Major General W. E. Kepner from 10 May 1945.

At peak personnel strength, the Air Force numbered more than two hundred thousand officers and men. At peak operating strength, it numbered 40½ Heavy Bomb Groups, 15 Fighter Groups, and 2 Photo/Recon Groups operating from bases in the U.K At this strength, a typical mission consisted of 1,400 heavy bombers escorted by 800 fighters, consuming 3,500,000 gallons of aviation gasoline, expending 250,000 rounds of .50 calibre ammunition, destroying 25 German aircraft in the air and on the ground for the loss of 4 U.S. fighters and 5 bombers, and dropping 3,300 tons of bombs on enemy targets of which on visual missions, 40% fell within one thousand feet of assigned MPIs and 75% within two thousand feet. A typical damage assessment report from photographs taken by Eighth Air Force photo aircraft after the attack reads as follows: "Very severe damage is seen in both the North and East Marshalling Yards. In the N. M/Y, both semi-round houses are severely damaged, one turntable is wrecked, many tracks obliterated in the center of the yard, all through-running lines cut, the large transshipment shed burning, large numbers of locomotives, wagons, and cars derailed, damaged and destroyed. In the E. M/Y, the locomotive depot is severely damaged, all through-lines cut, and all sidings un-

serviceable. The passenger stations in both Marshalling Yards are severely damaged." (From K report covering attack on Falkenburg M/Y, 19 April 1945)

This partial statistical record of the 459 days when bombing operations were carried out (with related fighter, photo and special operations) represents only a collection of facts and figures on effort, consumption, strength and costs. No attempt has been made—or can be made—to properly reflect in statistics the devotion to duty, heroism and sacrifices made by personnel of the Command to accomplish the mission of the Eighth Air Force. Behind the figures on these pages are the combat crews and fighter pilots who fought in the skies—46,456 of whom became casualties; the maintenance/ground personnel—who kept the airplanes flying—repaired 59,644 battle-damaged aircraft, loaded the 732,231 tons of bombs expended, and linked and loaded the 99,256,341 rounds of ammunition; and the planners who directed the missions.

HIGHLIGHTS

1942

28 JAN—Eighth Air Force activated at Savannah, Georgia.

FEB—First detachment of Eighth Air Force officers arrived in U.K.

4 JUL—Six Eighth Air Force crews in RAF Bostons participated in mission to DeKooy Air Field.

17 AUG—First mission in Eighth Air Force aircraft. 12 B-17s bombed Rouen.

9 OCT—B-24s joined the air assault. First mission of over 100 bombers (108 bombers attacked air fields in France).

NOV/DEC—4 Eighth Air Force Fighter Groups and 2 Heavy Bomb Groups transferred to MTO for "Torch" project.

1943

3 JAN—First use of "formation" (instead of individual) precision bombing.

27 JAN—First mission to Germany. 91 bombers dispatched to Wilhelmshaven and Emden.

JAN—48% of all bombers crossing enemy coast received battle damage.

18 MAR—First use of automatic flight control linked with bombsights.

13 MAY—3rd Division became operational. Air Force now had 12 heavy bomb groups.

14 MAY—First mission of over 200 bombers. 11 B-26s joined heavies in attacks on Kiel, Antwerp, Courtrai and Ijmuiden. 10 B-26s were MIA.

MAY—P-47s began regular escort up to 200 mile range.

24 JUL—Longest bomber mission to date and first mission to Norway.
28 JUL—P-47s, equipped with auxiliary fuel tanks, escorted bombers across German border for first time.
1 AUG—B-24s of 2nd Air Division on D.S. to MTO joined with Ninth Air Force to attack Ploesti oil fields. Of 102 Eighth Air Force B-24s dispatched, 30 were shot down.
17 AUG—First shuttle mission to North Africa bases after attack on Regensburg. 60 bombers lost on attack on Schweinfurt and Regensburg. 319 e/a destroyed by H/Bs.
27 SEP—First use of radar instruments to bomb through cloud—used over Emden.
SEP—P-47s range increased to 325 miles. Air Force dropped over 5,000 tons of bombs in one month.
7 OCT—First night propaganda leaflet mission.
15 OCT—VIII Air Support Command Medium Bomb Groups transferred to Ninth Air Force.
OCT—214 bombers were lost—9.2% of aircraft entering enemy territory.
3 NOV—First mission of over 500 bombers—574 dispatched to Wilhelmshaven.
25 NOV—First fighter-bomber mission carried out.

1944

JAN—Air Force dropped over 10,000 tons of bombs.
11 FEB—P-51s joined Eighth Air Force fighters.
20-25 FEB—Four devastating attacks on German aircraft plants and assembly factories crippled German aircraft production.
25 FEB—First fighter low-level strafing attack.
6 MAR—First major attack on Berlin. 69 bombers MIA on this attack—largest number MIA in one day.
MAR—First month over 20,000 tons bombs dropped.
7 MAY—First mission of over 1,000 bombers.
6 JUN—D-Day. 40½ heavy bomb groups were operational. 2,698 bombers dropped 4,778 tons of bombs on two missions. 1,966 fighters provided escort and cover.
21 JUN—First shuttle mission to bases in Russia.
22 JUN—GAF destroyed 47 U.S. aircraft on the ground at Eastern bases.
JUN—25,402 fighters were sortied—Greatest number in any single month.
28 JUL—First GAF jet/rocket enemy aircraft being used operationally encountered by U.S. fighters.
13 AUG—Fighters dropped 334 tons of bombs on fighter-bomber attack. Largest tonnage for one mission.
16 AUG—First jet aircraft destroyed by fighters.
29 AUG—Trucking operations to ground troops commenced.

18 SEP—Bombers dropped supplies to beleaguered Warsaw.
27 NOV—Fighters encountered 747 enemy aircraft—Greatest number sighted in one day—102 E/A destroyed.
NOV—Fighter effective strength averaged 1,031—Largest of any month.
24 DEC—Largest bomber mission to date—2,055 in the air at one time to attack targets in the "Ardennes Bulge" sector. 4,302 tons of bombs dropped on one operation.

1945

14 JAN—Fighters destroyed 161 enemy aircraft in the air—Largest fighter air claims in one day.
JAN—An average of 2,799 heavy bombers and 1,484 fighters were assigned—Greatest aircraft strength of the Air Force. Fighters destroyed 319 locomotives, 657 goods wagons, and 58 tank cars in strafing attacks.
FEB—Highly successful heavy attacks on Marshalling Yards in Berlin, Dresden and Nurenberg carried out on six days.
28 MAR—Last mission to Berlin—The most heavily bombed U.S. target (27,985 tons on Greater Berlin).
MAR—Greatest bomber effort for any month. 31,297 bombers were sortied. 73,878 tons of bombs dropped, 74,009,324 gallons of gasoline were consumed in 395,829 flying hours. 92.3% of bombers sortied were effective. Jet E/A shot down 24 bombers.
16 APR—752 enemy aircraft destroyed on one operation by fighters—34 fighters MIA on strafing attacks.
25 APR—Last bombing operation carried out.
APR—Bombing accuracy on visual operations—best of any month. 59% within 1,000 feet and 85% within 2,000 feet. Over 2,000 E/A destroyed in air and on ground.
1 MAY—First "Chow Hound" mission to Holland.
8 MAY—VE-Day.

HEAVY BOMBARDMENT EFFORT
17 AUGUST 1942 TO 8 MAY 1945

Total Sorties	330,523
Sorties less Spares	318,450
Credit Sorties	293,599
Effective Sorties	266,565
Tons on targets: Bombs	686,406
Tons on targets: Leaflets	2,807
Tons on targets: Gas and Supplies	6,184
Enemy A/C Claims: Destroyed in air	6,236

Of them who running on that last high place / Leapt to swift unseen bullets, or went up / On the hot blast and fury of hell's upsurge, / Or plunged and fell away past this world's verge, / Some say God caught them even before they fell.

(from "Spring Offensive," by Wilfred Owen)

But I must go and meet with danger there, / or it will seek me in another place / and find me worse provided.

(from *Henry IV, Part Two*, by William Shakespeare)

Enemy A/C Claims: Probably destroyed in air 1,826
Enemy A/C Claims: Damaged in air 3,198
Enemy A/C Claims: Destroyed on ground 3,079
Operational Losses: A/C MIA 4,137
Operational Losses: CAT E 1,556
Operational Losses: Missing 162
Personnel Casualties: MIA 39,007
Personnel Casualties: KIA 2,818
Personnel Casualties: Wounded Ser 1,933
Personnel Casualties: Wounded S1 3,015

AMMUNITION EXPENDITURE ON COMBAT OPERATIONS
17 AUGUST 1942 TO 8 MAY 1945

Bombers, .50 calibre 72,339,729
Bombers, .30 calibre 31,300
Fighters, .50 calibre .26,623,123
Fighters, .20 millimeter .262,189

ENEMY AIRCRAFT CLAIMS BY TYPE
17 AUGUST 1942 TO 8 MAY 1945

BY BOMBERS: IN THE AIR

Type	Destroyed	Probable	Damaged
FW-190	3,107	880	1,356
FW-189	1	3	1
FW-290	2	0	0
ME-109	1,955	459	1,022
ME-110	449	151	310
ME-210	182	63	140
ME-410	81	43	69
JU-86	0	0	1
JU-87	5	1	1
JU-88	299	94	164
DO-217	7	2	2
HE-111K	1	0	0
HE-113	0	1	0
AR-240	1	0	0
Other & unknown	110	93	87
Total	6,200	1,790	3,153
ME-163	2	3	3
ME-262	57	43	54
Total jet	59	46	57
Grand total	6,259	1,836	3,210

BY FIGHTERS: IN THE AIR

Type	Destroyed	Probable	Damaged
FW-190	1,948	137	584

ME-109	2,535½	159	639
ME-110	185	13	80
ME-210	40	4	20
ME-410	74	4	22
FW-200	8½	0	0
JU-88	82	7	21
JU-188	2	0	0
JU-290	1	0	0
HE-111	22	2	10
HE-177	6	0	2
DO-217	26	1	7
JU-52	0	0	0
Other & unknown	146	11	34
Total	5,076	338	1,419
ME-163	4	2	1
AR-234	12	0	4
ME-262	130	9	44
HE-280	0	0	0
U-I jet	0	0	1
Total jet	146	11	150
Grand total	5,222	349	1,569

BY FIGHTERS: ON THE GROUND

Type	Destroyed	Probable	Damaged
FW-190	664	5	340
ME-109	509	0	307
ME-110	185	0	130
ME-210	49	2	39
ME-410	192	0	120
FW-200	8	0	13
JU-88	637	11	427
JU-188	15	0	9
JU-290	0	0	0
HE-111	293	0	198
HE-177	216	0	104
DO-217	178	1	131
JU-52	89	0	54
Other & unknown	1,094	4	949
Total	4,129	23	2,821
ME-163	3	0	7
AR-234	14	0	2
ME-262	100	0	55
HE-280	3	0	0
U-I jet	1	0	1
Total jet	121	0	65
Grand total	4,250	23	2,886

FIGHTER GROUND CLAIMS
FEBRUARY 1944 TO APRIL 1945

Locomotives destroyed 4,660
Locomotives damaged 2,791
Oil tank cars destroyed. 1,500
Oil tank cars damaged 1,422
Trains destroyed 20
Trains damaged 226
Goods wagons & other RR cars destroyed 6,069
Goods wagons & other RR cars damaged 23,929
Armored vehicles & tanks destroyed 178
Armored vehicles & tanks damaged 253
Flak towers & gun positions destroyed 270
Flak towers & gun positions damaged 557
Motor trucks destroyed 3,858
Motor trucks damaged. 3,091
Other vehicles destroyed .1,021
Other vehicles damaged 720
Tug boats, barges & freighters destroyed 129
Tug boats, barges & freighters damaged. 853
RR stations & facilities destroyed. 51
RR stations & facilities damaged 234
Radio & power stations destroyed. 102
Radio & power stations damaged 294
Oil storage tanks destroyed. .73
Oil storage tanks damaged .127
Hangars & misc buildings destroyed. 234
Hangars & misc buildings damaged. 600

AIR SEA RESCUES
PERSONNEL SAVED
OF THOSE INVOLVED
JANUARY 1943 TO MAY 1945

B-17 CREWMEN
Number of men who ditched or
bailed out over water 3,336
Number of men rescued .1,266
Per cent rescued of those involved. 37.9

B-24 CREWMEN
Number of men who ditched or
bailed out over water 1,025
Number of men rescued 272
Per cent rescued of those involved. 26.5

P-47 PILOTS
Number of men who ditched or
bailed out over water 69
Number of men rescued 27
Per cent rescued of those involved. 39.1

P-38 PILOTS
Number of men who ditched or

bailed out over water 27
Number of men rescued 12
Per cent rescued of those involved. 44.4

P-51 PILOTS
Number of men who ditched or
bailed out over water 131
Number of men rescued 56
Per cent rescued of those involved. 42.7

AIRCRAFT ATTRITION
AUGUST 1942 TO MAY 1945

B-17
MIA 3,093
Cat E 1,025
Missing. 126
War weary. 180
Non-op salvage 386
Gains from previous losses 56
Net inventory losses 4,754
U.E. end of month 27,624
Attrition as per centage of U.E. 17.2

B-24
MIA. 1,099
Cat E 551
Missing. 36
War weary. 213
Non-op salvage 221
Gains from previous losses 8
Net inventory losses 2,112
U.E. end of month 12,720
Attrition as per centage of U.E. 16.6

P-47
MIA 529
Cat E 176
Missing. 44
War weary. 176
Non-op salvage 131
Gains from previous losses 13
Net inventory losses 1,043
U.E. end of month 7,950
Attrition as per centage of U.E. 13.1

P-38
MIA 266
Cat E 84
Missing. 2
War weary. 29
Non-op salvage 74
Gains from previous losses 4
Net inventory losses 451
U.E. end of month 1,800

Hold my hand, oh hold it fast— / I am changing!—until at last / My hand in yours no more will change, / Though yours change on. You here, I there, / So hand in hand, twin-leafed despair— / I did not know death was so strange.

(from "The Child Dying," by Edwin Muir)

Attrition as per centage of U.E. 25.1

P-51
MIA 1,235
Cat E 514
Missing 132
War weary 168
Net inventory losses 2,201
U.E. end of month 12,375
Attrition as per centage of U.E. 17.8

FLYING TIME COMPUTED TO THE NEAREST HOUR AUGUST 1942 TO MAY 1945

Operational flying time 3,192,081
Non-operational flying time 1,398,310
Total flying time. 4,590,391

GASOLINE CONSUMPTION (IMPERIAL GALLONS) AUGUST 1942 TO MAY 1945

Grade: 100/150 53,321,258
Grade: 100/130 811,466,295
Grade: 87/91 2,776,564
Total imperial gallons 867,564,117

DEFINITIONS
(Extracts from U.S. STRATEGIC AIR FORCES IN EUROPE REGS 80-6, 8 May 1944, 80-6A, 16 Jan. 1945, 80-6B, 20 Jan. 1945, and EIGHTH AIR FORCE MEMORANDA 15-15, 18 April 1945, 15-7, 14 December 1944 and 15-6, 10 December 1944)

OPERATIONAL DEFINITIONS

SORTIE: A "sortie" is an aircraft airborne on a mission against the enemy (synonymous with terms: aircraft dispatched, aircraft airborne and aircraft taking off).

A/C CREDIT SORTIE: An "aircraft credit sortie" is deemed to have taken place when an airplane, ordered on an operational mission and in the performance of that mission, has entered an area where enemy anti-aircraft fire may be effective or where usual enemy fighter patrols occur; or when the airplane in any way is subjected to enemy attack.

EFFECTIVE SORTIE: An "effective sortie" is a sortie which carries out the purpose of the mission. An aircraft, when loaded with bombs or markers, is considered an effective sortie when it has released one or more armed bombs or markers, either by individually sighting or upon that of the formation leader, such sighting being made with the use of sighting or radar equipment, in a deliberate attempt to destroy or mark a target. Aircraft not loaded with bombs or markers are considered effective sorties if they carry out the purpose of the mission, e.g., drop leaflets, drop chaff, carry out weather flights, take photos, provide escort, carry out diversion as ordered, etc. Lost aircraft, unless definitely known to have been lost before reaching the target, are to be considered as effective sorties.

NON-EFFECTIVE SORTIE: A "non-effective sortie" is a sortie which for any reason fails to carry out the purpose of the mission.

JETTISONED: Bombs are considered to have been jettisoned: (a) when they are dropped anywhere in safe condition, (b) when they are released, either safe or armed, in the interest of the safety of the aircraft or its crew rather than in an effort to destroy a target, or (c) when dropped on operations without attempting to destroy or mark a target, (d) when dropped either safe or armed by any other non-effective sortie.

OUR PERSONNEL CASUALTIES

MISSING: If personnel have not returned.

WOUNDED: (i.e. due to enemy action) qualified by such words as "slightly" or "seriously."

KILLED: (or FATALITIES when pertaining to aircraft accident deaths).

INJURED: (i.e., not due to enemy action) qualified by such words as "slightly" and "seriously."

ENEMY AIRPLANE LOSSES

DESTROYED: A. Enemy aircraft in flight shall be considered "destroyed" when: (1) seen to crash, (2) seen to disintegrate in the air or to be enveloped in flames, (3) seen to descend on friendly territory and be captured, or (4) pilot and entire crew seen to bail out. B. Enemy aircraft not in flight shall be considered "destroyed" when: (1) seen by photograph to have been blown apart or burned out, (2) seen by strike photo to have been within unobstructed lethal radius of a fragmentation bomb, (3) seen to sink in deep water, or (4) known to have been aboard carrier or other ship at time of confirmed sinking.

PROBABLY DESTROYED: Aircraft shall be considered "probably destroyed" when: (1) while in flight the enemy airplane is seen to break off combat under circumstances which lead to the conclusion that it must be a loss, although it is not seen to crash, (2) so damaged by bombing or strafing as to have less than an even chance of being repaired.

DAMAGED: Enemy aircraft shall be considered "damaged" when: (1) while in flight it is so damaged as to require repair before beginning another mission, but has better than an even chance of continuing its flight, or (2) so damaged by bombing or strafing as to require repair before becoming operational.

OUR AIRCRAFT LOSSES

OPERATIONAL LOSSES
MISSING IN ACTION: Airplanes which are known to be lost in enemy territory or at sea.

CAT E (SALVAGE): An airplane damaged beyond economical repair while engaged in or in performance of an operational mission.

MISSING (UNKNOWN): Airplanes reported as believed to have landed in friendly territory on the Continent, unlocated and/or unheard of during the month of loss or 30 days thereafter. (Applies only to operations after D-Day.)

NON-OPERATIONAL LOSSES
WW (WAR WEARY): Tactical aircraft which because of age, obsolescence, excessive repair requirements, or other reasons are classified as permanently unfit for combat.

NON-OP SALVAGE: An aircraft damaged beyond economical repair while not in performance of an operational mission (accidents not due to enemy action, training flights, etc.).

OTHER DEFINITIONS

MISSION: Any ordered flight. There are three types of missions:

SERVICE MISSION: A mission such as ferrying personnel, material or aircraft within or between theaters of operations when no enemy opposition is expected. ("Trucking" was a service mission.)

TRAINING MISSION: A mission for training purposes.

OPERATIONAL MISSION: (Combat operational mission or Combat mission.) An ordered flight with the designed purpose of operating against the enemy.

ENCOUNTER: An encounter is deemed to have taken place whenever unfriendly airplanes meet, whether a combat ensues or not.

COMBAT: Combat is deemed to have taken place whenever contact is made with opposing forces and fire is exchanged or developed by one side or the other.

DIVERSION: A diversion may be a real mission, and it is a movement regardless of size or composition to draw the enemy defenses away from the main effort.

DIVERSIONARY SWEEP: A non-attacking action designed to mislead the enemy and draw his defenses away from the area of the main effort.

DIVERSIONARY ATTACK: An action wherein a force actually attacks a target, other than the main target, for the purpose of drawing enemy defenses away from the area of the main effort.

MEAN POINT OF IMPACT (MPI): Assigned point on the earth's surface on which a formation of aircraft, bombing as a unit, is ordered to place the center of its bomb pattern.

LEAFLET DROPPING: The dropping of leaflets over enemy-held territory as part of the psychological warfare effort. (British term for leaflets is "nickels.")

AWARDS AND DECORATIONS
17 AUGUST 1942 to 15 MAY 1945

Medal of Honor 14
Distinguished Service Cross 220
Oak Leaf Cluster to D.S.C. 6
Distinguished Service Medal. 11
Oak Leaf Cluster to D.S.M. .1
Legion of Merit. 207
Oak Leaf Cluster to L. of M.. 2
Silver Star. 817
Oak Leaf Cluster to S.S. 47
Distinguished Flying Cross. 41,497
Oak Leaf Cluster to D.F.C. 4,480
Soldier's Medal. 478
Oak Leaf Cluster to S.M. 2
Purple Heart 6,845
Oak Leaf Cluster to P.H. 188
Air Medal. 122,705
Oak Leaf Cluster to A.M. 319,595
Bronze Star 2,972
Oak Leaf Cluster to B.S. 12

Unit Citation. 27
Meritorious Service Unit Plaque. 19